This book should be compulsory reading for men who want to understand contemporary Islamic cultures. It also contains great riches for women who are part of those cultures or who are relating with people of those cultures. And for people who want to think about the relationship between scripture, faith and culture. And for those who would like some fresh insights into the Bible.

Dr Ida Glaser, International Academic Coordinator and Founding Fellow of the Centre for Muslim-Christian Studies, Oxford.

In her latest book, Dr Moyra Dale opens diverse windows into the world of Muslim women, who "are talked about, rather than listened to." This important study reminds us that 50% of the world's Muslims are marginalised in various ways: both socially within their own cultures and in terms of the limited attention received in study programmes focusing on Islam. The author achieves a remarkable balance between scholarly rigour and practical relevance. Through the pages of this book, Muslim women gain a voice which is long overdue.

Professor Peter G Riddell, SOAS University of London

The author's many years living in the Middle East and building friendships with Muslim women from around the world, combined with her passion for both anthropological and theoretical research, have culminated in this very unique introduction to Islam and the diversity of Muslim cultures around the world. Reflecting the author's unique standpoint, this book is unabashedly a feminine reading of Islam for Christian readers, but it is much more than that. It is a tutorial in how to appreciate the diversity of expressions and experiences of a global religion, which serves as an important challenge to the essentialising and 'othering' tendency of many Christians, and indeed many people who have not much opportunity to live alongside Muslims. This is an important perspective for people interested in fields such as geopolitics, counter-terrorism, multiculturalism and migration.

Dr Kathryn Kraft, Senior Lecturer in International Development at University of East London

Muslim women are the most neglected demographic in Christian mission. This glaring gap in missiological thinking and practice has been crying out for a book like this. Moyra Dale combines the incisive insights of a serious scholar with the compassionate perspective of a woman practitioner to produce a very well-researched and balanced contribution. This should become the standard textbook in this field.

Dr Bernie Power, Melbourne School of Theology

I enthusiastically welcome the consolidation of Moyra's many years of observation, experience and research in Muslim countries and in the West. This book exposes the secret world of Muslim women that the majority of missiological texts are silent on and therefore fail to equip women effectively. As Moyra examines the culture and religion of Muslim women she shows how this impacts their beliefs and practices which in turn enables us to understand and connect effectively with our Muslim friends. This is essential reading for all women seeking to connect with Muslim women and is a helpful text for men as well that they might understand the Muslim world more accurately.

Margaret Powell, Practitioner-Trainer, Sydney Anglican Diocese

I simply love this profoundly important book. It gives unique voice to Muslim women and shines rare light into their rich, passionate, complex and often fraught lives. Oozing transparent love of neighbour, Dale skilfully weaves sensitive storytelling with expert research and penetrating questioning to produce an outstanding resource for anyone wishing to deeply engage with Muslim women on questions of faith - especially their Messiah.

Rev Dr Richard Shumack, Director of the Arthur Jeffrey Centre for the Study of Islam at Melbourne School of Theology

While the everyday life of Muslim women flows through many books, rarely do we hear how these women interpret the Qur'an. This book captures that elusive reality. Moyra Dale immerses herself in Arab women's worship groups to explore the vibrant diversity of their prayer and scripture interpretation. Another treasure trove in this volume is the rich data on women throughout Muslim history. Surprising facts and detailed stories spill from many pages. Finally, feminism appears, with a dizzying variety of social media, ecofeminism, international collaboration, even the justification of prostitution as a choice, evolving in four waves, from 1840 to 2021. Central to it all is Jesus, the core of the cosmos and the souls of Muslim women.

Miriam Adeney, PhD (Anthropology), Associate Professor, Seattle Pacific University; Author, Daughters of Islam: Building Bridges with Muslim Women

Moyra Dale has invested her whole life in serving the Lord Jesus Christ amongst Muslim women. This book is the distillation of those experiences: she has lived in three different Middle Eastern countries; raised her family alongside Muslim women, their families and communities; completed two doctoral degrees that have included extensive ethnographic research amongst Muslim women; observed and learned from a women's education and empowerment programme in a Middle Eastern mosque. She has taught Islamic Studies in seminaries and universities in Australia and the United States, articulating the forgotten and unheard perspective of women in Islam. This book is rich in both understanding and experience, presenting a deeply sympathetic portrait of women in the Islamic world. It shatters many stereotypes and brings a vital but neglected perspective to mission studies.

Rev Dr David Williams, Director of Training and Development, CMS-Australia

This book is essential reading for every Christian who is interacting with Muslim women. Men should read it to appreciate how much Muslim women's experience of the world differs from that of Muslim men. Distilled from a lifetime's experience of ministry among Muslim women, Moyra Dale opens our eyes to see the richness and challenges of women's lives in a distinctly gendered realm, as well as how women breach the boundaries of gender to participate in the world surrounding them.

Dr Evelyn Hibbert, Founder and Colloquium Chair, Angelina Noble Centre

Although there are nearly 1 billion Muslim women in the world, their voices often go unheard. This book offers readers the opportunity to hear how various Muslim women across the globe navigate, shape, and perpetuate the socio-cultural and religious landscapes in their communities. If we are to begin understanding the Muslim world, we must look beyond religious texts and start listening to the community of women who embody the texts. This book will give you the skills necessary to begin that process.

Trevor Castor, PhD, Managing Director and Professor, Zwemer Center for Muslim Studies, College of Intercultural Studies (CICS), Columbia International University

Dale's book provides an invaluable resource for anyone wanting to make friends with Muslim neighbours and probably essential reading for those going to live in a Muslim context. It provides not only a huge amount of information about the realities of life and faith for Muslim women but also careful, thoughtful reflection on how this might impact Christian understanding and reaction. The honest portrayal of the author's experience of life amongst her Muslim friends is a real bonus.

Dr Mary Evans, former Vice-Principal, London School of Theology

The Muslim world is largely a gendered society. Our contextual mission thinking and approaches are typically geared towards just one half of that society. Most Christians serving in the Muslim world are women. Most of their leaders and trainers are men. If you, like me, are one of those men, and you are serious about the Great Commission, then you need to read this book. Moyra draws us into a world that so many of us have been so ignorant of for so long.

I have lived in the Muslim world for over 20 years, yet I found new insights on nearly every page of Moyra's book that I am still meditating on. Moyra writes with a depth of understanding born from a sharp mind, a genuine sensitivity, and deep and genuine friendships with Muslim women. This is not just a book for women though. It is for all of us serving in the Muslim world, and in some ways, especially for us men.

Dr Stephen Bauer, Associate International Director, Operation Mobilisation

This book is a treasure trove of learning for those who are in any way engaged with or seeking to understand the world of Muslim women.

Having set the scene by sharing of her wide knowledge of the Qur'an and historical texts which shape the lives of Muslim women, the author goes on to generously share insights gained from her own study and experience of being immersed in Muslim communities and their cultures.

Questions inserted in the text encourage and enable reflection from the reader and the excellent appendix will support any practitioner who, inspired by Moyra's work, seek to become 'learners of culture and how people live within their culture(s).' Particularly helpful is the discussion on honour and shame and the ways that shame is embodied by women. The exploration of ritual purity, and the tracing of this concept through the Old Testament to its imperative being fulfilled in Christ is a highlight. Insights gained from rites of passage inform the discipleship needs of believers from a Muslim background as does the discussion on patronage and grace.

As one who shares Moyra's passion for informed cross-cultural living and engagement I am very happy to recommend this book.

Jan Pike, Creator of The Prophets' Stories, a resource for use with Muslim/Christian women in grass roots dialogue.2017. Co-author of Storying Christian and Muslim Faith Together. Grove Books 2018.
Recipient of the Archbishop of Canterbury's Hubert Walter Award 2019

In this book, Moyra Dale brings together years of experience with Muslim women, her deep reflections on the text of scripture, her love for Jesus and desire that people can come to know him. The result is a unique, refreshing and deeply personal account of the lives of Muslim women in the light of Islamic teaching. This is a book I will be recommending to my students and all interested in understanding Muslim women.

Rev. John L Bales, Past gospel worker in South Asia, visiting lecturer Moore Theological College, Sydney.

Invaluable! Accessible, scholarly, respectful and wise, *Islam and Women* immerses the reader in the richly textured world of Muslim women. I wish I could have read this decades ago. A must-read for Christians with Muslim friends. Moyra Dale knows Muslim women. Let her introduce you.

Dr Karen Shaw, Honorary Researcher, Angelina Noble Center; author, Wealth and Piety: Middle Eastern Perspectives for Expat Workers.

There is nothing quite *Islam and Women: Hagar's Heritage* to be found amongst resources for those wanting to relate well to Muslim friends. Moyra Dale writes as a discerning, empathetic intermediary, coaxing Christian readers into recognising their own starting points even as she provides tools for gaining deeper insights into the lives of Muslim women. Through a blend of careful scholarship and familiarity with everyday concerns a comprehensive range of topics are made accessible by this timely, much needed resource.

Carol Walker, formerly Tutor for Islamic Studies at All Nations Christian College, Ware, UK

REGNUM STUDIES IN MISSION

Islam and Women:
Hagar's Heritage

Series Preface

Regnum Studies in Mission are born from the lived experience of Christians and Christian communities in mission, especially but not solely in the fast-growing churches among the people of the developing world. These churches have more to tell than stories of growth. They are making significant impacts on their cultures in the cause of Christ. They are producing 'cultural products' which express the reality of Christian faith, hope and love in their societies.

Regnum Studies in Mission are the fruit often of rigorous research to the highest international standards and always of authentic Christian engagement in the transformation of people and societies. These are for the world. The formation of Christian theology, missiology and practice in the twenty-first century will depend to a great extent on the active participation of growing churches contributing biblical and culturally appropriate expressions of Christian practice to inform World Christianity.

Regnum is supported by the generosity of EMW

Islam and Women: Hagar's Heritage

Moyra Dale

First published 2021 by Regnum Books International

Regnum is an imprint of the Oxford Centre for Mission Studies
St. Philip and St. James Church
Woodstock Road
Oxford OX2 6HR, UK
www.regnumbooks.net

https://hagarsheritage.com/

09 08 07 06 05 04 03 7 6 5 4 3 2 1

British Library Cataloguing in Publication Data
A catalogue record for this book is available from the British Library

ISBN: 978-1-5064-8906-3
eBook ISBN: 978-1-5064-8907-0

Typeset by Words by Design

Cover image and pictures in text by Jacqueline Gad
Cover design by Matthew Brown – Tako Design Studio

Distributed by 1517 Media in the US, Canada, India, and Brazil

Dedication

In warm memory of
Stephanie Lockery,
with thankfulness for her courage, creativity, commitment,
and love for Muslim women.

Contents

Foreword

It is hard to say when Moyra and I first met. We have differing memories of that. For her it was when we were in the same Middle Eastern city, for me it was when she made a trip to Sydney to meet me. 2014, however, marked a fresh connection, one that has resulted in a shared journey. Moyra was good enough to come to where I was giving a lecture and listen to me share a crazy idea about connecting women, scholars and practitioners, who work among and share their lives with women living under Islam. Her response? Let's go for it. From there, When Women Speak…, first a conference and then a network was born.

Moyra is both a scholar and a practitioner, or a practitioner first and scholar, and this book reflects that. The two parts into which she divides the book reflect this tension which she holds together in life and practice, as well as in her writing.

There are several things that stand out about this book. Firstly, there is the concern that practitioners and scholars working among Muslims give consideration to the way women living under Islam experience their faith. For too long there has been an androcentric assumption underlying our interactions with Islam and, in particular, shaping the way the Church and mission construct their interactions with it. Moyra takes us on a journey to see, to think, to listen through the eyes, heart and ears of women in order to reshape those interactions.

A second thing that makes this book's contribution unique and necessary is the way it provides a framework for the reader to continue to explore these topics in their own stories of relationships with Muslims. I have had the privilege on a number of occasions, especially through the courses that the When Women Speak… network runs, of listening to Moyra help participants think about how to reflect on their everyday connections to enhance their learning. This has also been an integral part of the way she helps students she has been involved in training for cross-cultural work. The first part of the first chapter should not be skipped over. Nor should the questions throughout the book. The book does not just give learning. It invites the reader into a learning journey and gives them the tools to make everyday events a learning opportunity.

In addition to that, you will learn a lot about ethnography throughout the book. The examples and stories model how to do and interrogate ethnographic learning. Moyra is a passionate ethnographer and demonstrates how that can enable our relationships and work.

The third thing I was excited to find is Moyra's own ongoing learning. One of the things I have loved about having her as a colleague is her enquiring mind. That has resulted in many extended conversations peppered with thoughtful questions, explorations of nascent ideas, and a desire to expand her learning by inviting others into the conversation. Many times I have heard her say, "I hadn't thought of that", or "What a great thought". It is this readiness to enquire, listen and learn which will enrich your experience of reading this book.

There is one other thing: listening to the scriptures through the experiences of women. No learning experience with Moyra is ever complete without engaging with how the biblical narrative and its individual stories speak to the issue, event or idea. One of the riches of this book is the way it helps the reader let scripture speak to what is in front of us.

Not only is the book a rich dig into understanding Islam through women's lives, but it is also a rich missiological text. Moyra demonstrates for us a missiology of honour toward those with whom our lives intersect. When you read the passages that come from her cross-cultural experience, you begin to see how we ought to live as those who love God and love our neighbour as ourselves. Moyra models for us this missiology of honour, calling us to work at building relational connections in order to live out what it is to honour others across differences. She reminds us that there is no advantage gained by 'othering' our Muslim friends. We are called to love as Christ has loved us.

You will leave reading this book with an encouragement to a whole view of what shapes people's lives; the personal, textual, cultural, and historical, along with the way the biblical narrative helps us read and respond.

I love the fact that this book is readable, while at the same time being a rich resource in understanding Islamic texts, deciphering the everyday of a lived religion, and a tool to help you keep learning.

Cathy Hine
July 2021

Acknowledgements

I will always be grateful to the Muslim women – neighbours, friends, teachers – who have generously shared something of their lives with me in different countries and contexts, and for all I have learned through them.

Much of the material in this book has appeared in blog posts and webzine articles on the When Women Speak… website (https://whenwomenspeak.net). Some of it I have taught in courses in Australia and the USA. I am thankful for the opportunities to explore these topics, and for the questions, insights and corrections contributed by my students; and those who have been involved in the WWS…network. In particular, I have benefited from the women who, from many different backgrounds and with diverse experience in countries and communities around the Muslim world and among the diaspora, have shared their insights through the WWS…Women's I-View courses. To Cathy Hine, co-founder of When Women Speak…, I have appreciated travelling together in growing this area of research and learning with women around the world. My thanks to those who have offered helpful suggestions on the manuscript or offered examples, including Miriam Dale, Hertha Ganz, Deborah Gunthorpe, Evelyn Hibbert, Jan Pike, Margaret Powell, Mary Reside, Inneke Riddell and Louise Simon – and many more than I am able to list. In particular, I am indebted to Gina Denholm for all of her hard work reshaping the book into its current form. Peter Riddell has encouraged me to delve more into Islamic texts, and modelled collegial generosity. Jill Firth has been unstinting in her friendship and support. Thanks to Jacqueline Gad for her insightful illustrations. My gratitude to Dr Annette Rice, to the medical team led by Dr Ross Jennens, and for the prayers of more people than I can know, through whom God has given me unexpected years and energy. I am thankful to Terry Fanning for always reminding me that attention and responsiveness to God's presence and action is more important than projects or whatever else we measure our time by. To Tarek, Miriam and especially Lauren Dale, thank you always for your constant encouragement and companionship as we have shared so much along this journey.

Unless otherwise noted, Qur'anic quotes are taken from the al-Hilali and Khan 'Translation of the meanings of The Noble Qur'an in the English Language', *hadith* references from searchtruth.com, and Bible citations from the NRSV.

As We Begin

The mosque dominates the old city. Tourists visit the mosque, and men go there to pray. But far more of daily life and interactions take place in the surrounding *suq* (market), where there are a range of wares to browse and bargain over – shops selling textiles, clothes exotic and mundane, fine china and delicately-painted glass, tentmakers, carpet vendors, interspersed with coffee shops, bathhouses and smaller mosques linked with particular artisan guilds. At the core of the *suq*, the spice market overflows with sacks of different coloured spices, herbal teas, jars of condiments, metre-long cinnamon sticks, pyramids of soap, hanging gourds and strings of dried okra or chilli – all the substances that make up the flavours of daily life, health and community.

The apartment block in which we are living in this city is, like so many others, inhabited by extended families. The men go out to work each day, and when they return, they clap their hands as they enter the door into the building stairwell, to let any women on the stairs know that they need to be covered, or else back in their own apartments. During the day the women cook and clean, and visit one another to drink tea and talk, while the children play, or make their way to school and return. This space is the home: the engine room, or better, the beating heart of society.

This book seeks a stereoptic vision in learning about the Muslim world. The study of Islam is largely too blind to the perspectives of women. Their voices are unheard in Christian colleges, in training courses, and in the plans and programmes of Christian organisations. By exploring cultural and textual themes, history and everyday life from the perspective of women, we gain a better view of the issues faced by both Muslim women and men.

Muslim women are one of the most talked-about and pictured groups in the world. Almost every day we can find images of them in the media. Most often pictured as 'veiled', they are also often silenced and unheard, with little attention given to their own voices telling their own stories of who they are and how they live life. They are talked about, rather than listened to. When we meet Muslim women, we are meeting individuals, humans, made in God's image [Genesis 1:27], and we honour them as image-bearers of the Divine. While Judaism, Christianity and Islam all look to Abraham as their ancestor, Judaism and Christianity trace their line through Sarah. Islam has Hagar as its foremother, through Ishmael, Abraham's firstborn son, and so she gives her name to this book.

Muslim women comprise about 12% of the world population. Of the men and women in cross-cultural Christian work, including in Muslim contexts, about two-thirds are women. Muslim women face the same sort of issues, longings and questions, as other women around the world. There are significant numbers of women with post-graduate qualifications in Islam. Yet, despite all that, it is surprisingly rare to find women teaching courses on Islam, female authors in reference lists, or women in leadership who are involved in training and strategic planning. What are the implications of a dominant asymmetrical perspective?

"Religious studies tends to be a rather androcentric discipline," comment Kamila Klingorová and Tomáš Havlíček wryly in their article on religion and gender inequality.[1] Their comment rings true in the field of Islamic studies. While female authors writing on Islam are beginning to emerge, overwhelmingly the books and articles published on Islam are still written by male authors. Male teachers predominantly staff religious faculties and courses on Islam. Yet, surprisingly, there has been little discussion of how this bias shapes the way Islam is understood or taught. Surprising, because recognition of the importance of perspective in research is not new. It is nearly three decades since Patti Lather noted that "ways of knowing are inherently culture-bound and perspectival." For Patti, feminist research offered the possibility of correcting "both the *invisibility*

---

[1] Klingorová, Kamila, and Tomáš Havlíček. "Religion and Gender Inequality: The Status of Women in the Societies of World Religions." *Moravian Geographical Reports* 2 (June 30, 2015). https://doi.org/10.1515/mgr-2015-0006.

and *distortion* of female experience."[2] Feminist studies have contributed to deconstructing how 'rational knowledge' hides its gendered nature and male privileging under claims of neutrality and universality. *Women's Ways of Knowing* was first published in 1986, noting how women learn not just in classrooms, but also in relationships, juggling life demands and dealing with crises in families and communities.[3]

The researcher's perspective inevitably guides what they see and don't see, the questions they ask and don't ask. Men writing about religion tend to focus on official religious texts, formal religious rituals and public space. This is one viewpoint, a window through which to look into the house of Islam (*dar al-Islam*). But there are other windows, offering different perspectives, that need to be included to see the whole house. Women's frame of reference looks also at patterns of daily life, family space and rites of passage.

This pattern of restricted analysis is evident in anthropology, as in many other fields. Male anthropologists see the men's world. However, Lila Abu-Lughod suggests that in gendered societies such as the Arab world the flow of information between men's and women's worlds is asymmetrical. The hierarchy of power means that men would speak to each other in front of women, but not the reverse; young and low-status men would tell female relatives the news of men, but "a conspiracy of silence excluded men from the women's world." For example, in Yemen, Steven Caton was confined "almost exclusively in the world of men in this sex-segregated society. … His access to the domestic world of home and intimate gatherings of close friends and relatives was limited."[4] This asymmetry finds architectural expression in the traditional lattice windows in harem walls which allowed women to look out and see who came and went, but it was impossible for those outside to look in. Earl Sullivan, introducing his book on women in Egyptian public life, suggests that "when men view the roles of women in society, they often see little more than the reverse of their own self-

---

[2] Lather, Patti 1991:2,7.

[3] Belenky, Mary Field, Blythe Mcvicker Clinchy, Nancy Rule Goldberger, and Jill Mattuck Tarule. 1997:xi, 15. The authors list five major epistemological categories for women they interviewed in the United States: **silence**, a position in which women experience themselves as mindless and voiceless and subject to the whims of external authority; **received knowledge**, a perspective from which women conceive of themselves as capable of receiving, even reproducing, knowledge from the all-knowing external authorities but not capable of creating knowledge on their own; **subjective knowledge**, a perspective from which truth and knowledge are conceived of as personal, private, and subjectively known or intuited; **procedural knowledge**, a position in which women are invested in learning and applying objective procedures for obtaining and communicating knowledge; and **constructed knowledge**, a position in which women view all knowledge as contextual, experience themselves as creators of knowledge, and value both subjective and objective strategies for knowing.

[4] Abu-Lughod, Lila 1986:23, 31.

image. Women, on the other hand, frequently see a more objective picture of themselves *and* of men".[5]

This lack of binocular vision, of not knowing or understanding the women's world, affects both those teaching about Islam, and those leading Christian organisations.

Where women take training or study courses, they are being primarily equipped to answer the questions of Muslim men. Women studying in centres of Islamic studies tell me that 'the course doesn't relate to the questions Muslim women are asking me'. Or their experience and voices are invalidated. On more than one occasion I have heard of women being told bluntly: "You're wrong, your Muslim friend *can't* have said that because Muslims believe something different!" (Whereas perhaps Muslim *men* may believe something different.) They are not learning about the questions and issues that dominate the lives of Muslim women.

Leaders of organisations plan their programmes and recruiting around Muslim men, sometimes with a faulty understanding of patterns of social influence. For example, the approach which advocates reaching the men as head of the household, on the assumption that everyone else will follow their lead, is based on the assumption that patriarchal societies function with the husband–wife connection as a strong social bond as it is in the west. In many Muslim societies, the husband–wife relationship is not particularly strong. Blood relationships are stronger and, in particular, the mother–son relationship. A more focused analysis of patterns of control and communication might rather look to the older women, particularly mothers-in-law, as key centres of influence and relationship.

For over two decades I had the privilege of living among Muslim communities in different countries in the Middle East, and gaining friends also among Muslim women in the diaspora. For a few years I was able to attend a women's programme in a Middle Eastern mosque, and that time took me deeper into learning about the Qur'an and the *hadith*, and how women in the mosque programme read and interpreted the texts that helped to shape their daily lives.[6] My own understanding of being a woman has been deeply enriched by the Muslim women with whom I have shared life, talking over glasses of tea or small cups of coffee, with whom I have partied, laughed and cried. And the questions that I have encountered in the lives of my Muslim friends have changed and deepened how I read the Bible, bringing new questions to it which have enlarged my vision of the God who made and loves us, who works in history, and who has redeemed us in the Messiah.

My allegiance to Jesus Messiah as Lord shapes my life, my daily actions and my commitments. I believe that the message of the life Jesus brings is also deeply

---

[5] Sullivan, Earl L. 1986: xi.
[6] Some of this is written up in 'Shifting Allegiances: Networks of Kinship and Faith', Dale 2016.

important for Muslim women and men. What it looks like when Muslims from around the world give allegiance to the Messiah who was revealed in a Middle Eastern context and culture will almost certainly look different to the patterns with which I was raised in the west. This book asks what it might mean for Jesus to encounter Muslim women and men, stepping into their daily lives and the issues that preoccupy them.

This book, then, is for those who find themselves living among or seeking to understand Muslim communities. Because space and life are gendered in many Muslim communities; it is primarily women who will be relating to Muslim women, and so many of the illustrations and questions are relevant to women. However, men who have less access to Muslim women outside professional or perhaps political contexts also need to understand this essential part of life, home and community, and the themes that shape daily life and interactions. Each chapter introduces its topic through lived experience and references from the Qur'an and *hadith*, before exploring the topic through culture or history. I go on to ask what the Bible says on the subject, and conclude with suggested questions to help each reader explore the issue in their own context. Male readers may find it helpful to ask these questions of their male colleagues.

The book is in two parts. The first part, Texts, Cultures and Contexts, introduces more general themes that help shape communities and relationships across the Muslim world. An introduction to culture is followed by discussion of the place of the Qur'an and *hadith,* and ways of prayer. This leads into chapters which consider significant cultural themes including honour and shame, purity and power. The second section, Everyday Life, explores daily life activities and relationships, in family, marriage, life cycles and life rituals, and in education and society.

Part 1

Texts, Cultures and Contexts

1. Reading Cultures, Reading Texts

"How do you like your *qawah* (Arabic coffee)?" my hostess asks me. "With the crema on top or without?" I have recently come from Egypt, where the coffee is carefully brought to the boil and then removed from the heat, with the crema still on it. But I know that in Jordan and Syria it is more often stirred vigorously until the crema has disappeared. So how do I drink coffee here? I recall how some years earlier I was visiting Melbourne, which has become the coffee capital of Australia. Sitting down at a cafe with others in the group I was at a loss as to how to decipher the options: Flat white? Long black? Latte? Macchiato? Cappuccino? and the list continued. My hostess waits now for my answer as I sit, feeling lost in a maze of different cultures and coffee options.

It's not just coffee. I grew up in rural Australia drinking tea with milk and no sugar. In Egypt, tea was black, sweet and stomach-churningly strong, made by adding a spoon of tea and several spoons of sugar to a glass of hot water. In Jordan, tea was often served flavoured with a sage-like herb. In Syria and parts of North Africa, sweet mint tea was offered. In other countries, tea is always made with milk, adding different spices, such as ginger, cardamon or cinnamon. And each country has its speciality drinks: the sweet flower-based tea of Damascus, the popular tamarind drink sold through Middle Eastern markets, the hibiscus drink of Egypt and Ethiopia.

How do we drink? How do we dress? Differences in what we do grow out of underlying understandings of reality and what is important. What are the deeper values and beliefs about life, people and God that are the basis of our daily actions and reactions? These underlying beliefs and attitudes are shared with the people and communities to which we belong. They are often not in our daily consciousness, until something happens to disturb or challenge them – until people behave in ways that don't seem 'right' to us. These beliefs, attitudes and ways of behaving are tied to material artefacts (what we drink from, eat with or sleep in), and institutions of law, education, sport and government. Taken together, they make up the different cultures we inhabit. Before we engage with the texts of a culture, we need to be able to read the culture itself, which provides the lens through which texts are read and interpreted (and sometimes out of which the texts have come).

Culture is as pervasive and as invisible as the air we breathe: none of us operate outside of it. The existence of culture goes right back to the beginning of the world and the people within it. In Gen 1:27-8 we find the basis of culture – our relationships with one another, and with the environment around us.[1] Different groups of people have different cultures, and the Bible also introduces us to ethnicity and diversity. Gen 10:5 tells us: *From these the coastland peoples spread, in their lands, with their own language, by their families, by their nations.*[2] Ethnic distinction is defined here by family, nation, territory and language. As in the early chapters recounting creation, we see that God's nature is reflected in the world through diversity, including linguistic and cultural variety, rather than by a static uniformity of culture and language.[3]

Cultures shape and are shaped by particular societies and the subgroups within them. They are given visible form in the physical objects they produce and how they are used, the ways in which people interact with each other and with the physical world around them, including the clothes they wear, the food they eat, how they live, love, talk, negotiate conflict, work and worship. Culture then includes visible material products; behaviour, customs and institutions (how products are used, how people relate to one another); and values and beliefs (how products, events, texts, people and relationships are interpreted and the meanings they are given). Cultures are not static but are constantly changing, and shaped by the particular histories, social patterns, physical environments and other cultures by which they are impacted.

Rynkiewich summarises this versatility in his description of cultures as:
- Constructed (on a daily basis, and out of the materials, ideas, social relations and spiritual resources that are at hand),

---

[1] Further expanded in Genesis 2:15-25.

[2] See also Gen 10:20, 31, 32. The repetition underlines the significance of this statement of summary and definition. It is frequently returned to elsewhere in the Bible, as people are introduced, or called by God, within the context of their family, clan and land (for example, Jer 1:1).

[3] This continues into heaven itself: Revelation 7:9. It supports the possibility of diversity rather than unvarying unity within the Godhead.

- Contingent (on what is at hand in their environment), and
- Contested by others in the same society (At each step there are alternatives, and people will construct culture in ways that suit them).[4]

Cultures provide the context in which religious texts are interpreted and lived out, as women and men live out the daily implications of their faith, and seek answers to life questions within it. Cultures affirm particular sources as authoritative, and how we relate to the objects and people associated with those sources. Religious teachings can reinforce some cultural patterns, and be in tension with others. While we will spend some time looking at themes that are common across much of the Muslim world, the way in which these common themes are practised and worked out depends very much on local context. We all need to be learners of culture and how people live within their culture(s). There are some useful tools which can help us be better observers and learners in new contexts.

Ethnographic Observation and Theological Reflection

A. Learning to observe

i) **Observing myself** (fine-tuning the instrument)

Learning to observe begins with learning to observe ourselves. This is a way of tuning or calibrating the instrument of observation – ourselves. So, we can ask:

- What is going on in me at the moment? How am I feeling emotionally? What is happening in my body, where are my muscles tense?
- How is that affecting how I perceive things and how I relate to people?

We need to be aware of and guard against the tendency we all have to *negative attribution*. This is what happens when I see something and interpret it negatively, or assume that people are responding negatively to me. For example, I might see people talking together and laughing, and immediately assume that they are laughing at me.

ii) **Observing the scene** (We ask ourselves Who? Where? What? When? Why?)

Who? Males or females? What age? Background (ethnic, social, wealth). What are the power dynamics? Who can speak first? Who can interrupt? Who sits where? Who gets served first?

Where? Where is it happening? Who can come into this space? Who isn't allowed in here?

What? What is being done in this space? What can't be done in this space?

When? When does it happen? What can happen at other times?

---

[4] Rynkiewich 2011: 38f.

Why? Why is it happening? Especially if it seems comic, bizarre or uncomfortable. Our feelings of discomfort can often be keys to new cultural insights.

(Asking people 'why' something is done doesn't always elicit an answer. Sometimes we can ask, 'What might happen if this wasn't done?')

iii) How do people divide up space and time?

Calendar time. What calendars do people use? (For example, national, religious, agricultural, sporting.) How do they divide up days, weeks, years?

Lifetime. What are the different rites of passage? (such as pregnancy, birth, puberty, marriage, death). Who does what? Who is responsible for what? What is the rite trying to ensure, and for whom? (such as protection, growth, compliance?). What is valued and what is not valued? (such as independence? interdependence? safety? initiative? conformity?).

Space. Draw a map of the area. What are the different places? (including administrative, religious, recreational, judiciary, commercial). Who goes where? When?

Draw a map of a typical house. What are the different rooms/spaces? Who can go where? (Children, parents, visitors, males, females.)

B. Recording observations

Develop the habit of keeping a notebook or file on your computer, where each day (or as often as you can) you write down anything you've noticed, anything that was new or strange, questions that you have.

- What stood out? What struck me?
- What was surprising?
- What emotional reactions have I experienced?
- What questions do I have?

C. Learning to suspend judgement

We learn to assess something – not as right or wrong, but just different – until we are sure we have understood it deeply in its cultural context and how it functions in the community. Using the Theological Reflection Cycle opposite can help us grow in understanding.

This reflection cycle is best done in a group. The dotted squares are the insights, prayers or contributions of others in the group. However, it can still be taken up as an individual tool. And usually, we all learn new insights from the individual experience being reflected on.

People generally go straight from (1) experience to (4) [re-]action. Some jump straight to (3) the Bible, but not always to the appropriate passages. Some do (2) the analysis, but not the theological reflection. So, this takes us right through the steps, to appropriate reactions. Spending lots of good time on the second step – Cultural/Social/Personal analysis – is really important. The effectiveness of the rest of the cycle is in direct proportion to how thoroughly this is done. If it is not done well, it is easy to jump to the wrong passages for the theological reflection. That includes thinking about our own reactions and what was happening for us and our emotions, as well as cultural and social questions. It's always worth filling the board with this step.

Theological Reflection Cycle

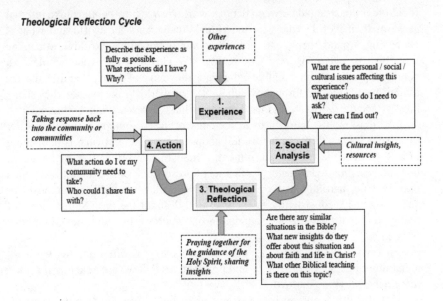

For the theological reflection, I usually encourage people to look for narratives/stories. When we go straight to teaching material, we often choose what just reinforces our own assumptions and cultural blinkers. It's by looking at the stories of people that our cultural assumptions get stretched and we gain new insights.

Of course, each story is treated in its place in the whole story of biblical revelation, taken in context. Within that, the stories of people in the Old Testament and New Testament serve to give us rich insights into God's redemptive work in our own lives and the lives of those we're interacting with.[5] At this stage, I encourage people to suggest a range of stories, and usually let the person whose experience it is to prayerfully/intuitively choose which one they think would best suit to help open up their experience.

The final step is often one that a number of members of the group can apply to their own situations.

I have done this with both mixed- and single-gender groups – it probably depends on the issue as to which is most useful. But it is sometimes good for

---

[5] See https://whenwomenspeak.net/blog/women-of-the-bible-what-do-they-teach-us/ for examples.

both groups to be aware of issues faced by the others. I have tried to model this theological reflection cycle for the topic in many of the following chapters.

Worldview

If culture is constructed between people, worldview is how people make internal sense of their world – the way individuals understand the world and what is happening around them, and how they interpret reality. Worldview can be described as a *map* or *model* of reality: "Worldviews are what people in a community take as given realities, the maps they have of reality that they use for living",[6] or the *glasses* through which we see the world. "Like glasses, they shape how we see the world around us. They are what we look *with*, not what we look *at*. Like glasses, it is hard for us to see our worldview; others often see it better than we do",[7] or the *narrative* we tell about who we are and what is happening to us: "A worldview is a commitment, a fundamental orientation of the heart, that can be expressed as a story or in a set of presuppositions (assumptions which may be true, partially true or entirely false) which we hold (consciously or subconsciously, consistently or inconsistently) about the basic constitution of reality, and that provides the foundation on which we live and move and have our being."[8]

Our own worldviews are not easy to perceive. It is often only as we learn about other people's worldviews and perspectives that we are able to gain some more perspective on our own.

As with culture, our worldview is not static, but is formed as we interact with the world around us, and can change as we face different contexts or new circumstances. Hence, I suggest a river as a model to understand our own worldview and that of others. The river is constantly moving, and it is both shaped by and shapes the terrain through which it flows. We see the surface of the river, but what happens at the surface is deeply influenced by what is going on underneath. The different levels are not separate from each other but rather, each level is connected to and affected by the others.

The visible level is that of behaviour – what people do. Underlying any pattern of behaviour are people's values, beliefs, and their (often subconscious) understanding of how the world ultimately operates.

At the surface level of behaviour, we ask what people do and how they act. While people pay attention to different aspects of behaviour as being important, we can begin with a focus on food, on feasts (and fasts), when people gather, what they celebrate and how they celebrate it. What are the rites of passage? How do people structure their time and space?

---

[6] Hiebert 2008:15
[7] Hiebert 2006: 27.
[8] Sire 2009: 20.

Worldview River[9]

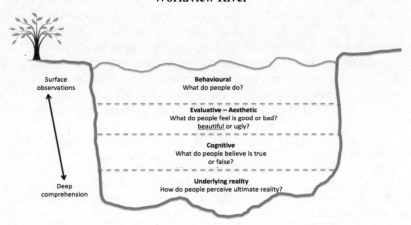

At the level of values, we ask what is considered good. When values collide, what is given priority or seen as best, and why? In particular, we ask what characterises a good person, and a bad person. No one will trust a message if the messenger is not considered trustworthy and a good person. We ask about belonging to a community, about loyalty and identity, and the place of family, and within it, the different roles across genders and generations.

As we explore beliefs, we ask about how right and wrong is understood, about how truth is defined, and how morality is constructed. And we ask about what happens at times of sickness and crisis.

When we come to the deepest level, the understanding of ultimate reality, we ask about how death is understood, and the rites around it. We compare different models of reality, of spiritual forces and beings, and the relationship between the seen and unseen worlds.

The questions that take us through the worldview levels may help us understand when we encounter attitudes or behaviours that are different from our own worldview. And they may suggest some of the issues that are significant at each level for the people we are learning about and from. Appendix 1 suggests questions that may be useful in learning about people's worldview at the different levels.

Texts and Cultural Themes

This first section of the book discusses themes which shape culture. We begin by looking at the authoritative texts within Islam. In particular, at the Qur'an and

---

[9] The author acknowledges the inspiration of Paul Hiebert's 'Levels of Culture,' in *Transforming Worldviews* (2008: 33), and the work of Geoff Morrow of WBT, for the four-interview structure.

hadith. We will ask how people respond to the manifestation of these texts in everyday life, and how they are interpreted as guidance for daily living. People's lives are shaped by these writings, according to which writings are given prominence and authority, and how they interact (intertextual relations). Their interpretation is also formed by the extra-textual contexts, the particular culture and history of where people are reading them.[10] We ask which texts have authority, and also who determines which texts are selected, and how they are interpreted. Khalid al-Fadl, a professor of Law in America, comments that:

> If one says, 'A Muslim woman ought to wear the hijab (cover her whole body except her face and hands),' or if one says it is immodest for a woman to reveal her hair, this assertion ... about modesty relies on a reference to a set of Qur'anic verses, prophetic traditions, reports about the Companions and most importantly, the cumulative juristic efforts in selecting, preserving and giving meaning to these textual sources.[11]

Islamic schools of law[12] contribute to regional differences in interpretation. Leila Ahmed, an Egyptian-American Muslim, comments on the impact of the different schools of Muslim jurisprudence in the cities where they were practised:

> In Medina, a woman couldn't contract a marriage but had to be given by her guardian, whereas Kufa gave her the right to contract her own marriage. One judge ruled that the Qur'anic injunction to 'make a fair provision' for divorced wives was legally binding: another judge stated that it was only directed at the husband's conscience and carried no legal weight.[13]

Hence, as we look at the Qur'an and *hadith* and what they contain on women and related issues, we find that there is not one reading. Local cultures and rulings affect issues of authority and interpretation, which will impact on how the texts are understood and applied.

Following on from the texts, we look at cultural themes which are reflected in the texts in different ways and help shape how people respond to them. People make sense of us and our message through their cultural lens. Richard Hibbert comments that "a person will more easily understand a message when it is framed in terms of the hearer's frame of reference or worldview."[14] And Don Richardson suggested that in each culture we may find what he has called 'redemptive analogies', patterns of behaviour or values that can point to what

---

[10] Barlas 2002: "Believing Women", p. 33, figure 1.
[11] El Fadl 2001: 98
[12] The four Sunni schools (*madhahib*) are the Hanafi, Maliki, Shafi'i and Hanbali. The Shi'ite follow Ja'fari. They constitute approximately 31%, 25%, 16%, 4%, and 23% of Muslims. Other minority schools include the Zayidi and the Isma'ili.
[13] Ahmed, 1992: p.89.
[14] Hibbert, 2008: p.344.

God has done through the life, death and resurrection of Jesus Messiah. As Christians across the world, our cultural themes or frameworks help us to interpret our world, and what we read in the Bible.

As we look at significant cultural themes in the context of Islam, we will also ask how they may help us read and understand the Bible better. From there we ask how the Bible may suggest ways of understanding or responding to these cultural values and behaviours. The theological reflection cycle gives us a way to reflect on these themes.

Does religion form the culture or the culture shape religious practice? The answer is 'yes' to both. What we sometimes think of as 'Christian' cultures are western cultures that have been formed by and have also shaped the expression of Christian faith. Faith practice and understanding of ancient Eastern Christians, for example, or even Jesus' practices and those of early Christians might look different to western individualist understandings.[15] This book offers some ways to read the Bible afresh through questions raised by our Muslim friends' faith practices.

Jesus was incarnate within a particular history, geography and culture. To be human is to be located in space, time, culture and relationships. Through Jesus we are empowered both to take culture seriously and, at the same time, be able to critique culture as insiders in our own cultural contexts.

- When have you encountered a situation where people from a different background to you behaved in a way that you found unexpected or surprising? What differences in culture might underlie it?
- What cultural themes have you noticed in your context?
- When have you reacted viscerally to something that is happening around you? What might your reaction suggest about your worldview, and that of the other people involved?[16]

---

[15] See Richard and Randolph's helpful discussion in *Misreading Scripture with Individualist Eyes,* 2020.
[16] Geert Hofstede (https://geerthofstede.com/culture-geert-hofstede-gert-jan-hofstede/6d-model-of-national-culture/) and Erin Meyers (https://erinmeyer.com/). Both offer helpful tools to understand some of these differences and our reactions.

2. The Qur'an: Present, Recited and Interpreted

I walk into the upper women's section of the mosque, a little before the starting time for the weekly lecture. A few women are performing *salah* prayer: more women are sitting in pairs, one reciting the Qur'an while the other listens to check the accuracy of her recitation and pronunciation. In a room off to the side, a group of women round a white board are just finishing a class on pronunciation of the Qur'an. On the walls of the main hall are framed texts, verses from the Qur'an in beautiful calligraphy.

The daily environment of people in the Muslim world is interwoven with the Qur'an. Recited in homes or mosques, heard over the radio or television, played on cassettes or discs from shopfronts, it is part of everyday aural surrounds. It is seen visually in beautifully decorated, carefully preserved books, displayed on a *kursi*[1] in a home or mosque or wrapped up on an elevated shelf. Qur'anic verses are inscribed in elaborate calligraphy winding around the domes of mosques or on other public buildings, set in frames in building interiors or fashioned into jewellery or amulets (often with protective intent). People sit swaying as they memorise it, or knee to knee[2] with a teacher who is hearing them recite it. Heard, seen, and memorised, the Qur'an forms an intrinsic part of Muslim life.

---

[1] 'Chair' stand for the Qur'an.
[2] Traditionally in memorising the Qur'an, the student/candidate would repeat the passages she or he has mastered or learned by ear, sitting on the floor knee-to-knee with

According to Islamic teaching, the Qur'an originates in a heavenly preserved tablet[3] eternally pre-existent[4] with God (*Al-Buruj* 85:22), which is also known as the 'Mother of the Book' (*Al-Zukhruf* 43:4: *Al-Ra'd* 13:39). All the sacred books are believed to derive[5] from this tablet. Muslims believe that it descended from the seventh, highest heaven where Allah resides, to the lowest heaven on the Night of Power in Ramadan. From there the Qur'an was given, revelation by revelation, and piece by piece to Muhammad, over about a thirty-year period.[6] This is an understanding of revelation transmitted directly from heaven to earth, given to Muhammad to recite:[7] this is not an understanding of God's word mediated through history and people's lives.

The Qur'an is made up of 114 *surahs* (chapters). After the first chapter (the *Fatihah* 'Opening'), the chapters generally go from the longest at the beginning to the shorter chapters. Most of the material in the longer chapters is ascribed to the years in Medina when Muhammad was political leader as well as Prophet, and contains more details about everyday life. The shorter chapters are generally linked to the earlier revelations in the Meccan years, and are more poetic.

Many Muslims interact foremost with the Qur'an as a source of power in its physical form, whether written (material) or recited (aural).[8] Memorising and reciting the Qur'an correctly in Arabic is the primary way of encountering it, and of receiving blessing (*baraka*). Constance Padwick, author of the book *Muslim Devotions*, describes how it is regarded as a source of divine power: "So the book lives on among its people, stuff of their daily lives, taking for them the place of a sacrament. For to them these are not mere letters or mere words. They are the twigs of the burning bush, aflame with God."[9]

In this chapter we discuss memorising and reciting the Qur'an, and then look at different traditions of interpretation. This is to help recognise and locate the commentators, both traditional and more contemporary, who are influential in interpreting the Qur'an and Islam in the communities with which you are interacting.

---

the teacher (Kahteran 2006:232).

[3] Prior mention of heavenly tablets occurs in the pre-Christian Book of Jubilees.

[4] Its eternal nature was disputed traditionally by Mu'tazilites, and now by contemporary neo-Mu'tazilites.

[5] Torah given to Moses, Zabbur (Psalms) given to David, Injil given to 'Isa (Jesus), and Qur'an given to Muhammad.

[6] This means that the Qur'an does not have within itself the same sense of history and God's progressive revelation as the Bible, cumulatively revealed over about 1500 years. Within some groups, this can manifest in a disregard for history and readiness to erase it.

[7] Some take *al-A'raf* 7:157 to suggest that Muhammad was illiterate, thereby emphasizing the miraculous nature of the revelation.

[8] See chapter 7 on Power.

[9] Padwick 1961/1996:119.

Reciting the Qur'an

The number of women and girls learning how to memorise the Qur'an has exploded in recent decades. In almost every urban settlement in the Muslim world, young and older girls with headscarves can be seen clustering around the doorways of street mosques, going to or coming from Qur'an classes. Memorising may begin at the end with the shorter chapters. For ease of memorisation and recitation, the Qur'an is divided not only into chapters of different length but also into equal sections: the most common division is 30 *juz* (sections).

Arabic in the Qur'an is considered the divine speech, an exact representation of its heavenly source. In this understanding of divine inspiration, translation into another language is impossible: any non-Arabic versions of the Qur'an can only be interpretations. For very many people in the Muslim world, being able to recite the Qur'an properly (in Arabic) is the primary concern and way of interacting with it; questions about its meaning and interpretation are secondary. The very first word that Muhammad is said to have received was *"Iqra'!"* (recite/read).[10] People learn the principles of correct recitation in Arabic through the rules of *tajwid,* a comprehensive set of rules governing pronunciation and timing, so that it is delivered in the way that Muhammad is believed to have received and recited it: "The intent of *tajwid* is the recitation of the Qur'an as God Most High sent it down, ... knowledge of it is a collective duty."[11] Both Arabic and non-Arabic speakers learn the same rules, that include but go beyond the rules of reading literary Arabic, so that *tajwid*[12] unites reciters of the Qur'an around the world, across barriers of language and geography, the reciters gaining merit through correct cantillation. However, about 85% of the Muslim world do not speak Arabic as their first language, and even for Arabic speakers, the sixth century Arabic of the Qur'an is very different to everyday speech, and even to the more formal Arabic of written materials. So, it is very possible to meet Muslims who have memorised and can recite the whole Qur'an, but do not know the precise meaning of what they recite.

The Qur'an is believed to bring blessings and merits through its presence and through its recitation. Beyond that, its content is authoritative as guidance for life for those who follow it, and its verses are read within particular communities of interpretation.

---

[10] *Iqra*! (read/recite) begins *Al-'Alaq* 96, traditionally believed to be the first revelation to Muhammad. To read was to recite aloud.
[11] Nelson 2001:14,15.
[12] For a description of *tajwid* classes, see Dale 2016:223-226: and Nelson 2001 on the rules of *tajwid*.

Interpretation

Tafsir is the exegesis or interpretation of the Qur'an. In the history of Islam, the authoritative teaching of *tafsir* and its application has been predominantly in male hands. So, it is male scholars who have determined the meaning and application of texts concerning women in Islam, including those which mandate the intimate details of women's lives. For example, Marion Katz records Muslim scholars' debate on whether the male scholars or the women themselves had authority to determine the nature of women's bleeding and the degree of uncleanness involved, with its consequent requirements for whether they could participate in practical piety, including *salah* and fasting.[13]

Many copies of the Qur'an are printed with the *tafsir* alongside or around the Qur'anic text. At a women's mosque programme in the Middle East, when women had completed memorising the Qur'an, they would then begin to memorise the *tafsir* of Ibn Kathir, an early and still influential conservative commentator. Other commentators were available to read in the women's mosque library.

One way of understanding the traditions of *tafsir* is to look at how they interpret a particular verse in the Qur'an. The verse *Al-Nisa'* 4:34 (below) can be controversial. Because of that, and also because it so particularly bears on the place of women, it will be a useful touchstone verse through which we can view the different traditions of *tafsir*.

> Men are the protectors and maintainers (quwwamun) of women, because Allah has made one of them to excel the other, and because they spend from their means. Therefore, the righteous women are devoutly obedient, and guard in the husband's absence what Allah orders them to guard. As to those women on whose part you see ill-conduct, admonish them, refuse to share their beds, beat them; but if they obey you, seek not against them means. Surely Allah is Ever Most High, Most Great. *Al-Nisa* 4:34.

While traditionally much of the discussion was about the meaning of *quwwamun*, in recent decades there has been extensive discussion and publications about the last clauses, particularly the clause that appears to sanction wife-beating.[14]

---

[13] Katz 2015.
[14] Recent discussions include: Hashmi, Taj. *Women and Islam in Bangladesh: Beyond Subjection and Tyranny.* London & New York: Palgrave Macmillan & St. Martin's Press, 2000, ch.2; *Comparative Islamic Studies,* 2/2, 2006 has an issue with four articles dedicated to this verse; Mahmoud, Mohamed. "To Beat or Not to Beat: On the Exegetical Dilemmas over Qur'an, 4:34." *Journal of the American Oriental Society* 126, no. 4 (2006); Ali, Kecia. "Religious Practices: Obedience and Disobedience in Islamic Discourses." *Encyclopedia of Women & Islamic Cultures.* Leiden-Boston: Brill, 2007; Ammar, Nawal H. "Wife Battery in Islam: A Comprehensive Understanding of Interpretations." *Violence Against Women* 13 (2007): 516. doi:10.1177/1077801207300658. 537–550; Scott, Rachel M. "A Contextual Approach

Traditional *Tafsir*

Historically, there have been two principal methodological approaches to *tafsir*. They are *tafsir bil-ma'thur* and *tafsir bil-ra'y*, and some mention a third, *tafsir bil-'ishara.*

The *tafsir bil-ma'thur,* or (or *bil-riwaya* [by transmission] as it is also called) is interpretation which predominantly draws from other authoritative sources. The Qur'an is interpreted by using other Qur'anic verses, *hadith, sunnah* and other sayings of those who were close to Muhammad. It also sometimes used what is called *Israi'liyat* (Judeo-Christian, mostly non-biblical sources, such as the Hebrew *midrashim* traditions). Persian al-Tabari (838/9–923) and later Syrian Ibn Kathir (1301–1373) both wrote this kind of *tafsir*, and their writings are still highly regarded and cited.

In the 12th century, *tafsir bil-ra'y (*also called *bil-diraya* [by knowledge]) developed. While this approach draws on authoritative traditions, it includes part or all personal opinion or interpretation. Persians Al-Zamakhshari (d.1144) and al-Razi (1149–1209) both wrote significant *tafsir* in this tradition. Some connect al-Razi[15] also to the *tafsir bil-'ishara* (by signs) tradition, which looks more for the inner meaning and concepts linked to words or verses of the Qur'an. The *bil-'ishara* approach is a more mystic approach. Al-Razi links *Al-Nisa'* 4:34 to *Al-Nisa'* 4:32:

> Know that Allah Most High has said [two verses previously], '… and not to long for that with which Allah has preferred some of you above others' (Al-Nisa' 4:32), a verse that we said was revealed because some women made remarks about Allah's favoring men over them in estate division inheritance [by certain male heirs receiving twice the share of their female counterparts]. So Allah mentions in this verse that He only favored men over women in estate division because men are the caretakers of women. For although both spouses enjoy the usufruct of each other's person, Allah has ordered men to pay women their marriage portion, and to daily provide them with their support, so that the increase on one side is met with an increase on the other – and so it is as though there is no favoring at all. This clarifies the verses arrangement and order.[16]

---

to Women's Rights in the Qur'an: Readings of 4:34." *The Muslim World* 99, no. January (2009): 60–85; Dunn & Kellison. "The Intersection of Scripture and Law. Qur'an 4:34 and Violence Against Women." *Journal of Feminist Studies in Religion* 26:2 (2010):11-36; Duderija, Adis. "A Case Study of Patriarchy and Slavery: The Hermeneutical Importance of Qur'anic Assumptions in the Development of a Values-Based and Purposive Oriented Qur'an-sunna Hermeneutic." *Journal of Women of the Middle East and the Islamic World* 11 (2013): 1–30.

[15] His commentary is known as *Tafsir al-Kabir,* or *Mafatih al-Ghayb* (Keys to the Unknown).

[16] *Tafsir al-Fakhr al-Razi.* 32 vols. Beirut 1401/1981. Reprint (32 vols. in 16). Beirut: Dar al-Fikr, 1405/1985, 10.90 Cited in http://masud.co.uk/what-is-the-meaning-of-qawwamuna-as-used-in-surat-al-nisa-verse-34/, accessed 12/1/2018.

By the end of the 13ᵗʰ century, commentators such as Ibn Kathir had returned to *tafsir bil-ma'thur* as the preferred approach. Ibn Kathir's commentary on *Al-Nisa'* 4:34 gives an extensive explanation of the verse, by invoking the authoritative statements of others. It is included here at length because of his continuing influence, and because the *hadith* that he quotes are often invoked in general discussion around the place of women.

> (*Men are the protectors and maintainers of women,*) meaning, the man is responsible for the woman, and he is her maintainer, caretaker and leader who disciplines her if she deviates.
>
> (*... because Allah has made one of them to excel the other,*) meaning, because men excel over women and are better than them for certain tasks. This is why prophethood was exclusive of men, as well as other important positions of leadership. The Prophet said "People who appoint a woman to be their leader, will never achieve success." Al-Bukhari recorded this *hadith*. Such is the case with appointing women as judges or on other positions of leadership.
>
> (*... and because they spend from their means,*) meaning the dowry, expenditures and various expenses that Allah ordained in His Book and the sunnah of His Messenger for men to spend on women. For these reasons it is suitable that he is appointed her maintainer, just as Allah said, "But men have a degree (of responsibility) over them" (*Al-Baqara* 2:228).
>
> (*Therefore, the righteous*) women, are obedient to their husbands, as Ibn 'Abbas and others stated.
>
> (*... and guard in the husband's absence.*) As-Suddi and others said that it means she protects her honor and her husband's property when he is absent, and Allah's statement (*what Allah orders them to guard*) means the protected (husband) is the one whom Allah protects. Ibn Jarir recorded that Abu Hurayrah said that the Messenger of Allah said, "The best woman is she who when you look at her she pleases you, when you command her, she obeys you, and when you are absent she protects her honor and your property." Then, the Messenger of Allah recited the Ayah (verse), (*Men are the protectors and maintainers of women,*) until its end. Imam Ahmad recorded that 'Abdur-Rahman bin 'Awf said that the Messenger of Allah said, "If the woman prayed her five daily prayers, fasted her month, protected her chastity and obeyed her husband, she will be told, 'Enter Paradise from any of its doors you wish.'"

Allah said (*As to those women on whose part you see ill conduct,*) meaning, the woman from whom you see ill conduct with her husband, such as when she acts as if she is above her husband, disobeys him, ignores him, dislikes him, and so forth. When these signs appear in a woman, her husband should advise her and remind her of Allah's torment if she disobeys him. Indeed, Allah ordered the wife to obey her husband and prohibited her from disobeying him, because of the enormity of his rights and all that he does for her. The Messenger of Allah said, "If I were to command anyone to prostrate before anyone, I would have commanded the wife to prostrate before her husband, because of the enormity of his right upon her." Al-Bukhari recorded that Abu Hurayrah said that the Messenger of Allah stated, "If the man asks his wife to come to his bed and she declines, the angels will keep cursing her until the morning." Muslim recorded it with the wording, "If the wife goes to sleep while ignoring her husband's bed, the angels will keep cursing her until the morning." This is why Allah said, "*As to those women on whose part you see ill conduct, admonish them* (first)". On Allah's statement (*abandon them in their beds,*) 'Ali bin Abi Talhah reported that Ibn 'Abbas said, "The abandonment refers to not having intercourse with her, to lie on her bed with his back to her." Several others said similarly. As-Suddi, Ad-Dahhak, 'Ikrimah, and Ibn 'Abbas, in another narration, added, "Not to speak with her or talk to her." The Sunan and Musnad compilers recorded that Mu'awiyah bin Haydah Al-Qushayri said, "O Allah's Messenger! What is the right that the wife of one of us has on him" The Prophet said, "To feed her when you eat, clothe her when you buy clothes for yourself, refrain from striking her face or cursing her, and to not abandon her, except in the house." Allah's statement (*beat them*) means, if advice and ignoring her in the bed do not produce the desired results, you are allowed to discipline the wife, without severe beating. Muslim recorded that Jabir said that during the Farewell Hajj, the Prophet said: "Fear Allah regarding women, for they are your assistants. You have the right on them that they do not allow any person whom you dislike to step on your mat. However, if they do that, you are allowed to discipline them lightly. They have a right on you that you provide them with their provision and clothes, in a reasonable manner." Ibn 'Abbas and several others said that the Ayah refers to a beating that is not violent. Al-Hasan Al-Basri said that it means a beating that is not severe.[17]

A New Move in *Tafsir*

In the 19th century, the Muslim world faced a crisis of engagement with the colonial western powers. The reactions to western thought and technology ranged from refusal to adoption. Among those responding, Egyptian Muhammad Abduh (1849–1905) was a notable pioneer of the modernist school of interpretation. This approach assumed the right to *ijtihad* (independent judgement, using reason and mind to interpret). It drew on and went beyond the *tafsir bil-ra'y*. Abduh and those who have followed him, while they were familiar with traditional *tafsir*, chose to de-emphasise the role of *hadith* and, particularly, medieval formulations of *fiqh* (jurisprudence). They sought rather to understand the value system of the Qur'an as a whole and apply it to the modern world. Abduh advocated the separation of *ibadat* (laws on religious duties) from the *mu'amalat* (laws on social transactions in the Qur'an and sharia). He argued that while *ibadat* were intrinsically beyond interpretative change, the *mu'amalat* should be interpreted by successive generations of Muslims according to the context of their own times. Abduh died before completing his commentary *tafsir al-Manar*, but it was continued and completed by his disciple Rashid Rida (1865–1935).

---

[17] https://archive.org/stream/TafseerIbnKathirenglish114SurahsComplete/
004Nisa#page/n99 (adapted punctuation).

Muhammad Abduh asserted that Islam was the first to recognise the equal humanity of women. He sought to renew Muslim society through 're-Islamicising' the family, teaching that the status of women directly affected the well-being or decay of society. Hence, he argued for reforms in polygamy, education for women and women's right to divorce. Barbara Stowasser offers a summary of the interpretation of *Al-Nisa* 4:34 in *tafsir al-Manar*:

> In the God-willed natural order of the family, the man is charged with leadership (*qiwama*) to protect domestic life and well-being. He is to the wife as the head is to the body. Men merit this 'superiority' because of qualities they alone possess, (they are) stronger, more perfect, more complete, and more beautiful in constitution, as is the case with the males in all species. This physical constitution is linked to a stronger mind and sounder perceptions, the ability to earn money and administer affairs in creative way. ... The husband's *qiwama* over his wife consists not of acts of tyranny but of guidance toward righteous behaviour, education, domestic efficiency, houseboundness, and fiscal responsibility to his budgetary guidelines. Then the woman can keep her house in safety and order, and bear and raise the children.[18]

Traditionalists, Modernists, Islamists

Three main streams of Qur'anic interpretation have emerged today: traditionalist, modernist and Islamist (fundamentalist). Their emphases overlap in different areas.

The **traditionalists** are conservative, opposing modernity and holding to Islam as a complete system based on scripture and interpretation through scholarly consensus. They retain a focus on the authority of traditional sources.

Both **modernists and Islamists** have developed from the teaching of Muhammad Abduh. **Modernists** use *ijtihad* (personal interpretation) and the separation of *shariah* law from its medieval formulations, looking to reinterpret the teaching of Muhammad and the early faith community in order to modernise the practice of Islam. **Islamists** also use *ijtihad* rather than the conservative approach of communal scholarly consensus, to interpret the Qur'anic message for the modern world. Yvonne Haddad comments that:

> Whereas the modernists focused their efforts on a reinterpretation of Islam in order to modernize its teachings and traditions, the Islamist movement at present is engaged in the process of Islamicizing modernity. Both groups have used the religious traditions in order to buttress their arguments, and both focus on women as one of the key elements in their respective platforms.[19]

---

[18] Stowasser 1998:35.
[19] Haddad 1998:7.

Both traditionalists and Islamists join in their view of women as having a role that is different and complementary to men in the Muslim community, deriving from a more literalist application of the Qur'an. Modernists hold a less patriarchal and more egalitarian view.

The **traditionalist** view of the complementary nature of the sexes, mediated through medieval scholars, was based on the 'deficiency' model of women. Haddad cites Egyptian Muhammad Atiya Khamis:

> There is no argument that the woman's work is inside providing for the comfort and happiness of the family and managing the house and keeping it in order ... If the woman competes and participates with the man in his work while she is exhausted by menstruation, pregnancy, childbirth, and raising the children, given the fact of her natural incapacity, she would have transgressed her condition and deviated from her nature. Then the family system would be undermined and its bond would disintegrate and there would be no love and mercy between them. ... Woman was created crooked, lacking in intelligence and religion.[20]

While there has been a shift from an emphasis on women's deficiency to a focus on women's spiritual equality with men, traditional cultural perspectives often work to reinforce the authority of men. At the same time, traditionalists (with Islamists) highlight the supposed emotional nature of women which makes them good mothers, against the purported rational nature of men which qualifies them to be the guardians of and providers for women.[21]

Modernists and Islamists both focus on women as central to society and its future.

Modernists seek a place for women according to social liberal values of emancipation and egalitarianism: they advocate higher education for women, and a place in the professional and paid working world. Pakistani Fazlur Rahman (1919–1988) is influential in modernist thinking, distinguishing between the Qur'an's literal laws which were given for specific situations, and the eternally valid reasons that lay behind them. According to Rahman, the interpreter's role is to determine the eternal principles embodied in Qur'anic rulings, and then determine how those values are to be applied in the present time. The Qur'an should not be viewed as a law book, but rather as the religious source of the law. For Rahman, men's superiority over women, as asserted in 4:34, was functional rather than inherent. If the woman is economically self-sufficient and contributes to the household expenditure, the man's superiority is reduced, "since, *as a human*, he has no superiority over his wife."[22] Palestinian-American Ismail Al-Faruqi (1921–1986) similarly argued that if the Qur'an teaches the fundamental

---

[20] Haddad (1998:9), citing Muhammad Atiya Khamis, *al-Shari'ah al-Islamiyah wa al-Harakah al-Nisa'iya,* Cairo: Dar al-I'tisam, 1987, p.56.

[21] However, in some SE Asian Muslim countries, men are seen as more emotional: and for that reason, women are given control of family finances.

[22] Rahman 1980:39.

equality of men and women, then hierarchy no longer applies if women are not dependent socioeconomically on their husbands.

Islamists also highlight the role of women in safeguarding Islamic society, but for them this happens through her adherence to a traditional role within the home. They do not say that women are inferior to men, but their adherence to conservative values of conduct, dress and domesticity is crucial in protecting religion, morality and culture according to the Islamic way of life.

Shehadeh analyses the writings of contemporary Islamist idealogues[23] for their understanding of women across countries and Shi'a and Sunni Islam, finding a focus in all of them on the role of the traditional patriarchal Muslim family in creating the ideal Muslim society, and three common elements:

> ... domesticity as women's primary role; gender differences, where the physical, physiological, biological, and psychological differences between the sexes are viewed as universal and immutable in the social and intellectual domains, dictating parallel differences in the respective roles of husband and wife, both, however, remaining spiritually equal; and the element of danger inherent in women's nature.[24]

Women's veiling (or *purdah*) is needed to safeguard women in their role, and to protect society from the danger inherent in women.

Pakistani Abul A'la Mawdudi (1903–1979) has been a major influence for conservative Islam in the Indian sub-continent. His interpretation of *al-Nisa* 4:34 follows:

> Men are superior to women in the sense that they have been endowed with certain natural qualities and powers that have not been given to women or have been given in a less degree, and not in the sense that they are above them in honor and excellence. Man has been made *qawam* (governor) of the family because of his natural qualities and woman has been made his dependent for her own safety and protection because of her natural drawbacks.

> ...In this connection, it is necessary to give a warning. Obedience to Allah is of far greater importance than obedience to the husband and has precedence over it. Therefore, it is the duty of the wife to refuse to obey her husband if and when he orders her to do a thing which amounts to Allah's disobedience. In that case it shall be a sin to obey him. On the contrary, if the husband orders her not to observe a certain voluntary religious devotion, she must obey him, otherwise her devotion will not be accepted.

---

[23] She includes Egyptians Al-Banna (1906–1949), Sayyid Qutb (1906–1966), and Zaynab al-Ghazali (1917–2005: the only woman in Shehadeh's book), Pakistani Abul A'la Mawdudi (1903–1979), Iranians Ruhollah Khomeini (1902–1979) and Morteza Mutahhari (1919–1979), Sudanese Hassan al-Turabi (1932–2016), Tunisian Rached al-Ghannoushi (born 1941) and Lebanese Mohammad Hussain Fadlallah (1935–2010).
[24] Shehadeh 2003:219.

If the wife is defiant and does not obey her husband or does not guard his rights, three measures have been mentioned, but it does not mean that all the three are to be taken at one and the same time. Though these have been permitted, they are to be administered with a sense of proportion according to the nature and extent of the offense. If a mere light admonition proves effective, there is no need to resort to a severer step. As to a beating, the Holy Prophet allowed it very reluctantly and even then, did not like it. But the fact is that there are certain women who do not mend their ways without a beating. In such a case, the Holy Prophet has instructed that she would not be beaten on the face, or cruelly, or with anything which might leave a mark on the body.[25]

Women's Readings, and Women's Roles in Islam

As women gain more access to education and religious studies, how do they read the Qur'an? We can identify four ways in which Muslim women today approach understanding their roles within Islam. They are Traditionalist, Secular, Islamist, and Islamic Feminist.[26]

Traditionalist

For Traditionalist women, religious teaching is mediated through cultural traditions, and according to the teaching of established historical scholars. They hold a generally patriarchal understanding of the teachings of Islam for family and society. The Qur'an and *hadith* are authoritative, and followed according to the tenets of the established schools (*madhahib*) of Islam. The majority of women throughout the Muslim world could be categorised as traditionalist, living their faith according to the traditional instructions that have come through their culture and the local sheikhs. Some have joined the growing movement of women to memorise the Qur'an, and may do so primarily for merit or blessing, particularly if they memorise without further instruction in how to understand it.

This group includes women in the women's mosque movement who mediate their reading of the Qur'an through the *tafsir* of traditional scholars. However, by their presence bringing women's reading and women's questions to the text, they are changing traditional ways in which the Qur'an is interpreted and applied, opening up the possibilities of new models. There is a growing number of women who, by their teaching the Qur'an and modelling female Muslim leadership (even within all-female gatherings), bring an implicit challenge to the damaging *hadith* that women are lacking in intelligence and piety.

Suad Salih (b.1945) is an Egyptian professor of *fiqh* at Al-Azhar Islamic University in Cairo, who has written numerous books and also hosted a TV programme called 'The Woman's Fatwa' to answer Muslim women's questions.

---

[25] http://www.searchtruth.com/tafsir/tafsir.php?chapter=4
[26] I am using the term 'feminist' in describing this position, however because it is seen to have western secular overtones, some Muslim women prefer to avoid it.

She takes a conservative view.[27] On the other end of the scale is 'Umm Faris', described by Saba Mahmood in her book on Muslim women's piety. As a popular teacher at a neighbourhood mosque in Cairo, while 'Umm Faris' lacked formal religious training, she regularly invoked the Qur'an and *hadith* as she had learned them through local sermons, orally transmitted stories, and popular devotional materials.[28]

Another ME *shaykah*, Anisah Huda, discussing the term *'quwwamun,'*[29] chose to interpret it in singular locational terms: "The man is the protector/authority over the <u>house</u>" (*al-rajul quwwam 'ala al-bayt*), rather than in plural gendered terms according to the Qur'anic text: "Men are protectors/in authority over <u>women</u>" (*quwwamun 'ala al-nisa'*):

> This means that he is responsible for the house, fixing things, children's study, the needs. It's best (seen) in action and not in the self. I wish men knew the meaning of *quwwam* – the right of the women for the man to be responsible for the house, (to provide) the woman's income. It was once thought that women are *min an-najasah* ([originating] from uncleanness) – this isn't in Islam.

Thus, she interprets the verse in terms of role responsibilities, in behavioural rather than ontological terms of men versus women, and challenges popular linking of women with uncleanness. However, she doesn't mention the ways to deal with women "on whose part you see ill-conduct," and I heard no discussion of this part of the verse on any other occasion within that mosque community. This is in contrast to the wider contemporary discussion around that verse. It may have been too controversial in that social and cultural context.[30] Thus, the women

---

[27] Suad Salih attracted criticism in a 2014 interview when she suggested that rape was legitimate for women taken as prisoners of war: "The female prisoners of wars are 'those whom you own.' In order to humiliate them, they become the property of the army commander, or of a Muslim, and he can have sex with them just like he has sex with his wives." https://www.memri.org/tv/al-azhar-professor-suad-saleh-legitimate-war-muslims-can-capture-slavegirls-and-have-sex-them/transcript. For a fuller and more sympathetic interview with Salih, see Maher 2010.

[28] Mahmood 2005:92–99.

[29] The word *quwwamun* is variously translated as 'protectors and maintainers' (al-Hilali & Khan, Yusuf Ali), 'authority' (Dawood), 'overseers' (Malik), 'in charge of' (Pickthall). Wehr's dictionary suggests 'manager, director, superintendent, caretaker, keeper, custodian, guardian.' (1974:800) See Wadud 1999:71–74 for further discussion of this term.

[30] See, for example, the vehement rejection by clerics of laws against domestic violence in Lebanon in 2013, on the basis of this verse. http://www.al-monitor.com/pulse/originals/2013/07/womens-rights-activists-lebanon-domestic-violence-law.html Accessed 5/8/2013.
Clerics in some Muslim countries have drawn on *Al-Nisa'* 4:34 and other texts to oppose laws which restrict domestic violence against women. http://www.al-monitor.com/pulse/originals/2013/07/womens-rights-activists-lebanon-domestic-violence-law.html#. http://www.aljazeera.com/n ews/2016/03/religious-leaders-slam-

in that mosque programme operate within the permitted cultural space, but seek a re-reading that is more balanced, within the framework of gender complementarianism.

Secular

As the Muslim world came increasingly into contact with the post-enlightenment and growing secular western world, some women[31] drew on secular rather than religious writings to chart their understanding of what it meant to be a woman, believing that they could not find equal position for women within Islam. Iranian Mahnaz Afkhami commented, "The epistemology of Islam is contrary to women's rights. ... I call myself a Muslim and a feminist. I'm not an Islamic feminist – that's a contradiction in terms."[32] Saba Mahmood from Pakistan, introducing her influential book on the women's piety movement in Egypt, described how secular Muslim women experienced "profound dis-ease with the appearance of religion outside the private space of individualized belief. ... the slightest eruption of religion into the public domain is frequently experienced as a dangerous affront, one that threatens to subject us to a normative morality dictated by mullahs and priests" along with a conviction that our way is the best way out for these "unenlightened souls" who are caught up in religious superstitions, and that religious truth is just a way of being manipulated by political and economic forces.[33]

While some of these women had previously held senior posts in Muslim countries (for example, Afkhami, born 1941, was Minister for Women's affairs under the Shah's government in Iran 1975–1978), with the increasing shift to conservative religion in most Muslim societies, most of them are now living and writing from western countries.

Nawal al-Sadawi (1931–2021), born in Egypt, became a doctor, and then Director of the Ministry of Public Health 1966–1972. She lost her job through the publication of her book *Al-Marah wa Jins* (*Women and Sex*). She continued to write and teach prolifically on the place of women in the Muslim world, including through novels and plays. Al-Sadawi was imprisoned under President Sadat for a while and moved to the USA to live and teach after persecution and death threats from Islamists and the government in 1988.

Islamist

Islamism (Islamic fundamentalism) became a growing force as people in Muslim countries grew disenchanted with the results of socialism and westernisation: a

---

women-protection-act-pakistan-160303160705361.html,
https://www.rt.com/news/336025-pakistan-womens-law-unislamic/.
[31] While a few have chosen to reject Islam, many of these women still self-identify as 'Muslim', retaining it in its ethnic rather than religious sense.
[32] From an interview in 1999, cited by Moghadam 2002:32.
[33] Mahmood 2005: xi.

trend accelerated by Israel's defeat of Egypt in 1966. As more young people, often from traditional or more rural backgrounds, were coming to the cities for education, life there confronted them with a sense of moral breakdown. Wealth and luxury goods were available, but only for the elite and those with foreign connections. There was a move to seek for solutions within Islam. In 1979, the revolution against the Shah in Iran ushered in a contemporary Islamic republic.

Women within the Islamist movement sought an Islamic definition of their place in society, turning away from answers derived from western and secularist movements and turning to Islam. In this view, woman was a partner in the Muslim family unit, which would underly a moral and stable Islamic society. Where women had education and leisure time (in the growing middle classes), they were encouraged to be involved in religious and charitable activity. While these women positioned themselves as religious over against secular movements, at the same time they were taking up the space made for women in the public sphere by the earlier secularists. This trend had been there from the earliest days of feminism in Muslim countries, but it is perhaps best exemplified in the life of Zaynab al-Ghazali in Egypt (1917–2005). In her teens she joined the Egyptian Feminist Union, but left it to found the Muslim Women's Association (*Jamaa'at al-Sayyidaat al-Muslimaat*). The association taught women (al-Ghazali's weekly lectures at the Ibn Tulun Mosque are said to have drawn thousands of women), published a magazine, ran an orphanage, offered assistance to poor families, and mediated family disputes. Al-Ghazali gave a personal oath of loyalty to Hassan al-Banna, founder of the Muslim Brotherhood, and helped regroup the Brotherhood after al-Banna's assassination (1949). She was herself imprisoned from 1965, but released in 1971. She encouraged women to be educated, and at the same time to be obedient to their husbands and stay at home while rearing their children. Some have suggested that her divorce of her first husband contradicts her teachings on the place of women. However, she insisted that her call to the Islamist cause and *da'wa* ('call' – mission) would always come before her marriage, and described her own childlessness as a 'blessing' because it freed her to participate in public life.

Da'wa, the call to Islam, has become a significant part of contemporary Islamism, including in much of the Muslim women's mosque movement. Women teachers are known as *da'iyya*s. The call is first to other Muslims, to embrace the teachings and practices of Islam more completely, and then beyond, calling non-Muslims to Islam.[34]

While extremist Wahabi Islam is violently against Sufism, there are significant Sufi links underlying Islamism. Hassan al-Banna came out of the al-Hassafiya Sufi order, and there are suggestions that Zaynab al-Ghazali was also

---

[34] This view of mission has parallels to the Old Testament prophets who called Israel back to true worship of Yahweh, and the Old Testament model of attractive, or centripetal mission.

influenced by Sufism.[35] The Naqshbandi order was well connected to the Damascus mosques out of which the Qubaysi women's movement and also Huda al-Habashi's classes developed. Islamist teaching does not embrace all the tenets of Sufism. However, Sufi orders may well have contributed structural elements to the growth of Islamism, such as routinised piety in the context of a wider religious body, the emphasis on teaching and its application in personal life, and strong allegiance to the wider religious group and to devotion to teachers within it. *Dhikr*s or *wird* (litany) were part of the practice of al-Banna and of the Damascene movements mentioned.

Islamic Feminist

The Islamic feminist movement is rapidly gaining momentum, particularly in publications and, principally, in the western world.

Fatima Mernissi can be seen as a forerunner of this movement and Amina Wadud is a notable exemplar of it today. Amina Wadud takes *al-Nisa'* 4:1 as setting the hermeneutic context, from which all other verses should be read:

> O mankind, fear your Lord, who created you from one soul and created from it its mate and dispersed from both of them many men and women. And fear Allah, through whom you ask one another, and the wombs. Indeed, Allah is ever over you, an observer.

Wadud, in her book *Qur'an and Woman*, explored a Qur'anic hermeneutic inclusive of female experiences and the female voice,[36] pioneering the first of what has in the past decade become a spate of publications in the area. However, in relation to verse 4:34, having tried to read it "with different methods for two decades," Wadud finally concludes in *Inside the Gender Jihad* that she "cannot condone permission for a man to 'scourge' or apply *any kind* of strike to a woman." For her it is necessary at this point to "*acknowledge that we intervene with the text.*"[37] To do so, she invokes Fadl's "conscientious pause"[38] in relation to its reading and application.

When Christians come to the Bible they want to know what it says, its meaning, and the implications for our faith and life. However, this is not necessarily the first question on the mind of Muslims approaching the Qur'an. The Qur'an occupies a place of popular reverence in daily life for its power and healing. A Muslim's primary engagement may be seeking to access power through the Qur'an's aural or written manifestation. Perhaps an analogy could be the place of the tabernacle in the Old Testament, which was seen as a physical manifestation of God's presence and glory, based on the heavenly original (Acts

---

[35] Lewis 2007: 1–47.

[36] Wadud 1999: x.

[37] Wadud 2006:200, 204. Original emphasis.

[38] El Fadl 200: 213.

7:44, Hebrews 8:2, 9:23).[39] Or they may seek merits in heaven based on its correct recitation. So, we need to take our hermeneutic hat off, to appreciate the power the Qur'an is believed to offer in this life and merit for the next life, through its written or recited realisation, common across the Muslim community.

However, it is also relevant to ask about the community of interpretation. The importance of the tradition of interpretation can be compared to the way in which Christians with opposing perspectives on issues such as baptism or the place of women, discuss the same verses in validating their position. How the Qur'an is interpreted, and which commentators are looked to as authoritative, has immediate consequences in the lives of Muslim women and men. This chapter has mapped the main positions and traditions in interpretation. Some questions that may be useful in exploring this for the community with which you are interacting are found below.

It can be tempting in looking at Christianity and Islam to compare Jesus and Muhammad. However, the more apt comparison is between Jesus as eternal Word of God and the Qur'an as eternally pre-existent Word from God. While giving Jesus the special title of Word of God, the Qur'an asserts that he is only a messenger.[40] John 1:1 insists that Word of God necessitates deity. Jesus as Word, Message from God, is not a document or list of instructions to be followed or even doctrines to be affirmed, but rather by living among us, shows us the fullness of who God is (Col 1:15; Heb 1:1–3), inviting us into a relationship with God (John 1:12-14).

- Ask your friends what they have memorised of the Qur'an. Are there particular verses or chapters they recite in *salah* or at other times? (e.g., when someone is sick). How do they benefit from reading/reciting the Qur'an? When do they do it? Alone, or with others? How much do they understand of what they recite?
- As we talk with Muslim women, we can ask which Qur'anic verses are most influential in their lives and daily activities in what they can and can't do. And who are the religious teachers or authorities that influence their lives?
- What Muslim commentator(s) are promoted by your local mosque or used by your Muslim friend in reading the Qur'an?
- Among the different ways that women engage with the Qur'an (Traditionalist, Secular, Islamist, Islamic Feminist), where would you place the Muslim women in your context?

---

[39] See the beginning of this chapter, on belief and references that the Qur'an derives from a heavenly original.
[40] The Qur'an describes Jesus as a Word from God, and Word (*al-Imran* 3:39, 3:45: *al-Nisa'* 4:171). Other Qur'anic titles for Jesus include Spirit from God (*al-Nisa'* 4:171), Saying of Truth (God) (*Maryam* 19:34), and Messiah (*al-Imran* 3:45, *al-Nisa'* 4:157, 172; *al-Ma'ida* 5:17, 72, 75; *al-Taubah* 9:31).

3. *Hadith*: Shaping Daily Life

It is the Night of Vigil, the most special night in Ramadan, when many Muslims spend the whole night at the mosque in prayer, believing that their prayers that night will be answered. I have joined women at the mosque across the city early in the evening. At about 1.30 a.m. I find a text message on my phone, which has arrived twenty minutes earlier, to say that my husband has come and is waiting to collect me. The women are packed in rows to pray, standing shoulder to shoulder. I begin to make my way out, with difficulty, through the rows of women. It is soon apparent from their expressions that I am doing the wrong thing in walking over the space where they are about to prostrate in prayer. One woman puts her hands on my shoulders and thrusts me back physically. I should have waited another fifteen minutes for the next break in the cycle. Later I find the *hadith* about walking in front of someone's prayer space:

Narrated Abu Salih (Following a description of a man who was repulsed and complained to Marwan): Abu Sa'id said, "I heard the Prophet (PBH)[1] saying, 'If anybody amongst you is offering *Salat* (prayer) behind something as a Sutra and somebody tries to pass in front of him (between him and his Sutra), then he should repulse him and if he refuses, he should use force against him for he is a Satan.'"

---

[1] Peace be upon him. *Sala Allah 'alayhi wasalam.* صلى الله عليه وصلم.

Narrated Abu Juhaim: Allah's Messenger (PBH) said, "If the person who passes in front of another person in *Salat* (prayer) knew the magnitude of his sin, he would prefer to wait for 40 (days, months or years) rather than to pass in front of him."[2]

Hadith – What Are They?

A *hadith* (tradition) recounts something that Muhammad said or did or that he approved or disapproved of, or what was said or done by his Companions. Making up a vast corpus, the *hadith* are influential in shaping the details of Muslims' daily lives and actions. Because of their impact, people find different ways to establish their validity or to challenge them. This chapter introduces *hadith* and some of the early female transmitters, and the basis of establishing their authenticity. It notes their impact on daily life and ways to dispute them.

As the Muslim community expanded in numbers and into new countries and cultural contexts,[3] they faced the urgent question of how they should behave, of where they could find a code that would guide their conduct in matters great and small. The Qur'an does not offer detailed guidance of how to live out everyday life and faith. However, Muhammad is seen as the perfect exemplar of how to live as God wants, and his words and actions are believed to be inspired, and thus normative for Muslims. So, all questions were resolved by appealing to the authoritative example and words of Muhammad, or failing that, of the example and words of his Companions who were closest to him, or their immediate successors. Things that may only be alluded to in the Qur'an, including the details of everyday worship (*ibadaat*) and life (*mu'amalaat*) are found in the *hadith*, which recount the words and actions of Muhammad and of his Companions. For example, how often to pray each day, with the detailed actions and words required to properly carry out prayer and pre-prayer washing, as well as countless other details of daily life.[4]

Over the first two or three hundred years of Islam, the number of *hadith* grew exponentially, as people sought new examples of what Muhammad had said or done to validate their actions. So, in the eighth and ninth century CE, scholars began to painstakingly build their collections of *hadith* that they considered authentic. Al-Bukhari (d.870) is said to have looked at about 600,000 *hadith*, and

---

[2] Az-Zubaidi, Al-Imam Zain-uk-Din Ahmad bin Abdal-Lateef, ed. *The Translation of the Meanings of Summarized Sahih al-Bukhari, Arabic-English*. Translated by Dr Muhammad Muhsin Khan. Riyadh: Maktaba Dar-us-Salam 1994:195–196.

[3] The revisionist view suggests that it was at this time of Arab expansion that the person of Muhammad and religion of Islam were developed to provide a unifying figure and faith to help control the growing empire. This is the opposite to the traditional understanding that the Arab expansion out of the Arab peninsula was a result of Muhammad's leadership and the advance of Islam.

[4] See Bernie Power's discussion of the relationship between the Qur'an and *hadith* in terms of abrogation or reinstatement of particular Qu'ranic verses or *hadith* (2016:33-43).

retained 7,275 as authentic. Some of the other great collections are al-Muslim (d.875), Abu-Dawud (d.888), the Muwatta' of Malik (d.795), al-Nasa'i (d.915) and al-Tirmidhi (d.892).

The Shi'ite collections include those of al-Kulayni (d.939), al-Qummi (also known as ibn Babawayh: d.991) and al-Tusi (d.1067). A later and influential collection is al-Majlisi's Bihar al-anwar (Ocean of Lights), which was completed about 1674.

Authority of the *Hadith*

The authority of Muhammad's words, example, and prohibitions as recounted in the *hadith* is supported by Qur'anic verses such as *Al-Nur* 24:52:

> Whoever obeys Allah and His Messenger, fears Allah, and keeps his duty, such are the successful.[5]

This immediate connection between obedience to Allah and to Muhammad for many suggests equal authority for both the Qur'an and the *hadith*.

Al-Ghazzali (1058–1111), the revered medieval theologian of Islam, describes the relation of Qur'an and *hadith*:[6]

> "God has but one word which differs only in the mode of its expression. On occasions God indicates His word by the Qur'an; on others, by words in another style, not publicly recited, and called the prophetic tradition. Both are mediated by the Prophet."[7]

Describing the closely-connected authority of the Qur'an and Muhammad's example, a Muslim *shaykhah* twice told the women attending her lectures that "The *sunnah* of the Messenger came to us in the same way the Qur'an came to us." However, some contemporary writers, aware of the contradictions and variation in credibility and acceptance of different *hadith*, see the Qur'an as more authoritative. Wadud writes:

> "While I accept the role of the Prophet both with regard to revelation, as understood in Islam, and to the development of Islamic law on the basis of his sunnah or normative practices, I place greater significance on the Qur'an. This is congruent

---

[5] See also *Al-Nisa'* 4:80, *Al-Ahzab* 33:21, *Al-Fath* 48:10, *Al-Hashr* 59:7.
[6] The Qu'ran and *hadith* are mediated further by the *sunnah* (recommendations for daily life, based on Muhammad's words and actions), and the *tafsir* (commentaries interpreting the Qur'an). They are codified by different schools of jurisprudence into the Shari'ah (Muslim jurisprudence) laws which guide application of principles into laws of religion, family life, economics and criminal code, for all the details of daily life.
[7] Cited in R. Peters 1990:192.

with the Orthodox understanding of the inerrancy of Qur'anic preservation versus historical contradictions within the *hadith* literature."[8]

Women Transmitters

In this authoritative area which determines so many of the daily precepts of Islam, women have always been recognised as *muhaddithat* (female transmitters of *hadith*). Among Muhammad's wives, Aisha is most commonly cited as a notable transmitter of *hadith*, and also Umm Salamah. The Shi'ite discount Aisha because of her opposition to Ali (Muhammad's cousin and the fourth caliph), and take Fatima (Muhammad's only surviving daughter and the wife of Ali) as more authoritative. Among Muhammad's female Companions, Naseebah and Umm Sulaym are described as narrators of *hadith*.[9] Abdel-Halim adds the names of Al-Khansa' and 'Umara bint Abdel-Rahman in the first century of Islam, together with 'Aishah 'Abd-al-Hadi and Nafissah (great-granddaughter of Muhammad), and Rabia'a al-Adawiyya in the following century, as significant early women scholars.[10] In the early years of the Islamic empire, women were part of a revival in *hadith* scholarship in Syria, learning and teaching *hadith* in some of the main mosques in Damascus, in gardens and private houses.[11] They included Umm al-Darda', a famous female *muhaddithat* and jurist.[12]

Nadwi's introductory book on the *muhaddithat* examines the role of women narrating *hadith* throughout the centuries since the time of Muhammad until the present. He suggests that the first and second centuries A.H. (the early emergence of Islam), followed by the sixth–ninth centuries A.H. (which included defeats from the Crusaders and the Mongols),[13] were the most significant times for women scholars within Islam. It seems that times of disruption allow more space for women to flourish. At times of consolidation they are found again in traditional confines.[14]

Hadith and Women's Daily Lives

In the daily arena of Muslim women's lives, *hadith* are most commonly invoked to determine what women may or may not do. We encountered a number of them

---

[8] Wadud 1999:xvii.

[9] 'Ali Qutb 2007:189, 212.

[10] Abdel-Halim 2008:19.

[11] Deeb 2007:335; Nadwi 2007:248 266–7; Roded 2008:49.

[12] See chapters 10, 13 & 17 for more details on some of these women.

[13] 6th and 7th centuries and 12th–15th centuries CE.

[14] Nadwi 2007:246, 255. Mernissi, viewing the social disruptions of the Gulf War, asked: "Traditionally, women were the designated victims of the rituals for re-establishing equilibrium. As soon as the city showed signs of disorder, the caliph ordered women to stay at home. Will it be we, the women living in the Muslim city, who will pay the price…?" (1992:9).

in Ibn Kathir's commentary on *Al-Nisa* 4:34 in the previous chapter. Because there are so many *hadith*, it is possible to find both positive and negative material on almost any topic – including women. Asma Barlas comments:

> "Finally, it is ironic that even though there are only about six misogynistic Ahādith[15] accepted as Sahīh (reliable) out of a collection of 70,000, it is these six that men trot out when they want to argue against sexual equality, while perversely ignoring dozens of positive Ahādith. Among the latter are Ahādith that emphasize women's full humanity; counsel husbands to deal kindly and justly with their wives; confirm the right of women to acquire knowledge; elevate mothers over fathers; proclaim that women will be in heaven, ahead, even of the Prophet; record women's attendance at prayers in the mosque during the Prophet's lifetime, including an incident where a girl played in front of him as he led the prayer; affirm that many women (including women from the Prophet's family), went unveiled in the later years of Islam; and record that the Prophet accepted the evidence of one woman over that of a man."[16]

However, as Barlas suggests, it is often the more misogynistic *hadith* that are most quoted about and at women. One of the most widespread and cited *hadith* includes two devastating critiques of women: that they make up the majority of people in hell, and that they are lacking in intelligence and piety.[17] Other commonly-quoted statements about women include describing them as crooked like a rib:

> Narrated Abu Huraira: Allah's Apostle said, "Treat women nicely, for a woman is created from a rib, and the most curved portion of the rib is its upper portion, so, if you should try to straighten it, it will break, but if you leave it as it is, it will remain crooked. So, treat women nicely."[18]

Or as a harmful affliction:

> Narrated Usama bin Zaid: The Prophet said, "After me I have not left any affliction more harmful to men than women."[19]

Or including them with donkeys and dogs:

> Abu Huraira reported: The Messenger of Allah (may peace be upon him) said: "A woman, an ass and a dog disrupt the prayer, but something like the back of a saddle guards against that."[20]

---

[15] *Ahadith*: Arabic plural of *hadith*.
[16] Barlas, 2002:46. Also Mernissi 1994.
[17] This *hadith* is quoted in full in the chapter on Purity & Defilement.
[18] Book #55, *Hadith* #548), Also (Book #62, *Hadith* #113, 114.
[19] Al-Bukhari, Book #62, *Hadith* #33.
[20] Al-Muslim, Book #004, *Hadith* #1034.

However, this *hadith* was indignantly rebutted by Aisha in another authoritative *hadith*:

Narrated Aisha: The things which annul the prayers were mentioned before me. They said, "Prayer is annulled by a dog, a donkey and a woman (if they pass in front of the praying people)." I said, "You have made us (i.e., women) dogs. I saw the Prophet praying while I used to lie in my bed between him and the Qibla. Whenever I was in need of something, I would slip away, for I disliked to face him."[21]

The *hadith*: "Take half your religion from this Humayra" (redhead – Muhammad's nickname for Aisha), endorsing the authority of Aisha, is often quoted, but its authenticity is doubtful; it is classified as 'Fabricated' (see following section).

A *hadith* ascribed to Umar, third caliph of Islam, demonstrates both how the events of life and inspiration of Qur'anic revelation are seen as interwoven, and also Umar's sometimes more unsympathetic attitude to women:

Narrated 'Umar (bin Al-Khattab): My Lord agreed with me in three things:

1. I said, "O Allah's Apostle, I wish we took the station of Abraham as our praying place (for some of our prayers). So came the Divine Inspiration: And take you (people) the station of Abraham as a place of prayer (for some of your prayers, e.g., two Rakat of Tawaf of Ka'ba)". (*Al-Baqarah* 2.125)

2. And as regards the (verse of) the veiling of the women, I said, "O Allah's Apostle! I wish you ordered your wives to cover themselves from the men because good and bad ones talk to them." So the verse of the veiling of the women was revealed.

3. Once the wives of the Prophet made a united front against the Prophet and I said to them, "It may be if he (the Prophet) divorced you, (all) that his Lord (Allah) will give him instead of you wives better than you." So this verse (the same as I had said) was revealed. (*Al-Tahrim* 66.5).[22]

Further *hadith*, as well as relevant Qur'anic verses, will be included in the following chapters, and others can be found in Appendix 2. You might like to

---

[21] Al-Bukhari, Book #9, *Hadith* #490.

[22] Al-Bukhari, Book #8, *Hadith* #395. The following *hadith* recounts the second incident recounted:

Narrated 'Aisha: The wives of the Prophet used to go to Al-Manasi, a vast open place (near Baqia at Medina) to answer the call of nature at night. 'Umar used to say to the Prophet, "Let your wives be veiled," but Allah's Apostle did not do so. One night, Sauda bint Zam'a, the wife of the Prophet, went out at 'Isha' time and she was a tall lady. 'Umar addressed her and said, "I have recognized you, O Sauda." He said so, as he desired eagerly that the verses of Al-Hijab (the observing of veils by the Muslim women) may be revealed. So, Allah revealed the verses of "Al-Hijab" (a complete body cover excluding the eyes) (Sahih Bukhari, Book #4, *Hadith* #148).

add there any other *hadith* which are particularly significant for the women with whom you are interacting.

Authentication of *Hadith*

Given the multiplication of *hadith* in the early centuries of Islam, it became crucial to establish a way of testing their validity, and the science of *hadith* developed.

Each *hadith* is made of two parts: the *isnad/sanad* (support: chain of reporters) and the *matn* (text: the substance of the report). Most sources give only the first narrator, with whom the *isnad* begins. In the above *hadith*, Umar is the narrator. The *isnad* is followed by the *matn*, or main content of the *hadith*. For a *hadith* to be authenticated, it should have a trustworthy origin, a strong train of transmitters (*isnad*), and content (*matn*) that is supported by other *hadith* or the Qur'an. If any of them are doubtful, it can invalidate the *hadith*. Below are some of the following categories used to assess the *hadith*.[23] Each category is in descending level of veracity. Most of the categories of authentication focus on the transmitters, on the *isnad*.

1. The first category is according to the <u>source</u>, or from whom the *hadith* is said to have originated.

Qudsi (Divine)	Attributed to God
Marfu' (Elevated)	Attributed to Muhammad
Mawquf (Stopped)	Attributed to a Companion
Maqtu' (Severed)	Attributed to a successor of a Companion

2. Another influential category assesses the <u>trustworthiness and character of the reporters</u>. If one of the key transmitters was shown to be untrustworthy in some way, such as refusing to give his horse a drink when it needed one, then that casts doubt on his trustworthiness in passing on authentic *hadith*.

Sahih (Correct)	Reporters have a reputation as being trustworthy
Hasan (Good)	The reporters are known
Da 'if (Weak)	Chain not great
Maudu' (Fabricated)	It contradicts confirmed *hadith*

---

[23] See http://www.islamic-awareness.org/Hadith/Ulum/hadsciences.html. This site helpfully explains the different categories.

Two further categories look at the <u>chain</u> (*isnad*) of reporters. If the chain of transmitters is broken, or has only one or two paths of transmission at some points, then it is more doubtful.

3. The strength or number of people in the chain at each level.

Mutawatir (Consecutive)	Multiple narrators at each level, more than can be counted	
Had (Isolated)	A countable number of narrators at any point in the chain. This grouping is further divided into:	
	Mash'hur (Famous)	More than 2 narrators at each level
	Aziz (Strong)	Only 2 narrators at a point in the chain
	Gharib (Rare)	Only 1 narrator at a point in the chain

4. Another category evaluates the continuity of the chain back to its source.

Musnad (Supported)	From a well-known Companion
Muttasil (Continuous)	A continuous chain back to a Companion or successor
Mursal (Hurried)	Gap in the chain between Muhammad and a successor
Munqati' (Broken)	A gap between the successor and the last narrator
Mu'adal (Perplexing)	The narrator misses a number of consecutive links
Mu'allaq (Hanging)	The chain is not cited

5. A further category evaluates both the <u>reporter and the content</u> of the *hadith*.

Ziadatu Thiqah (Sound)	The reporter is known to be trustworthy
Munkar (Denounced)	A weak reporter, and the content is against other *hadith*
Mudras (Interpolated)	Words have been added by the narrator

Even weak *ahadith* that are unreliable with regard to its origins or transmitters, can be justified on the grounds that they encourage pious or moral behaviour. Sabah Mahmood describes a woman teacher making use of a weak *hadith*:

> Prophet said to Ali, if he recited Surat *al-Ikhlas* three times before going to sleep, it was as if he had recited the whole Qur'an. ... (but the sheikh says this is a weak *hadith*) ... "But since in all the *ahadith* there is goodness, we should abide by them.

So even if it's a weak *hadith*, there is good in it because it calls upon us to recite the Qur'an."[24]

The preceding categories are the approved basis on which women or men may challenge *hadith* behind the customs and edicts that shape their lives. Fatima Mernissi carefully investigated the *hadith* on women in leadership:

> Narrated Abu Bakra: During the battle of Al-Jamal, Allah benefited me with a Word (I heard from the Prophet). When the Prophet heard the news that the people of the Persia had made the daughter of Khosrau their Queen (ruler), he said, "Never will succeed such a nation as makes a woman their ruler."[25]

She explores the circumstances in which Abu Bakra is reported to have narrated this *hadith*, and the integrity of his daily behaviour, to suggest that its influence has been overweighted (using category two above: Trustworthiness of the reporter). However, engaging with the science of authentication is a complex task, requiring access to the commentators on the *hadith* collections and the circumstances in which they were transmitted. Mernissi comments that:

> "Going through the religious literature is no small task. First of all, one is overwhelmed by the number of volumes, and one immediately understands why the average Muslim can never know as much as an imam. ... Now, without a very good commentary a non-expert will have difficulty reading a religious text of the ninth century. ...The vastness of the task and the rather limited reading time is enough to discourage most researchers."[26]

Such detailed access to and scrutiny of sources is not possible for most people. *Hadith* can have a strong influence in a community independent of how authentic they are assessed to be. So, women are finding alternative means to question troublesome *hadith*. A Middle Eastern *shaykhah* modelled ways to question the application or authority of *hadith* on the common *hadith* describing women as being the majority in hell. She explained to me that its textual context referred to women who cursed frequently and were ungrateful to their husbands; women who didn't have those characteristics didn't need to worry. On the description of women as "deficient in intelligence and religion," she commented that some didn't accept it as a valid *hadith,* which was her understanding. She argued this (about a well-authenticated *hadith*) on the grounds that it was contrary to Muhammad's own example, because he took advice from his wives, which he wouldn't have done if all women lacked intelligence and religion. This was supported by the example of when Muhammad's troops rebelled against him over the conditions of the truce of Hudaibiya and refused to obey his order to

---

[24] Mahmood 2005:94, 97.

[25] Al-Bukhari: Book #88, *Hadith* #219.

[26] Mernissi 1998:113–4. See Chapter 18 on Women in Society.

offer sacrifices. He told Umm Salamah what had happened and she advised him to offer sacrifice himself, whereupon his Companions rushed to follow his example.[27] She also quoted the *hadith* where Muhammad is said to have told people to take half their religion from Aisha (this little redhead).[28]

But if the *hadith* was accepted as authoritative, she suggested that there were three possible interpretations:

- The Prophet was referring to a particular group of women in a particular context.
- He was saying that women had incomplete mind and religion, but were still smarter than men.
- While both men and women had both mind and affection, you could say that men were lacking with regard to affection, as they were more guided by the mind. Conversely, women were lacking with regard to the mind as they were guided more by affection. For example, if as women we were guided only by our minds, we wouldn't embark on all the effort and labour of having and raising children. Another argument against this *hadith* is that as both men and women receive education now, it can no longer be said that women are deficient in intelligence and the knowledge of religion. Hence the situation has changed, and the original text no longer applies.

Being 'deficient in religion,' is also often taught as a mercy from God in lightening the religious load on women when they were carrying so many other loads in their work with children, house and other responsibilities; their monthly period absolves them from having to carry out the religious duties also. The *shaykhah* preferred to reinterpret the injunction against praying and fasting during menstruation as God's mercy, rather than indicating women's deficiency:

> Now fasting and *salah* are tiring and exhausting and the woman during her monthly period loses a lot of her blood and her time; and fasting and even *salah* becomes extra exhausting, and so she isn't ready to pray and the blood which issues from her is unclean. But this matter is to do with worshipping God, so during her menstruation she doesn't pray.[29]

However, while some may regard this taboo as a mercy, others are more sceptical! One woman notes:

> "I have little interest in what an all-male body of scholars has to say about my monthly cycle and what invalidates my prayer. That the scholars were all men and issued rulings from a deeply male experience (that, too, a very specific sort of male

---

[27] See Sahih Bukhari Book#50, *Hadith* #891.
[28] As noted above, this *hadith* is not supported.
[29] Dale 2016:136.

experience – based on class, region, age, etc.) needs to stop being ignored in the mainstream."[30]

Taken together, *hadith* play a strong role in shaping the practice of Islam and the daily lives of Muslim women and men. Given the extent and variety of *hadith*, there is a developed science around their authentication. However, the significant influence of *hadith* in the daily lives of women and men operates at a popular level, almost independent of the carefully developed criteria.

Islam is a religion of orthopraxis – right practice rather than orthodoxy – right doctrine. In fact, there can be considerable flexibility in what people believe so long as they do the right things.[31] Hence the emphasis on the *hadith* as guiding every aspect of life and the practice of faith in minute detail. If we are to compare Jesus and the Qur'an, we recognise that there are some similarities between an understanding of the *hadith* with the Bible, which tells us about Jesus' words and actions (John 21:25), and the activity of God through history and people. Recognising the power of *hadith* in shaping people's lives can give us confidence in the power of telling Bible stories, which demonstrate God's faithfulness in the lives of women and men – in particular, Jesus' attention to women and care for their needs in daily life and faith. It can be tempting to claim Christianity as a faith of orthodoxy, affirming the right doctrine. While we recognise the importance of right understanding and belief, God's self-revelation in the incarnation of Jesus Messiah reminds us that Christianity is primarily about a faithful relationship with God.

- Ask a Muslim friend about any common *hadith* she knows. Which does she esteem more? Are there some about women that she knows? Which does she find more challenging? Or encouraging?
- Which *hadith* are more important in shaping the lives of women in the community around you? Which are most quoted? Why? How supported are they according to the criteria of authentication?
- Often topics which are mentioned in the Qur'an are expanded and amplified in different ways in the *hadith*. You might like to use one of the internet search engines[32] to do a search on a given theme to see how it is described in the Qur'an and in the *hadith*. Examples of possible topics could be Muhammad, Jesus, Prayer, Fasting, Women, Pilgrimage, Cleanliness or Purity, Alms. Notice how the topic is treated in the two different sources.

---

[30] https://orbala.wordpress.com/2016/07/01/menstruation-ramadan-and-the-muslim-woman-beyond-the-whole-its-a-break-from-prayerfasting/.
[31] The five pillars/foundational practices of Islam include saying the creed (there is no god but God, and Muhammad is the Messenger of God), praying *salah* five times a day, fasting the month of Ramadan, giving the set percentage of income, and making the pilgrimage to Mecca at the set time, if they are able to.
[32] Possibilities include Searchtruth.com, https://www.searchquran.com, and there are others.

4. Patterns of Prayer

Through the upstairs hall, the women's section of a Middle Eastern mosque, comes the sound of a youthful male voice sounding the call to prayer. Women in the hall rise and walk through to the balcony, form quickly into ranks and wait silently. Numbers of women appear now from inside rooms off the hall – the last few pass through almost at a run. No curtain offers a barrier here between the balcony and the men's space below: there is just a railing.

'*Allahu akbar*' (God is great) – and they bend at the waist.
Rise, kneel and bow their head to the ground, sit up, bow, sit up.
Stand, bend, rise, kneel and bow, sit up, bow, sit up.

The voice croons the '*Salam 'alaykum wa rahmat Allah wa barakat*' (Peace and the mercy of God be with you) and the kneeling women look to their right and then their left shoulders.

While the five times of *salah* prayer are not detailed in the Qur'an, there are references to daily patterns of prayer:

Establish prayer at the decline of the sun [from its meridian] until the darkness of the night and [also] the Qur'an of dawn. Indeed, the recitation of dawn is ever witnessed. *Al-Isra'* 17:78 (Sahih International)[1]

---

[1] See also *al-Baqarah* 2:43, 238; *al-Nisa* 4:103; *Hud* 11:114; *al-Rum* 30:17; *Qaf* 50:39.

The *hadith* offer more details of prayer times, and other pious duties of Islam, such as:

Narrated Talha bin 'Ubaidullah: A man from Najd with unkempt hair came to Allah's Apostle and we heard his loud voice but could not understand what he was saying, till he came near and then we came to know that he was asking about Islam. Allah's Apostle said, "You have to offer prayers perfectly five times in a day and night (24 hours)." The man asked, "Is there any more (praying)?" Allah's Apostle replied, "No, but if you want to offer the Nawafil prayers (you can)." Allah's Apostle further said to him: "You have to observe fasts during the month of Ramadan." The man asked, "Is there any more fasting?" Allah's Apostle replied, "No, but if you want to observe the Nawafil fasts (you can.)" Then Allah's Apostle further said to him, "You have to pay the Zakat (obligatory charity)." The man asked, "Is there anything other than the Zakat for me to pay?" Allah's Apostle replied, "No, unless you want to give alms of your own." And then that man retreated saying, "By Allah! I will neither do less nor more than this." Allah's Apostle said, "If what he said is true, then he will be successful (i.e., he will be granted Paradise)."[2]

Once 'Umar bin' Abdul 'Aziz delayed the prayer and 'Urwa bin Az-Zubair went to him and said, "Once in 'Iraq, Al-Mughira bin Shu'ba delayed his prayers and Abi Mas'ud Al-Ansari went to him and said, 'O Mughira! What is this? Don't you know that once Gabriel came and offered the prayer (Fajr prayer) and Allah's Messenger (ﷺ) prayed too, then he prayed again (Zuhr prayer) and so did Allah's Apostle and again he prayed ('Asr prayers and Allah's Messenger (ﷺ) did the same; again he prayed (Maghrib-prayer) and so did Allah's Messenger (ﷺ) and again prayed ('Isha prayer) and so did Allah's Apostle and (Gabriel) said, "I was ordered to do so (to demonstrate the prayers prescribed to you) Allah's Messenger (ﷺ) at the stated times of the prayers?" Urwa replied, "Bashir bin Abi Mas'ud narrated like this on the authority of his father." Urwa added, "Aisha told me that Allah's Messenger (ﷺ) used to pray 'Asr prayer when the sunshine was still inside her residence" (during the early time of 'Asr).[3]

Patterns of prayer tell us something fundamental about how those who pray see the connection between themselves and God. People's descriptions of prayer offer a window into how they view God and humanity: it is a glimpse into the heart of faith. While many textbooks talk about God in Islam as fundamentally unknowable, surprising numbers of Muslim women around the world talk of God in terms of relationship and their desire to be close to God, to sense God's nearness, of feeling when they pray "as if we were between the hands of God."

Most of the discussion of prayer in Islam is around *salah* (better known in some places as *namuz*), the five times of daily ritual prayer mandated for all Muslims. But because of restrictions of purity, women do not have as much

---

[2] Al-Bukhari Book #2, *Hadith* #44.
[3] al-Bukhari https://sunnah.com/bukhari/9#!

access to God through *salah* as men. Other forms of prayer can also be important in approaching God. In this chapter we explore different forms of prayer and their place in the lives of women, including the three overlapping areas of *salah*, *du'a* and *dhikr*. We look at the place of women in Sufism, the mystical apprehension of God in Islam.

Salah

Salah (formal liturgical prayer) five times a day is one of the five duties of Islam for all Muhammad's followers.[4] With set actions (standing, bowing, kneeling, prostrating), set words to be recited in Arabic at set times, it is the basis of Muslim prayer, earning points of merit towards the afterlife. The pray-er needs to be in a state of ritual purity, through ritual washing (*wudu'*) or complete immersion in water (*ghusl*).[5]

The steps and order of *wudu'* are carefully prescribed:

- Say (silently) your intention to pray, and say '*Bismillah*' ('In the name of God').
- Wash hands to wrists, three times.
- Rinse mouth and nostrils out, each three times.
- Wash the whole face three times.
- Wash the arms to the elbow three times.
- Wipe the whole head once.
- Wipe the ears.
- Wash both feet to the ankles three times.

The appointed times of *salah*, marked by the muezzin's call and beginning before dawn, give rhythm to each day as they stretch and contract with the seasons through the daylight hours. A *shaykhah* described them to me:

Fajr (sunrise) Dawn prayer begins when the sun begins to rise, and finishes when the sun is risen.

Dhuhr (midday)

Asr (afternoon) When a shadow is about twice the length of the object and it lasts until sunset.

Maghrib (sunset) From the going down of the sun, lasting as long as there is still a red glow or red line in the sky.

Isha (night) When the sun is completely gone.

Originally based around the movements of the sun, now the times are regulated and displayed on electronic devices in mosques and homes around the world for the observant faithful. Each prayer call signals the beginning for the next prayer time: if the *salah* has not been completed by the end of the allotted

---

[4] A well-known tradition tells of Muhammad's night journey to heaven, and of his going back and forwards between Allah and Moses multiple times until the required times of daily prayer for all Muslims were reduced from 50 to 5. See Appendix 2.

[5] See the chapter on Purity.

period, then it can no longer be said, and the merits gained through that performance of *salah* have been missed.

Salah consists of set actions with set words: yet there is also flexibility within its performance. For those travelling, *dhuhr* and *asr* can be combined, and also *maghrib* and *isha* prayers, bringing the required number to three.[6] And for the devout there is also the *tahujjud* night prayer, ideally prayed between midnight and *fajr*. At each prayer time, the obligatory (*fard*) *raka*[7] are required, and the recommended (*sunnah*) is strongly suggested, following Muhammad's example. And then there is the optional (*nafil*) for those who want to linger. The table shows the number of *raka* prescribed for each *salah*.

No. of *raka*	*Fajr*	*Dhuhr*	*Asr*	*Maghrib*	*Isha*
Fard	2	4	4	3	4
Sunnah	2 before	4 before, 2 after	2 or 4 before	2 after	4 before, 2 after
Nafil		2 after		2 after	4 after

The phrases recited for each action include passages from the Qur'an and prescribed prayers.[8]

The act of *salah* is mandated five times daily for our Muslim sisters and brothers. Even if not everyone can manage all five every day, the call to prayer is a constant invitation to stop and be mindful of God. In Muslim countries, the muezzin call punctuates the daily hours, a recurring auditory evocation of the summons to prayer. *Salah* finds its way without drama into everyday life. Whether preparing a meal, working at an office desk, or having a cup of tea with a neighbour, the Muslim pauses to perform *salah*, and then returns seamlessly to the kitchen or conversation.

The image of Muslims standing, bowing, prostrating is familiar to us, either together in rhythmic lines, or the solitary worshipper making the office or sidewalk into a place of prayer, as in Kenneth Cragg's evocative description:

---

[6] Also, for a woman who is experiencing continual bleeding beyond normal menstruation: Narrated Aisha, Ummul Mu'minin: A woman had a prolonged flow of blood in the time of the Apostle of Allah (peace be upon him). She was commanded to advance the afternoon prayer and delay the noon prayer, and to take a bath for them only once; and to delay the sunset prayer and advance the night prayer and to take a bath only once for them; and to take a bath separately for the dawn prayer. I (Shu'bah) asked AbdurRahman: (Is it) from the Prophet (peace be upon him)? I do not report to you anything except from the Prophet (peace be upon him) (Al-Bukhari: Book #1, *Hadith* #0294).

[7] Each prescribed sequence of standing, bowing, standing, prostrating, kneeling, prostrating and kneeling, with the accompanying words.

[8] For details, https://whenwomenspeak.net/article/vol-7-no-1-november-2020-salah/.

...everyone's prayer mat is a portable mosque and wherever they choose to spread it they can find their *Qiblah*[9] and worship God. ... Nevertheless, the noon prayer on Fridays is to be said as far as possible in the place of corporate prayer.[10]

But here Cragg writes only about Muslim men. Khattab begins her book for Muslim women by noting that:

In Islam, religious duties are to be performed by men and women alike. All Muslims, whether male or female, are required to pray five times daily, to fast in Ramadan, ... Having said that, however, there are some differences in the ways in which men and women are to go about performing these acts of worship, which sisters need to be aware of.[11]

What are some of these differences? Women who are menstruating (about a quarter of every month) are not able to pray *salah* (or to fast or hold and read the Qur'an), until the flow has ceased and they can purify themselves again. Requirements of modesty constrain place as well as time for women, who cannot turn public places into prayer spaces with the same freedom as men. Women are encouraged to pray at home rather than in the mosque:[12] when they do go to the mosque they pray in a separate space or behind the men.[13] Even if there is a women's space in the mosque, it is often taken up by the men for the corporate Friday prayer.[14] Worship offered in the mosque gains more merit. Saqib assures us, "wherever a Muslim might be he can offer his *(sic) salah* but the reward of a *salah* offered in a mosque is far greater than that offered in an ordinary place." Yaya Emerick quotes it as twenty-five times better.[15] However, home is the preferred space for women's *salah* prayers within Islam.

As the primary models of faith for children in their earliest years, women have a crucial role as purveyors of faith to the next generation. Going to visit my Muslim neighbour one day, I knocked on her door and she opened it, dressed in the all-covering prayer skirt and top – they were always kept beside the door to pull on quickly for modest covering in case a man was at the door. As we sat and talked together while we drank sweet Arabic coffee, her young son took up the prayer clothes and pulled out the prayer mat, in a play imitation of what he saw

---

[9] Direction of prayer, towards the Ka'aba in Mecca.
[10] Cragg 1985, p.99.
[11] Khattab 1994:1.
[12] It was narrated from 'Abd-Allaah ibn Mas'ood that the Prophet (peace and blessings of Allah be upon him) said: "A woman's prayer in her room is better than her prayer in her courtyard, and her prayer in her cabinet is better than her prayer in her room." (Narrated by Abu Dawood, 570; al-Tirmidhi, 1173.
[13] See Asra Nomani's account challenging this separation in *Standing Alone* (2006).
[14] Narrated Tariq ibn Shihab: The Prophet (peace be upon him) said: The Friday prayer in congregation is a necessary duty for every Muslim, with four exceptions; a slave, a woman, a boy, and a sick person. (Bukhari: Book #3, *Hadith* #1062).
[15] Saqib 1997:17; Emerick 1997:122.

his mother do so often. As women do *salah* at home or even in the women's section in the mosque, their children often climb and tumble over them as they pray.[16]

Beyond *salah*, there are also other forms of prayer, not part of the five pillars of Muslim duty, not mandatory (and not subject to the same restrictions of purity and language), that are also part of popular piety for Muslim women and men.

Dhikr

Women are sitting in silent concentration in an upper room of the mosque. It is quiet, just the sound of their lips moving in time with the prayer beads, and someone's periodic murmur. A few of the women are rocking, some passing the prayer beads through their fingers. There is slight movement as women adjust their position: one woman takes off her coat. The noises of cars, voices, come in from outside. Inside, the women are quiet, still, concentrating. The girl beside me is crying. She swallows, continues to pass the prayer beads through her fingers. A low voice begins to recite something, and others join in quietly for a little while. Then there is silence again, with only the muted sound of voices whispering to themselves, lips moving. A woman in the front row begins to sing quietly, a song of worship. "I knew you, O Lord, in my heart and my thoughts." She sings this a few times, and some other phrases. Others sit silently, some moving their lips, some rocking their bodies a little.

Dhikr is the practice of recollecting God through recitation and meditation. Associated originally with Sufism,[17] it is linked in popular thought with vigorous movement and chanting, particularly with the spinning Mevlevi *darawish*.[18] However, *dhikr* is now part of the practice of many Muslims who are not associated with Sufi movements. It is characterised by the use of prayer beads[19] to count the number of repetitions of phrases. And movement, whether the gentle

---

[16] Wensinck (1974: 495) describes Muhammad performing *salah* with Zainab's little daughter hanging around his neck, and on another occasion Muhammad's grandsons Hasan and Hussein jumping on his back as he prostrated. Although Wensinck suggests that Muslim jurisprudence since then has ruled that such antics invalidate the *salah,* Muhammad's example can be seen repeatedly re-enacted as women do *salah.*

[17] Mystic form of Islam, seeking the apprehension of God through recitation of God's name or characteristics. Sufism offered the devotee a sense of union with God. It also offered a pattern of social life in socio-religious cults, which afforded some security against uncertainty, and changes in state authorities. Sufism tended to compromise with local forms, enabling the spread of Islam through popular practices more quickly in India, Central Asia, Turkey and Africa. However, the preeminent Muslim theologian al-Ghazali (1058–1111) claimed Sufism as a legitimate expression of Islam, in his book *The Revival of the Religious Sciences* (*'ihya' 'ulum al-din*).

[18] Or 'whirling dervishes' as they are often known in the western world.

[19] Counting (in multiples of eleven) on the joints of one's fingers, or mechanical counters, or counting off dried beans, can also be used.

passing of beads through the fingers, or more intense swaying or spinning, helps to focus the mind on what is being recited. As a mystical practice outside the five pillars, *dhikr* has always had its critics within Islam. *Dhikr* and the use of prayer beads are opposed by some Muslims as an innovation, and therefore heretical.[20] But those who practise *dhikr* point back to Muhammad meditating in a cave, and to Qu'ranic verses.[21] The most quoted verse is *Al-Baqarah* 2:152 with its promise: "So remember Me, I will remember you." Padwick notes on this verse: "In all the devotional comments and prayers based on the promise, the meaning hovers between 'remembrance' and 'mention.'"[22]

Dhikr is most often verbal recitation,[23] with *dhikr* phrases drawn from the Qur'an, *hadith* and other sources to draw the reciter to reflect on God's names and nature. Sometimes the recitation can include extended songs by the leader, or lively chants led by a chorus, often accompanied with a frame drum. Alliteration, rhythm and rhyme are used, drawing on the formative impact of music on people's minds and lives.[24] Whether repeated phrases, or actual songs or choruses (*tarnim* or *anashid*), *dhikr* draws deeply on the formative effect of music, with rhyme and rhythm, on people's minds and lives. *Dhikr* is also closely linked with the phrases and sentiments of *salah* (formal) daily prayer.[25]

For Muslim women, more restricted by purity requirements from pious activities such as *salah* and fasting, *dhikr* can offer a way to access God and his power for daily life. For some women in the mosque movement, *dhikr* is an

---

[20] One writer comments poignantly that: "'Salafis' accuse us of deviation and heresy because we sit and recite *dhikr* – loud or silently ... Some of them object because it is loud and they claim it should be silent; others object because it is silent and they claim it should be loud; others object because it is in a group and it should be individual; others because they claim our emphasis on *dhikr* is excessive and we should raise funds or study or hold conferences or make jihad instead; others object because some people are affected by the *dhikr* so as to sway or move this way or that instead of sitting still, so they want everyone to sit absolutely still; others because we sometimes perform *dhikr* in dim surroundings rather than in a glaring light; others yet object to reciting the name ALLAH by itself and claim it is an innovation, so that we should only say: YA Allah. Finally, they also accuse us of innovation and misguidance because we use *dhikr* beads which we carry in our hands." http://sunnah.org/ibadaat/dhikrtable.htm

[21] Some verses refer to the coming of Gabriel (*An-Najm* 53:1–18; *At-Takwir* 81:19–25) and Muhammad's night journey (*Al-Kahf* 17:1). Other verses suggest a mystical consciousness of God (*Al-Baqarah* 2:115, 186; *Al-Taubah* 9:123; *Al-'Ankabut* 29:20; *Qaf* 50:16), and especially the famous verse of light (*Al-Nur* 24:35). The word *dhikr* appears often in the Qur'an (such as *Al-Ma'idah* 5:91; *Al-Jum'ah* 62:9; *Al-A'la* 87:15 and, more particularly, *Al-Baqarah* 2:200; *Al-'imran* 3:41; *Al-A'araf* 7:205; *Al-Muzzammil* 72:17).

[22] Padwick 1961:16.

[23] *Dhikr lisani* (*dhikr* of the tongue). There is also silent *dhikr*, referred to as *dhirk qalbi* (*dhikr* of the heart).

[24] https://whenwomenspeak.net/blog/tune-the-song-of-our-hearts-to-the-music-of-creation/.

[25] For a more detailed discussion, see Dale 2016:180–201.

essential part of preparation before lectures, allowing them to put aside the preoccupations of home, family and work, in order to focus and take in the teaching. As in oral recitation of the Qur'anic text, in *dhikr* the reader's mind is stilled and quietened.

Du'a

Before the mosque lecture, the women have joined in *dhikr* together. Now women shift in position, leaning forward slightly, hands together, palms up. The *shaykhah* leads in the *du'a*. There are about five minutes of petition for Muslims throughout the world, for our sisters in Iraq, in Palestine. She asks God to heal us, our land, our society. Don't cut us off from your service. God, purify us from our sins and trespasses. The women join in with 'Amin' after each petition. The *shaykhah* finishes by saying, 'The *Fatiha*,'[26] and the women murmur it quietly with her. At the end, a number of them wipe their faces with their hands, bringing the flow of blessing (*baraka*) from what they have recited back on themselves.

Du'a (supplicatory prayer) is a deep river of pious practice that runs through the daily life of all Muslims. It is less constrained by the restrictions of purity and modesty, and by language. It is often characterised by hands held up together, palms facing the pray-er: and at the end of prayer, the person praying may make a gesture of wiping the face, in order to bring the power of the recited phrases (particularly the name of God) back onto the worshipper. *Du'a* can be set phrases or spontaneous, group or individual, in Arabic or in the heart language of the speaker.

Small books of *du'a* prayer can be found throughout the Muslim world, in bookshops and mosques, with set prayers to be recited. Situational rather than specific, they include the recommended phrases to be said when getting out of bed or before sleeping, when stepping into or out of the toilet, when hearing a dog bark or seeing the first dates of the season or getting into a car, for example. The prayers are often written in Arabic and transliterated in the local script as well as translated, to enable them to be said in Arabic.

Du'a is usually prayed after *salah* (or *dhikr*). When *du'a* takes place in a group, people join in with *"amin, amin!'"* after the leader prays each supplication. Some situations make it more powerful or efficacious, such as praying in places associated with power, or particular phrases at particular times. My neighbours would sometimes tell me that praying a particular phrase for a set number of repetitions each evening or morning on a given month would bring a benefit such as the forgiveness of sins. The Night of Vigil[27] in Ramadan is believed to be a time when all prayers are answered.

---

[26] The first chapter of the Qur'an: its recitation seals or sanctifies occasions.
[27] This is believed to be when the Qur'an descended from the 7th heaven into the lowest (1st heaven), whence it was then revealed piece by piece to Muhammad. It is one of the

But *du'a* can also be prayed anywhere, by anyone, expressing the heart longings of the person praying. It includes invocations for rewards in the next life, but is perhaps even more important for seeking power and protection for the needs of this life. While observing guidelines of purity and language (saying *du'a* in Arabic) may be viewed as making the prayer more effective, both *dhikr* and *du'a* are accessible to Muslims anywhere, any time. Hence, they have an important place in the lives and practices of Muslim women, who must find a way to access divine power to fulfil their responsibilities for family harmony and welfare, amid the restrictions of bodily purity which are so weighted against them. Group *dhikr* and *du'a* is often concluded by reciting the *Fatihah* – the first chapter of the Qur'an.

Similar phrases and themes can characterise *salah, dhikr* and *du'a*. They overlap rather than being three distinct modes of prayer, which together are part of the devotional life of Muslim women and men.

Women in Sufism

The importance of prayer for women, of seeking a connection with God, can be seen in how Sufism has always been a fertile place for women within Islam, offering a way to access God. Some famous examples include:

Rabia of Bosra (717–801), one of the well-known early Sufi mystics. She is reputed famously to have gone through the streets with a flaming torch and a bucket of water, saying that the torch was to burn down paradise, and the bucket to put out the flames of hell, so that we would love God for Himself alone, not from fear of hell or for the reward of paradise. Rabia wasn't an isolated example. Sha'wana (d.792) of Persia, was known for her beautiful voice, and her devotion to God, characterised by constant weeping. She used to say, "The eyes, prevented from beholding the Beloved, and yet desirous of looking at Him, cannot be fit for that vision without weeping." Nafisa (d.208/824), descendant of Muhammad, born in Mecca, brought up in Medina, lived in Egypt with her husband. Imam Shafi'i (who founded the Shafi'i school of jurisprudence) used to meet Nafisa for discussion and prayer, especially during Ramadan. When he was ill, he would ask for her prayers, and when he died, he asked that Nafisa perform the funeral prayers for him. Because she was so constantly fasting in worship, she was too weak to go to him, so his body was brought to her house for her to perform the prayers. Halima of Damascus (mid-ninth century), also a descendant of Muhammad, taught another Rabia, bint Ismail of Syria (d. c.850) to whom this verse is attributed:

A Beloved unlike all others:

---

last ten odd nights of Ramadan (21st, 23rd, 25th, 27th or 29th, starting with sunset the night before), with most people focusing on the 27th. It is also known as the 'Night of Power'.

He alone has touched my heart.
And although absent from sight and touch,
He is ever present in my heart.[28]

Fatima (d.223/838) was one of a number of prominent women Sufis from Nishapur (modern-day Iran). The shaykh Dhu an-Nun said of her, "I have never seen anyone more excellent than a woman I saw in Mecca who is called Fatima of Nishapur. She used to discourse wonderfully on matters pertaining to the meaning of the Qur'an." She died on pilgrimage. There were some well-known Sufi sisters in Baghdad, including Zubda and Mudgha, sisters of Bishr al-Hafi (d.226/840); and Abda and Amina, near Damascus, sisters of Abu Sulayman (d. 215/830). In the tenth century, Al-Sulami wrote a book with 231 entries on women Sufis. Women functioned as formal directors in the early period. Unayda (early 10th century) is reported to have had 500 male and female students. They also had less formal roles as mentors and preachers. Early Sufis would gather for religious discussion and to do *dhikr* (reciting the names or attributes of God in order to focus on Him more fully). They emphasised love for God, together with purity, abstinence and piety, seeking to gain *tawhid* – oneness with God – gained through a *tariqa* (pathway), together with *tawakkul* – reliance on God.

Ibn al-'Arabi (1165–1240), a controversial Sufi teacher, was influenced by women teachers, and is notable for the amorous imagery with which he describes love for God in his poetry. Ibn al-'Arabi was convinced that women could reach the highest ranks in the hierarchy of the saints, and chose women as fourteen of the fifteen individuals to whom he gave the *khirqa:* the patched frock of the dervishes.[29] Fatima bint al-Muthanna of Seville said of herself that she was 'Ibn al-'Arabi's spiritual mother. Ibn al-'Arabi was also influenced by other women, including Zaynab al-Qaliyya. He described her: "She was of those devoted to the Book of God, the foremost ascetic of her day. ... When she sat down to practice invocation [of the Name of God] she would rise into the air from the ground to a height of thirty cubits; when she had finished, she would descend again. I accompanied her from Mecca to Jerusalem and I have never seen anyone more strict in observing the times of prayer than she. She was one of the most intelligent people of her time."[30] The famous poet and mystic Rumi (1207–1273) mentions Sufi women holding meetings in their homes to which he was invited. Helminski comments:

> There have often been Mevlevi shaykhas (female teachers) who have guided both women and men. Mevlana (Rumi) himself had many female disciples, and women were also encouraged to participate in sema, the musical whirling ceremony of the

---

[28] Schimmel 2003:38.
[29] Schimmel 2003:47.
[30] Ibn 'Arabi, *Sufis of Anadalusia*:154-55, in Helminski 2003:74.

Mevlevis. (Women usually had their own semas, but sometimes performed semas together with men.)[31]

There were women's sufi convents in Mecca, Medina, Baghdad, Syria and Cairo as early as the 12th century. Women who were directresses of convents would preach, lead the women in prayer, and teach them in wisdom.[32] In North Africa, wealthy women endowed women's refuges (*ribaat*) as homes for single women, usually widows or divorcees. These refuges were also associated with religious practices and teaching. Sabra describes how:

> ... not only the patrons and beneficiaries but also the administrators, or *shaykhas*, were women. The *shaykha* was charged with the responsibility of leading the women in the *ribaat* in prayer and *dhikr*, and with giving them lessons in Islamic law. ... Although some of the women who lived in these institutions were impoverished, others came from elite families and chose to live out their final years in pious poverty.[33]

Umm Abdullah lived with her husband in Tirmidh on the Oxus River (bordering Afghanistan, Tajikistan and Turkestan. In his autobiography, her husband, at-Tiridhi, writes of his wife's dreams which contained mystical messages for him: "Now my wife kept dreaming about me, dream after dream, always at dawn. It was as if she, or the dreams, were messengers for me."[34]

By the 12th and 13th centuries, the more formalised Sufi orders were developing. These were characterised by the use of *dhikr*, or *wird* (litanies), and prayer beads, along with music, dancing and body movement to contribute to an ecstatic state. Saints' tombs and relics became venerated and places of pilgrimage. Entry to the Sufi order was through initiation ceremonies, and blessing was transmitted through the leader,[35] who had total authority over the disciple. "Thou shalt be in the hands of thy Shaykh like a dead body in the hands of its cleanser."[36] As Sufi orders grew more structured, women were usually connected through their husbands or brothers, with only occasionally more formal teaching roles. However, many of the orders also had women's circles that were (and continue to be) led by women. Some suggest that perhaps a quarter of the participants involved in these orders were women.

Women continue to be involved in Sufi orders today, in Muslim countries and among Muslim women in the western world also. Helinski mentions the Naqshabandi, Chishti, Bektashi and Mehlevi orders among those with women

---

[31] Helminski 2003:xxiv.
[32] Schimmel 2003:49.
[33] Sabra 2007:491; also Schimmel 2003:48-9; Ahmed 1992:110.
[34] Helminski 2003:64.
[35] *Shaykh, pir/murshid* in Persia, India or *muqaddam* in North Africa.
[36] Rahman 1979:154.

leaders as well as participants.[37] North African Sufi groups where women are involved include the Tijanni, Qadiri, Rahmani, Isawi and Nasiri, among others. Women make pilgrimage to the tombs of saints (both female and male saints) seeking blessing or healing, and perform *dhikr*s there or in their own homes, in places such as Chechnya and Dagestan.

Some elements of Sufi orders have been taken up into the *da'wa* movements that are part of contemporary piety for many Muslim women.[38]

The Bible, Christians and Prayer

When we just use the one word 'prayer', our Muslim friends usually interpret it as *salah*. But in fact, the spontaneous prayer regularly practised by many western Christians is closer to a Muslim understanding of *du'a*. When we read the Bible, we find a wide variety of different words used to describe prayer and ways of praying. Patterns of prayer in Judaism or among Orthodox Christians, may also help us understand some elements of what prayer means for our Muslim friends (and may also enrich our own prayer practice).

We can find similar patterns to formal liturgical *salah*, including praying aloud and using set prayers: prayer that is both physical and communal. People offer murmur prayer or recite scripture aloud, both in community and as individuals pray in their own homes.[39] Jesus himself would have recited the set Jewish prayers three times daily. The Psalms, through offering each of us words to respond individually to God and our circumstances, have become the prayer book for Jewish and Christian communities. The Lord's Prayer is foundational to Christian prayer (particularly to Orthodox Christians). Physically articulating, speaking, singing or chanting prayer and scripture aloud can help to impress the meaning into us.

The physical position of those praying can express their prayers. I have seen Orthodox Christians as they repeatedly stand and bow during the Easter vigil, expressing their worship of Jesus through their bodies as well as their words. In his book on discipleship, C.S. Lewis famously had the senior demon write to the junior demon: "At the very least, (Christians) can be persuaded that the bodily position makes no difference to their prayers; for they constantly forget, what you must always remember, that they are animals and that whatever their bodies do affects their souls."[40] Young western Christians, seeking to live out the reality

---

[37] https://sufism.org/sufism/writings-on-sufism/women-and-sufism-by-camille-adams-helminski-2.
[38] See Chapter 2, and the description of women Islamist movements.
[39] Psalm 1:2 describes the righteous man who 'murmurs (God's teaching) day and night' and Robert Altar comments that the verb (*hagah*) in that psalm "means to make a low muttering sound, which is what one does with a text in a culture where there is no silent reading. By extension … it has the sense of 'to meditate'." Alter 2019:27.
[40] *Screwtape Letters,* C.S. Lewis, Letter IV.

of their relationship in prayer to God among their Muslim friends, began to use kneeling and prostrating as part of their prayers, and found themselves encountering God as sovereign, almighty, in a way they had not experienced before.

Prayer can be oriented in particular time and space. Many Orthodox Christians face towards the east as they pray, where the direction of the rising sun points us towards our focus on the risen Son. For Jewish, early Christian and monastic communities, the day is structured around prayer times with the intervals between prayer times extending and contracting as the daylight hours extend and contract through the seasons of the year. When prayer times mark the passing of the hours, prayer is allowed to interrupt the passage of daily life.

We pray, not just as individuals, but as members of a community of faith. Orthodox Christians join with others to pray if they are together; if they are at home, the common time and words unite them with the wider community.[41] Each time we pray '*Our* Father' we are reminded that we pray as part of a wider community, not just on our own. As we pray as part of a community, we are strengthened and upheld by the wider community: as we spend time consciously in God's presence, we ourselves are transformed.

The primary characteristic of Christian prayer is that it is our response to God's initiative (it is not to gain merit, nor is it manipulative), and it is in the name of Jesus. As we join in prayer with believers from different cultures, our own practice and understanding can be enlarged to respond more fully to what God has done for us in Jesus Messiah.

The activities we see in *dhikr,* being mindful of God, meditating on Him, and memorising and reciting God's Word, are activities deeply rooted in ancient Judeo-Christian practice. And as in Muslim *du'a* we recognise the possibility of God who is present to, and who may intervene in, every part of our lives as we seek Him. In Jesus we meet someone who was always accessible to those who came to him for help, available with healing power for both women and men, no matter how socially peripheral they were: an old hunchback, a defiled and anaemic woman, a foreigner with a devil-possessed daughter, a spurned woman from his people's adversaries.[42] While women's voices can be seen as unsafe, part of their *awrah*,[43] in the Messiah, God honours and dignifies the voices of women by his attentiveness and response to their *du'a*.

The history of Sufism, as well as acknowledging Muslim women's desire to find closeness to God, reminds us of the importance of offering women opportunities to gather together in groups as women (as well as with men), for practical teaching on faith, and for structured prayer, worship and meditation on

---

[41] The famous painting of *The Angelus* shows two peasants pausing in the field to pray the prayer of the Angelus, marked by the ringing of the church's bell for prayer and the end of the day's work.

[42] Lk 13:10ff, Lk 8:43ff, Mark 7:24ff, Jn 4.

[43] See chapter 5 on Shame and Honour, Embodied Shame, and chapter 16 on Modesty.

the Word. It also brings into focus the significance of the relationship between learner and teacher, within the wider women's group to which they belong. This pattern of teaching in the context of people's everyday life issues, of relationship between teacher and learner, and of community, with group worship and prayer, is a way of discipleship that reflects and builds on the lives and environments of Muslim women. And it echoes Gospel patterns, modelled by the Messiah who taught women and men.

Muslim women around the world talk of God in relational terms, seeking nearness to God. We can tell stories of God who answers the prayers of all who call to him, and listens and responds also to women: who heard and responded to the heart-felt petitions of Hagar, destitute with no means of caring for her son; of Hannah, longing for a child of her own; of widows who had lost their only sons.[44] When we are with our friends we can also pray for them. It is often through our prayers that they sense God's closeness and power, the intimacy that God invites us into, and the intimacy and power for which they seek.

- What do you know of the prayer habits of your Muslim friends? What kinds of prayer activities do you observe in their lives?
- What Sufi groups exist or have existed in your area? What is the involvement of women in these groups?
- What do they think is happening between them and God when they pray? What are they doing? What is God doing?
- What opportunities do you have to pray for them, when you are with them? In what forms might you express your prayer?
- What stories can you tell from the Bible and from your own life of how God hears and responds to our prayers?

---

[44] Gen 21:14ff, 1 Sam 1:9ff: and 1 Ki 17:17ff, 2 Ki 4:17ff, Luke 7:11ff.

5. Honour and Shame

We are settling into a new town, and our upstairs neighbour has become our guide in the community. We mention to him the name of a family that has been friendly, and his face changes. "Don't make friends with them!" he cautions us. "Their women are too loud …" He leaves unspoken further information, the details of what had happened to that family to bring them a place of shame in the community, shame that would stick like physical contagion to anyone who was friends with them.

As an immigrant in a western country, Eman finds her husband is getting increasingly violent. To go to the police for help is too shameful. At length, a woman who has befriended her is able to help her escape with her two children to a women's refuge, and then to get her own home. But having left her husband, Eman is now disgraced in the eyes of the wider community of migrants from her country. Her only friends are a couple of other women who had also left their husbands, and one or two local western women.

A *hadith* sheds light on the power of shame in many Muslim cultures, and its place in women's conduct:

Narrated Abu Mus'ud: The Prophet said, "One of the sayings of the prophets which the people have got is, 'If you do not feel ashamed, then do whatever you like.'"[1]

---

[1] Al-Bukhari, Book #56, *Hadith* # 690. 691.

Being ashamed is linked to the word for shame, *haya'*. As well as shame, it carries the meaning of diffidence, shyness, modesty.[2] It is sometimes translated as 'positive shame', a term I have only heard in relation to women.[3] The theme of shame and honour has gained increasing attention in the last decade. Much missiological writing on shame and honour[4] describes men, whose experience is centred around ways of gaining honour. In contrast, for women, a significant theme of their daily lives is the avoidance of shame. Lila Abu-Lughod suggests that *"men's honor tends to take the form of valor and independence whereas women's honor takes the form of modesty, which can be defined as voluntary deference to social superiors and the sexual propriety that is one aspect of this deference."*[5] In many societies, the notion of honour encodes shame with femaleness.

Muslim societies are generally collectivist and relationship-based.[6] Such communities then involve the social dynamics of shame and honour: shame carries the meaning of broken relationships. The mechanisms of public shame and honour govern people's behaviour and morality. Children are not taught about appropriate conduct through wrong and right: rather, morality is enforced through sanctioning what brings shame. Both honour and shame are relational, constructed publicly between people, rather than intrinsic to individuals. Honour is grounded by the group publicly recognising that the honourable person is a valuable member of that group – someone who behaves honourably, embodying the values that they esteem. Honour may be ascribed (by birth or family connections,[7] or bestowed by someone in authority) or acquired (through demonstrating valued traits such as courage, generosity or piety, or excelling in language such as poetry or challenge–response verbal duels).[8]

Shame is acquired through a person behaving in ways that are against group norms of behaviour, or losing face before someone significant. Whereas public praise can be life-giving, public shaming can be deadly. An expression such as, "You're free," in English affirms the value of individual initiative and action. However, in the language of a collectivist culture, it may suggest that the person has absolutely no regard for other people and the community, but is

---

[2] See also Chapter 16 on Modesty and the Veil.

[3] See Richard and James' good discussion of this. 2020:174–189.

[4] Cultures are popularly described Shame–Honour, Guilt–Innocence or Fear–Power. These tropes can be found in all societies. They have different expressions, and different degrees of social significance, according to each culture.

[5] Abu-Lughod 2005:494.

[6] See further discussion on this in Chapter 11. Also, Hofstede on Collectivism: https://geerthofstede.com/culture-geert-hofstede-gert-jan-hofstede/6d-model-of-national-culture/.

[7] See the emphasis in the Bible on genealogies.

[8] See, for example, the verbal jousting recorded in the NT between Jesus and the Pharisees.
Before the Gulf war broke out, poets from the rival Arab nations had been duelling across the airwaves for months. Australian sarcasm has some similar characteristics in how it functions.

contemptuous of the accepted values and behaviours that bind them together; hence a popular version of the *hadith* above: 'He who knows not shame does whatever he likes', regardless of community expectations. And shame is contagious: when a person does something shameful, it brings down the powerful miasma of public shame on their family and community. Shame may be enacted at rites of passage, when the community refuses to come together for events such as a wedding or, more importantly, to bury the dead. Its expression can look very different in different places. For example, in sub-Saharan Africa and the Pacific, the person who has caused the shame may need to leave the community for a time. In the Far East, the one who is shamed may kill themselves, whereas in Central Asia and the Middle East, the group may respond by killing the person who has shamed them.

Christopher Flanders helpfully suggests some differences between sin understood in terms of guilt and of shame, in his book, *About Face*.[9]

Dimension	Guilt	Shame
Focus of evaluation	I *did* that *thing.* What I *did* was wrong.	*I* did that horrible thing. *I* am bad, defective.
Nature of problem	Discrete acts	Global inadequacy, falling short
Self as agent	Required	Agency not required
Type of responsibility	Causal responsibility	Responsibility possible but not required
Type of solution	Solution involves retribution, repayment and/or punishment	Solution involves change of state of self
Experience	Feelings of self-condemnation, regret, remorse	Feelings of inadequacy, failure, compromised state, unworthiness, shrinking, and powerlessness.
Phenomenological reaction	Desire to confess, apologise, or repair	Impulse to hide, escape, or strike back
Focus of failure	Infraction or neglect of duties, responsibilities, and/or obligations; concern with wrong done	Failure: not measuring up; concern with the kind of person one is
Type of attribution	Localised/specific	Absolute/global
Possibly vicarious?	No	Yes
Relation with the self	Self disfigured by deed(s) but remains essentially the same; thinks of self as doer of the deed; focus on deed or omission	Self viewed as a piece with what has been done (i.e., fits well with what I am)
Degree of distress	Generally less painful than shame	Generally more painful than guilt

[9] Flanders 2011:61.

Language

How we use language has important dimensions in Shame–Honour cultures. Languages where the concept of honour is important usually include a number of words for honour and for shame, reflecting different dimensions of meaning within the culture.[10]

In a Shame–Honour community, affirmation is given by publicly telling others about a person, their virtuous actions or honourable behaviour, and what they are good at, rather than speaking personally and privately to the individual. If you want to verbally reward or praise someone, it is more powerful to publicly tell others how well they've done or how honourably they've behaved (particularly if the person is present), than to thank them quietly. Conversely, if you are negotiating in a situation of conflict, an appeal to shame and honour, and an affirmation that you are an honourable person may be better understood and effective than arguing in terms of right and wrong.

Gossip is the means of public shaming. To be gossiped about brings social ruin, regardless of whether the gossip is true or not. Musk describes how:

> "Social control … is essentially exercised by the dynamics of shaming, for it is through shame that honour is quickly eroded. Such a form of social control depends on everyone knowing everything about anyone. This is quite easily achieved in a community-oriented society. 'Gossip' becomes the public expression of the shaming mechanism. Saving face – preventing gossip – is all-important within such a culture. A single shame experience threatens to expose and damage the whole self, or family."[11]

Typically, in shame cultures, the passive voice is widely used, rather than claiming agency. For example, 'it was fated,' or 'it became broken.' The need to maintain harmony in relationships also means that collectivist cultures make more use of indirect speech. People prefer to say things indirectly rather than through direct confrontation (unless they are deliberately provoking a peer to a verbal duel). 'No' is rarely used, as it is disrespectful to disagree with the person you are addressing, whereas 'yes' has a variety of meanings, ranging from 'Yes, I can hear what you are saying,' (whether I agree with it or not), through to 'Yes, I absolutely agree/will do it.'

Edward Hall's description of 'high-context' and 'low-context' cultures is useful here. In a low-context culture, the content of what is being said is almost all in the actual verbal communication and the words that are used. In a high-context culture, the actual words are only a small part of the meaning of what is being communicated. Far more of the meaning is contained in the context – who is and isn't present; where it is being said; what else is happening at the time; the relationship between the people involved; and also the body language, gestures

---

[10] See further discussion at https://whenwomenspeak.net/article/vol-6-no-1-july-2020-shame-and-honour-blunt-instrument-or-useful-lens/.
[11] Musk, 2004, 92,3.

and, perhaps most importantly, in what *isn't* said. As with music, the silences or pause marks are as important to the final score as the musical notes. When my daughter was working for someone from an indirect speech culture, he told her what she was doing well. She thanked him, and kept working. A little later he told her again what she was doing well. Then she realised that she needed to think about the parts of her work that he wasn't commenting on, and improve them. She needed to hear the silences.

In an honour–shame culture, I learned never to give information about someone else, unless I knew that the person I was talking to was already aware of it. When talking about someone who has done something wrong, it is especially important to pick up the non-verbal cues, so that neither you nor the person you are talking with can be accused of telling others. Similarly, in an indirect speech culture, it is important to be gentle and less direct when confronting or criticising others. Showing raw emotions may be considered immature, so it is essential to be calm, especially when you are cross or upset. When I was in a local organisation where I had responsibility to oversee a number of literacy workers in different villages, I asked a colleague how he would deal with a worker who wasn't carrying out their responsibilities. I knew that public confrontation was wrong; would he take the person aside and talk to them privately, I asked. He smiled and said, "I would tell the group a story about a person in another context who wasn't doing their work. Then that individual would know that I know, and he would begin to do his work properly."

Women's Shame

Women can experience shame both socially and physically.[12]

Shame is ascribed proportionally more to women in many situations: even sometimes when they are the victims. Traditionally, women carried the responsibility when a couple were unable to have children (or only produce daughters instead of sons). Women bear shame after a divorce, even when it was the man who walked out of the marriage or instigated the divorce.[13] In New Testament times, it was almost impossible for women to initiate divorce: that

---

[12] Eating disorders have been linked with shame. External shame, feeling of less value than others, is associated with anorexia nervosa symptoms. Internal shame, believing that we have not lived up to our own standards or expectations, is connected with bulimia nervosa symptoms. While both women and men experience this, it is more prevalent in the female population. Troop NA, Allan S, Serpell L, Treasure JL, Shame in women with a history of eating disorders. 2008, https://www.ncbi.nlm.nih.gov/pubmed/18240123.

[13] See also http://www.dailymail.co.uk/news/article-2589429/How-divorce-carries-stigma-21st-century-Half-couples-split-say-feel-sense-shame-failure.html.

power belonged to men.[14] Yet the Samaritan woman[15] who had had five husbands is often described by commentators or preachers as an 'immoral woman', despite the fact that in her situation Jesus makes no mention of sin or forgiveness. A group of Muslim women, hearing the story, commented, "She was probably unable to have children, which is why they kept divorcing her."[16]

Around the world, women carry the responsibility for men's desire or violent actions. This is used to justify some of the required rules of women's covering in different cultures. In western countries also, by preferring language which describes a woman as 'hot' rather than talking about his own sexual desires, the man is placing the locus of control within the woman's body, thus absolving himself of responsibility for his sexual feelings – making it 'her fault' if he gets turned on, or if he doesn't. When desire is wrongly directed it can demean and distort human relationships, and by ascribing to women the responsibility for creating desire, shame becomes embedded in women as female bodies.[17]

Even in situations of violence such as rape, women are frequently told it was their fault because of how they dressed or behaved. Some commentators ascribe blame to Bathsheba for David's actions. However, the Bible attributes responsibility to David.[18] Similarly in domestic violence, it has often been assumed that the woman provoked the violence or was responsible for it. More frighteningly, women are encouraged to remain within the lived fear and shame of experiencing violence in the home – often even in the name of religion.[19]

Community honour, and in particular male honour, is closely linked to female sexual propriety. The proverb that *'a man's honour lies between the legs of a woman'* locates the honour of men, families, even of nations, in a woman's sexual chastity.[20] This contrasts with male sexuality, where the expression of virility can be valorised, or at least not sanctioned in the same way. The strength of this association governs not only what happens to women in sexual terms, but also shapes where and how women may move, what they wear, and what they can or cannot do. When shame is located in the woman's body, if she is thought to have transgressed community expectations for female behaviour, then family honour may be restored by killing her. The UNPF estimates that 5,000 women are killed each year in 'honour' killings (almost all in the Muslim world). Authors Nicholas Kristof and Sheryl WuDunn estimate that the real figures are

---

[14] Hence Jesus' warnings to those men who took too easy advantage of their power: Matthew 5:31–2.
[15] John 4.
[16] Limited life expectancy in those days means that she could also have been widowed, even more than once.
[17] So Tamar: 1 Samuel 13:1–20.
[18] 2 Samuel 12:1–14, 1 Kings 15:5, Matthew 1:6.
[19] This can occur from religious leaders within Christianity as well as Islam.
[20] This oft-quoted Arab proverb is also found in other countries, including Latin America. Hudson et al. 2012:8.

at least 6,000 annually.[21] Beyond honour killings, women are also victims of
'honour rapes'. Allying women's sexuality with shame allows the use of rape as
a weapon to disgrace the victim's family, clan or nation. Militias in many
countries have recognised that the most effective way to terrorise a civilian
population is to commit brutally savage rapes. Rape, formally recognised as a
'weapon of war' by the United Nations in 2008, is now so widely used that one
commander suggests "It has probably become more dangerous to be a woman
than a soldier in an armed conflict."[22] I heard of stories from Syrian women
refugees of unspeakably sadistic rape at the hands of occupying militias.
Mukhtar Bibi[23] in Pakistan has given other women courage by her refusal to
suicide after a gang rape 'punishment'[24] of her family, but rather being willing
to face public shame to see her rapists charged, and provide help for other
women.[25]

A related dimension of embodied shame is the injunction for Muslim women
to cover or hide their '*awrah.*' *Awrah* is 'that which must be concealed'.[26] While
it is often translated as 'nakedness,' in literary Arabic it means 'defectiveness,
faultiness, deficiency, imperfection; genitals; weakness.'[27] What constitutes
awrah differs according to different Muslim schools of law, and also context. It
includes some parts of men's bodies, but it is more extensive in relation to
women's bodies and can include their voices, and even their whole body form.
Gabriele vom Bruck comments about Yemeni women: "On attaining physical
maturity, a woman is said to be '*aurah*, literally, that which is indecent to reveal.
… One of the guiding principles of learning to be female is to conceal one facet
of identity – the surface of the body –from *non-mahram*[28] both at home and in
the street." In early twentieth-century Indonesia, Ahmad Dahlan (1868–1923)
asked his female students, "Aren't you ashamed of showing your *awra* to men?"
"It would be a deep embarrassment, Sir!" they replied. "Then why do you go to
male doctors when you are ill, even when you deliver your baby [and let them

---

[21] They suggest that many of the executions are disguised as accidents or suicides.
Kristor and WuDunn 2010:82.

[22] Kristor et al. 2010:84.

[23] https://www.theguardian.com/global-development/2016/jun/03/mukhtar-mai-
pakistani-woman-gang-rape-punishment-hope-belated-justice.

[24] https://www.theguardian.com/world/2005/mar/04/pakistan.declanwals

[25] https://www.theguardian.com/global-development/2016/jun/03/mukhtar-mai-
pakistani-woman-gang-rape-punishment-hope-belated-justice,
https://www.theguardian.com/world/2005/mar/04/pakistan.declanwalsh.

[26] See discussion in chapter 16.

[27] Wehr (1974). *Awrah* is a term used within Islam which denotes the intimate parts of
the body, for both men and women, which must be covered with clothing. Exposing the
awrah is unlawful in Islam and is regarded as sin. The exact definition of *awrah* varies
between different schools of Islamic thought. http://islamic-
dictionary.tumblr.com/post/5658467793/awrah-arabic-
%D8%B9%D9%88%D8%B1%D8%A9-is-a-term-used.

[28] Males who are not closely related, and are therefore potential marriage partners.

see your *awra*]? If you are ashamed, then continue studying and become doctors, so that we have female doctors for women."[29] Fedwa Malti-Douglas quotes Egyptian Nawal El-Saadawi's childhood "sensation that my body was '*awra*."[30] The English version of El-Saadawi's book translates it as "Shameful! Everything in me was shameful, and I was a child of just nine years old."[31] El-Saadawi grew up to study medicine and become a doctor, and eventually Director of the Ministry of Public Health in Egypt.

The enforced hiddenness of women's bodies reflects hierarchies of gender and power, which embed shame in women as bodies. This hiddenness allows abuse and violence to be perpetrated on them. When women's sexuality is understood as the property of men, then control or removal of the female body can be justified in order to prevent it causing shame. The embodiment of shame in women makes rape an effective weapon of warfare, which is used to demonstrate the shame and weakness of the enemy, and their failure to preserve or defend their honour in their women. Family or national weakness, with shame, is made female in form.

Embodied shame finds particular and universal female form in women's reproductive fluids, especially menstruation. Menstruation is both a specific and all-inclusive aspect of how shame may be embodied in the natural cycles of being women. Most women have either experienced, or fear, the intense shame associated with menstrual blood leaking and becoming evident to those around. Used sanitary objects evoke far more visceral disgust than something like a bloodstained bandage. Menstrual blood is one of the few substances around which there is widespread, almost universal taboo, with different meanings, around the world.[32] Beyond the personal dimension of associated shame, in Islam menstruation involves ritual uncleanness, and women being unable to participate fully in communal piety. Muslim women cannot perform the daily *salah* prayers, join in fasting, or hold or recite the Qur'an when they are menstruating. In many Muslim communities, they are not allowed to enter the mosque during this time.[33] While the categories of minor impurity in Islam are not gender-specific,[34] most of the categories of *major* impurity concern women: menstrual flow, emission of sexual fluid or sexual intercourse, and childbirth (for about six weeks).

---

[29] Aryanti 2012:83–92.
[30] Malti-Douglas 1991:121.
[31] El Saadawi 1988:10.
[32] Buckley and Gottlieb (Eds.)1988.
[33] However, there is also a *hadith* in support of menstruating women attending the mosque: 'A'ishah said: The Messenger of Allah once told me to get his mat from the *masjid* and I said, "I am menstruating!" He replied, "Your menses is not on your hands." (Sunan Abu Dawud vol.1, no. 261 and Sahih Muslim vol.1, no. 587)
[34] See Chapter 6 on Purity.

Honour and Shame in the Bible

David deSilva affirms that, "The culture of the first-century world was built on the foundational social values of honour and dishonour."[35] Christine Mallouhi, describing the Muslim community and relationships that she encountered in the Arab world, reflects on how its focus on family has helped her to understand more deeply both dimensions of the Fall in Genesis, and also Jesus' saving work for us:

> In biblical morality, practices such as gender separation show that behavioral controls exist in the social situation, not in the individual conscience. Group members control the situation with the full force of custom. The individual conscience is not an internalized norm. Parents teach children how to behave by using shame. They don't usually say, "Don't lie because it's wrong." It *is* considered wrong, but they are more likely to emphasise that it's "shameful". This reflects the same understanding of sin that Adam displays in the story of the Fall. He hid from God because he was ashamed and he was subsequently put out of the 'home'. In Arab society the consequences of sin are shaming your father and family, and being put out of the house. The only way you get back into the house is when an intermediary comes and takes you home to reconcile you with your father. The Gospel story directly speaks to these societies and the good news is that Christ took our blame *and* shame and is the intermediary taking us back to the Father's house.[36]

DeSilva suggests that we need to understand honour and shame in the NT in order to know "what the New Testament has to tell us about where our own personal value – our self-respect, our validation – comes from, about what gives us our worth. (The same word in Greek, *timē*, meant 'worth, price, value,' as well as 'honour'.)"[37] The understanding of sin or wrongdoing as global (see Flander's table on p. 63), due to personal defectiveness, rather than simply wrong acts, can reflect the biblical understanding of sin as something inherent in and due to our nature as sinful people. The language of being agents of reconciliation used in 2 Corinthians 5:18–21 speaks into a shame–honour understanding of sin as broken relationships. We are now new creatures (no longer fundamentally defective), appealing to people on behalf of the Messiah to be reconciled to God.

The place of women in New Testament society was "embedded in the identity and honour of some male (her father, if she is unmarried, her husband after she marries)."[38] Bruce Malina, in his book on the New Testament world, comments that "In the area of individual, concrete behavior, *honor and shame are gender specific.* ... individual males symbol honor and individual females symbol shame. ... feelings of 'shame' to reveal nakedness, modesty, shyness, blushing,

---

[35] deSilva 2000:23.
[36] Mallouhi 2004:133–4.
[37] deSilva 2000:86.
[38] deSilva 2000:34.

timidity, restraint, sexual exclusiveness – all this is positive shame (*sic*) for the female and makes her honorable."[39] This is similar to some Muslim cultures.

How, then, does the Bible suggest ways to deal with shame?

Shame causes us to want to hide, omit facts, lie or keep secrets, thinking that we will be rejected if people know the truth about us.[40] When dealing with people carrying shame, we may seek to talk with them secretly, wanting to protect them. However, in collectivist cultures, shame is about the public perception of people.[41] As Jesus deals with people ascribed shame by the community, he unmasks the harmful hiddenness of shame in a public statement of acceptance, forgiveness (when needed) and vindication, allowing the communal restoration of relationships and status. In a stunning reversal of ascribed honour and shame, he affirms the love and forgiveness of the sinful woman at Simon the Pharisee's house in front of everyone present. In the synagogue he calls the crippled woman over to where he is teaching everyone, and heals her. And the woman who is healed of the flow of blood, he again calls out in front of everyone to name her affliction – and healing.[42] Rather than colluding with shame's hiddenness, he exposes the situation for public vindication, exposing the shame and publicly restoring their status.

The Bible tells the tales of people who have been ascribed communal shame: but then continues with their stories and how God went on to use them in his purposes! Their stories include that of Rahab (a prostitute), Bathsheba (a victim of rape), and also Peter (denying his Lord). The Bible also tells the story of women who are abused (including the terrible accounts of the Levite's concubine, and David's daughter Tamar).[43] Unlike every other culture, it does not hide these stories or pretend that the women do not exist, even when the perpetrators are men of power. Instead, it reports them, naming the fact that abuse happens rather than excusing or downplaying it. In naming it, in how the story is told, the victims are vindicated. In the same way Mukhtar Bibi has challenged the public narrative of her rape (see above).

---

[39] Malina 2001:49. My italics.

[40] However, Travis Stewart suggests that: "When we allow ourselves to be known, especially at our worst, we experience true acceptance and intimacy. Shame is grounded on the belief that if we are fully known we will not be accepted. Only by being fully known and accepted will we defeat shame."
https://www.eatingdisorderhope.com/information/bulimia/shame-and-bulimia.

[41] The concept of shame embodied particularly in women finds communal form in some Muslim societies. Bennett and Davies describe how if a couple in Bugis South Sulawesi are involved in extramarital sexual relations, while both extended families are shamed, it is the woman and her extended family who are ascribed shame, and must defend their honour. The link between sexuality and shame is linguistic, with the word for genitals (*kemeluan*) coming from the root word for shame (*malu*). Davies 2015:29–50, 33.

[42] Luke 7:36–50, 13:10–17, 7:40–48.

[43] Jud 19:14–30; 2 Sam 13.

Women experience socially ascribed shame, and also shame embedded in their bodies. Redemption begins at the point of incarnation, where God all-powerful emptied himself of divinity to take on human form in Jesus Messiah. As the eternal Word took shape in human flesh, all flesh receives dignity and meaning. Dualisms of good and evil described in terms of flesh and spirit, or female and male, are disrupted. The very objections that some have to God Incarnate as One who had to sleep, eat, go to the toilet – these are precisely the point of incarnation in bodily form, as the divine Word lived among us, taking on our flesh, entering into and so transforming what is perceived as shameful within human systems.

But Jesus Messiah went beyond incarnation, even to the point of shameful death on a cross. Brittany Wilson examines how Jesus' life and death challenge masculine norms of his time, in particular, his crucifixion. She describes crucifixion as:

>...a form of execution that particularly 'unmanned' its victims because it involved a series of bodily invasions that disfigured and disempowered the one being crucified. ... victims could be beaten, flogged, tortured, and then stripped naked. ... Death itself was protracted and painful, with the powerless victim suffering bodily distortions and experiencing a loss of bodily control. ... In the ancient world, crucifixion equated to bodily violation in its most gruesome form.

Cicero described it as a "cruel and disgusting penalty," and claimed that "the very word 'cross' should be far removed not only from the person of a Roman citizen but from his thoughts, his eyes and his ears."[44] Jesus Messiah broke the 'manly' norms of his time, particularly through his publicly exposed, bodily-penetrated, most shameful death. It is then through that shame, suffering and death that he is now publicly vindicated in his resurrection, and highly exalted in his ascension, given the name above all names. He continues now to undergo suffering and physical abuse through his followers who are his body on earth.[45] Through Jesus' incarnation in flesh and his endurance of suffering and the public dishonour of the cross, those who follow him experience their own shame and violation taken by him,[46] as they are redeemed to share his exalted life above. In Jesus Messiah, we also are now reconciled with God and exalted, seated with him in the heavenly places.

What of the ascribed shame and ritual uncleanness that women experience through their body fluids, menstruation or childbirth? God's good news in Jesus brings a further dimension to impurity and shame as it is embodied in women, and in their reproductive fluids. In the Gospel of Luke we hear that the first announcement to the cosmos of God Omnipotent being present in human form occurs, not with a blast of trumpets from the Temple, but through a conversation

---

[44] Wilson 2015:202–3.
[45] Wilson 2015:240. Acts 8:4–5, 22:8, 26:9–11.
[46] Isaiah 53.

between two pregnant women.[47] However, for a Middle Eastern Muslim-background colleague of mine, in his deeply-felt cultural understanding of the ritual uncleanness and shame of women's bodily fluids, he could not accept that God had taken human form and been born in the messy uncleanness of a woman's womb and birth canal. For him, it was impossible that God could become incarnate in that dimension of impurity and shame. His reaction helps us appreciate how startling is the news of Divine Incarnation that we read in the Gospels. The Bible tells us that in Jesus Messiah, God took human flesh and was born – of a woman. This means that women's bodies, with all the ritual uncleanness of menstrual fertility and birth, are made the vehicle of God's incarnation. So then, through God's own inhabiting, women's bodies are made holy and honoured forever.

Shame is part of the lived experience of men and particularly women in the Muslim world. We see how shame and honour are part of biblical cultures also, and how Jesus helps us respond to shame ascribed and embodied in women.

- What are the different words for shame in the language(s) of the people to whom you are relating? What meanings do the different words carry? What are the words and meanings associated with honour?
- What brings shame? And how is reconciliation achieved (if it can be)?
- How is honour acquired for men or women in the cultural context in which you are living?
- How is an 'honourable woman' described?

---

[47] Luke 1:39–55. In the same way the news that God incarnate had defeated death forever and was raised to new life, was given first to and through women (Luke 24:1–11).

6. Purity and Defilement

It is past midnight, in a block of flats in a poor quarter of Cairo. A woman is calling out for her sister, who lives in an apartment above her, to come – she is having a miscarriage and she urgently needs help. Everyone in the building can hear her, but it seems an age before her sister appears at her door. Next day, the friend who lives next door asks the sister, "Why did you take so long? We could all hear her calling for help!" The sister explains, "I'd just had sex with my husband. If I'd gone out in that state and anything had happened to me, I wouldn't have got to Paradise." So in the middle of a winter night, she had gotten up, poured several buckets of cold water over herself – and then felt able to go down to help her sister.

I am visiting a Muslim friend in hospital. As we talk, I comment on the Qur'an on her bedside locker, and ask if she is reading it. "I can't," she tells me, "I've got my monthly period. And you? Do you read your Bible when you're menstruating/impure?!"

Hibbert describes standing outside the meeting place for a church of people of Muslim background:

… when a young (unmarried) man arrived late and came up to me. After greeting me, he whispered in my ear that he had just had sexual intercourse, but that he had not washed. Could he go into the meeting, he wondered. He did not think so, and I realised that in his mind the problem was not the illicit sex itself, but the fact that he had not washed to ritually remove the uncleanness before approaching God.[1]

Ritual purity is a major category of life and faith for Muslim women and men. Categories of purity and defilement affect daily life and pious practice, with particular impact on women. We can easily dismiss purity concerns as ritualistic. This chapter discusses the significance of purity, and suggests a response from the Bible. Rules of purity are not abrogated in the NT: rather they find fulfilment in Jesus.

The Qur'an has numerous verses emphasising the importance of purity. These three illuminate the accounts described above.

al-Taubah 9:108: Allah loves those who purify themselves.

al-Waqi'ah 56:79: The Qur'an: a Book well-guarded, which none can touch but the purified.

al-Baqarah 2:222: Allah loves the repentant and those who purify themselves.[2]

The *hadith* also abound with references to ablutions, or related terms such as purity or cleanliness, including:

* Cleanliness is half of faith.[3]
* The key to Paradise is prayer and key to prayer is purification.[4]
* If anyone performs the Wudu[5] completely, his sins will come out of his body, even coming out of his nails.[6]
* My people will be summoned on the day of resurrection with shining faces, hands and feet from the marks of ablution. If anyone of you can extend his brightness, let him do so.[7]

Verses and *hadith* on purity are developed into detailed rules of practice by scholars of jurisprudence (*fiqh*) enumerated in multiple books. And these rules determine whether or not Muslims can participate in routine acts of piety, gaining merit towards the hereafter, such as ritual prayer (*salah*), holding the Qur'an to read it, and fasting. Every Muslim is in a state of either defilement or ritual purity every moment of every day.

Ritual Purity

For people in western societies, talk of purity usually evokes the idea of moral purity, or perhaps cleanliness and antibacterial hand washing soap. From a context where purity is defined in terms of personal morality or hygiene, how

---

[1] Hibbert:2008.

[2] Other verses include *al-Ma'idah* 5:6, *al-Muddaththir* 74:4-5, and *al-A'la* 87:14-15.

[3] Book #002, *Hadith* #0432, Sahih Muslim.

[4] Chapter #1, *Hadith* #4, Book of Taharah, Sunan at-Tirmidhi:
http://ahadith.co.uk/chapter.php?cid=34.

[5] Pre-washing ablutions required before Muslim prayer.

[6] Book #002, *Hadith* #0476, Sahih Muslim.

[7] Book #4, *Hadith* #138, Sahih Bukhari.

can we understand ritual purity and its implications? I suggest we begin by listing the substances which, if we touched them, would make us want to wash immediately before doing anything else, and even after washing we would still feel somewhat 'unclean'. Typically, such lists include faecal matter or urine, pus, vomit, sexual discharge and blood – particularly menstrual blood. Reflecting on our own reactions helps to give some sense of the ways in which purity and defilement are commonly experienced as embodied or felt reality, rather than an issue understood in terms of moral purity or bacteria.[8]

We notice that the list includes a number of bodily substances – in other words, things that are normally *in* the body, and when we encounter them *outside* the body we experience them as dirty or defiling. Sometimes dead bodies (things that should be alive and now are not) are included: or slugs (which seem to cross the boundaries between animal, reptile and insect without neatly fitting into any of them). This sense of unease or disgust around displaced substances was neatly described by anthropologist Mary Douglas in her famous definition of 'dirt' as 'matter out of place'[9] – matter which contravenes the 'natural' order by existing in a different place or state to that in which it should belong.[10] The list includes many substances categorised as defiling within other religions, including Islam.

Purity and Defilement in Islam

The Arabic word for purity is *taharah* (also used as a synonym for circumcision), and its opposite is defilement, *najasah*. There are two categories of defilement, minor and major (*al-Ma'idah* 5:6).[11]

Minor defilement (*hadath*) is caused by the following activities:

- Passing wind, urine or faeces
- Vomiting
- Sleeping or losing consciousness (in which case some of the previous activities might occur without the person being aware of them)

---

[8] For discussion of existing unwritten purity codes in contemporary western society, see deSilva 2000:244–5 and Malina 2001:162–5.

[9] Douglas notes that such a definition "implies two conditions: a set of ordered relations and a contravention of that order. Dirt then, is never a unique, isolated event. Where there is dirt there is system. Dirt is the by-product of a systematic ordering and classification of matter, in so far as ordering involves rejecting inappropriate elements." (1966:36)

[10] In a later publication, Douglas discusses how the social body reflects how the physical body is perceived, so that a social system concerned with social boundaries implies a concern for bodily boundaries, requiring strong body control (1970:72, 78ff). The physical body then becomes a map for social organisation, for relationships and hierarchy within the wider social community.

[11] This verse (5:7 in some translations) describes first the washing (*wudu*) before *salah* prayer for minor defilement: and then the requirement for purification (*ghusl* – full washing) for those in a state of *janaba* (major defilement). It also details the *tayammum* cleaning with earth, if there is not water.

- Non-menstrual vaginal discharge, secretion from the penis
- Touching women[12]
- Emission of blood or pus from the body
- Touching one's sexual organs
- Touching anything that is unclean: this includes urine, faeces, semen, blood, vomit, pus, corpses; dogs and pigs; intoxicating drinks. For all Shi'ites, non-Muslims are unclean,[13] including People of the Book (*Al-Taubah* 9:28).[14]
- Kilinc (with others) adds 'Laughing aloud' to the list of defiling activities[15]

The person who becomes impure is prohibited from participation in ritual prayer, from touching the Qur'an[16] or going around the *Ka'ba* (sacred stone at Mecca); and requires ritual washing[17] (*wudu*) to regain a state of purity.[18] *Wudu* is required in order to do *salah*, or to go around the *Ka'ba*. And it is desirable to do it before touching or reciting the Qur'an, before *du'a* (supplication), before going to bed to sleep, before each of the five daily prayers, even if your purity has not been broken, and having intercourse with your spouse.

Major defilement (*janabah*) is incurred through
- Menstrual flow[19,]

---

[12] From *Al-Ma'idah* 5:6. The four sunni schools of law differ on this. Shafi'i agrees that just touching a woman breaks *wudu*. Maliki and Hanbali say that it is only if the touching is done with carnal intent: and the Hanafi school doesn't agree that it breaks *wudu*.

[13] Dehqani-Tafti describes his family's reaction after he became a Christian: "At home I was like one 'unclean', not allowed to eat with them from the same dish. Yahya (older brother) especially adopted a strange procedure to mark my 'uncleanliness'. When prayer-time came he would bundle 'clean' garments under his arm and ostentatiously go and change into them lest any contact of mine with him or his other clothes had contaminated him." (2000:37)

[14] Safran (2003) examines debates by Maliki scholars about whether Christians are polluting.
Some suggest that non-Muslims are banned from mosques (*al-Taubah* 9:17-18).

[15] Kilinc 2011:50.

[16] From *al-Waqi'ah* 56:78–79

[17] Washing hands, feet and face, and rinsing out the mouth, ears and nostrils before praying. This must be repeated before each time of *salah,* unless nothing has occurred to defile the individual since their last ablution. See preceding chapter on Patterns of Prayer for details of performing *wudu.*

[18] Douglas's (1966) understanding of pollution as derived fundamentally from boundary transgression ('dirt is matter out of place') has been challenged by recent writers as not being applicable in detail to Sunni purity laws: see Gauvain's discussion of Reinhart, Maghen and Katz's work (2005). However, al-Ghazali's [d.505/1111] explanation of the impurity of various body excretions supports Douglas's general theory.

[19] Qur'anic exegetes debate the place of Mary, mother of Jesus, and whether she had prophetic status. The purity given to her by God was exceptional, and al-Razi implicates this with "the necessary absence of menstruation in Mary which is also linked to her sinlessness." (Rippin 2007:268)

- Emission of sexual fluid
- Sexual intercourse
- Childbirth
- Post-birth bleeding

Any of these conditions preclude the person from *salah,* holding the Qur'an and circumambulating the *Ka'ba*, as with minor defilement; and also, from fasting. Some authorities hold that it also prohibits entering a mosque, and reciting the Qur'an. It requires a complete bath (*ghusl*) to restore purity. *Ghusl* is also recommended, but not mandatory, before entering Mecca for the *hajj* or minor pilgrimage (*'umrah*).

Dry ablution (*Tayammum*: washing with pure sand or dirt) is permissible when there is no access to water, to substitute for *wudu* or *ghusl*. (*Al-Nisa'* 4:43)

Muslim Women and Purity

I encountered the subject of ritual purity as a frequent part of Muslim women's discussions in domestic gatherings, sandwiched among recipes and household concerns, with its constant impact on their daily lives and religious practices.

While both men and women need to be pure in order to complete their religious duties, the conditions of purity apply differentially. Gauvain, discussing the egalitarian nature of Sunni Islamic purity, notes, "According to Sunni Islam, no human being is deemed purer than any other, and none – *with the arguable exception of women* – is isolated or disadvantaged in any way through purity strategies."[20] Of the causes of major defilement (listed above), four fifths (80%) apply to women,[21] and only two fifths (40%) to men. Hence, we may estimate that for at the very least a quarter of their lives, between about thirteen and sixty years of age (menarche to menopause), women are in a state of ritual pollution, and thus proscribed from participating in pious duties described above. And that is for women who are not engaged at all in sexual relations or childcare.[22] The

---

Menstruation is linked with defilement in many different cultural and religious contexts. Within Christianity today, in many eastern churches, menstruating women may not take communion or enter behind the iconostasis. Women in contemporary indigenous African churches also face role restrictions on the basis of ritual purity (Crumbley 2003). De Troyer et al (2003) discuss issues of bleeding and purity for women in Jewish and Christian traditions. Diamant's (1998) compelling narrative of Dinah's story deals with defilement and fertility in the context of the Genesis records. Other contributions on menstruation and pollution include Hoskins (2002) in Indonesia, Stewart & Strathem (2002) in Papua New Guinea, and Churchill (1996) among Southeastern Indians in the USA.

[20] Gauvain 2005:350, italics added.

[21] The impact of stringent rules of purity may be a partial explanation of the more prominent involvement of Muslim women in rites of life passage, where restrictions of purity are less applicable than they are to rites of intensification such as *salah* and Friday *khutbah* attendance.

[22] Reflecting on Muslim women in China, Jaschok and Shui write: "Women... are faced

daily activities of caring for young children involve contact with defiling substances.[23] Buitelaar notes that although "this only means that women are more often impure but certainly not inherently more impure than men, in practice women tend to be more strongly associated with impurity than men."[24]

Intricate details among the different schools of Islam, determined by medieval male scholars, determine women's practice of daily piety. *Hadith* collections include detailed sections on issues of impurity, as do collections of *fatwa,* and multiple *fiqh* classes. There is careful enumeration of the various *najasah,* and the kinds of water offering different degrees of purity. And for women, there are also scrupulous descriptions of what constitutes states of impurity and purity, particularly with regard to degree and colour of menstrual flow and other bodily emissions, detailed analysis of different conditions of discharge and what pious practices are permitted in each condition. The prohibition on pious practices during menstruation is linked to the notable *hadith* about women's deficiency in intelligence and religion:

> Narrated Abu Said Al-Khudri: Once Allah's Apostle went out to the Musalla (to offer the prayer) of 'Id-al-Adha or Al-Fitr prayer. Then he passed by the women and said, "O women! Give alms, as I have seen that the majority of the dwellers of Hell-fire were you (women)." They asked, "Why is it so, O Allah's Apostle?" He replied, "You curse frequently and are ungrateful to your husbands. I have not seen anyone more deficient in intelligence and religion than you. A cautious sensible man could be led astray by some of you." The women asked, "O Allah's Apostle! What is deficient in our intelligence and religion?" He said, "Is not the evidence of two women[25] equal to the witness of one man?" They replied in the affirmative. He said, "This is the deficiency in her intelligence. Isn't it true that a woman can neither pray nor fast during her menses?" The women replied in the affirmative. He said, "This is the deficiency in her religion."[26]

Al-Faisal links women's imputed deficiency with fertility:

> Women's deficiency lies in the fact that she becomes pregnant, gives birth and menstruates. This clearly means that motherhood is the cause of her deficiency! ... these writers have forgotten to tell us whether we should deduce from all this that

---

with an in-built contradiction: in order to be a good Muslim, they must be good wives and mothers. The Muslim's duty of increasing her religious knowledge to attain perfect faith, to attend to the daily duties of purification and praying, are in daily life at odds with her inability to reconcile time-consuming domestic duties with the time-consuming task of learning, ablution and prayer." (2000:28)

[23] The urine of a male child is also less impure than that of a female child: defilement is further gender-specific (Gauvain 2005: 354, Note 68).

[24] Buitelaar 2007:542; also Roded 2008:98–101.

[25] al-Baqarah 2:282.

[26] al-Bukhari, Book #6, *Hadith* #301; and Sahih-Muslim, Book #001, *Hadith* #0142.

the barren woman is more complete than the one that is fertile, and whether women who do not menstruate are more complete than the other women.[27]

Women have to determine whether they are in a state of impurity or not, according to the conditions and length of their *hayd* (menstruation), and other factors.[28] My neighbour in the Middle East described how she had taken a pill to avoid menstruating during Ramadan. However, its impact on her body was severe enough to dissuade her from doing it again. Like most Muslim women, she returned to not observing the fast during her menstrual period, and making up the missed days at another time of the year.[29] Devout women will wear make-up and nail polish only for special occasions, or when menstruating: as face make-up washes off with each ablution and must be reapplied; and nail polish is viewed as a barrier between the water and the person, preventing proper *wudu'*. Wynn comments, "Thus piety is constructed and enacted through bodily practices."[30]

There exists wide-ranging debate and disagreement around defining the finer details of *taharah* (purity) in traditional *fiqh* (jurisprudence),[31] so that some negotiation among different schools of opinion is possible on issues such as whether menstruating women can recite some of the Qur'an, and[32] attend the mosque.[33] *Shaykhah* Huda al-Habashi explained:

> The woman, when she is menstruating, some of the (theological) schools and sayings of the scholars prohibit her entering the *masjid* (mosque), but some others say she can enter for essentials. So for me, coming to learn is essential; for others, it's not so essential that they always come and they don't safeguard learning sessions or worry too much about them; such a person would say that she wouldn't come during her menses. But for those who are never absent and who safeguard and follow (the sessions) with us, for such a one you could say that coming to the mosque is essential. We don't say to the girls to come; neither do we tell them not to come: she needs to decide, it's her decision.[34]

---

[27] Al-Faisal 1995:232–3.

[28] Anwar 2006:27; Philips 1995.

[29] Fasting outside the month of Ramadan, without the community participation and support, is more challenging (Jansen 2007:274).

[30] Wynn 2007:271.

[31] Maghen, as a generally sympathetic expositor, notes the "internal inconsistency and tortuous abstruseness of *tahara* jurisprudence and the bewilderment it occasions even among its own exponents," leading us to join them in the conclusive phrase: "*wa-Allahu a'alam!*" – "and God knows best!" (1999:353-4).

[32] Philips cites al-Bukhari and Ibn Taymiya to support the position that a menstruating woman can recite a Qur'anic verse (1995:16-17).

[33] A commonly mentioned *Hadith* by 'Aisha in the literature in support of menstruating women attending the mosque is cited in Chapter 5 Honour and Shame, Women's Shame, note 171.

[34] See Mahmoud's discussion of how women in the *da'iya* movement in Egypt use the

A woman attending al-Habashi's lectures told me that coming to the mosque during one's menstrual period depended partly on the time and whether men were present or not, adding "some scholars say it is permitted and some say it isn't, so you choose what you think." Another teacher corrected her comment: "It doesn't depend on the time or on the presence of men except if she means that in the time of the Prophet there was no means to keep clean, but in our times we have more than one means to keep ourselves and the mosque clean."[35] This supports Maghen's reading of impurity derived through the actual *najasah* (unclean substance) coming in contact with the place or person.[36] In a contrary ruling, an Australian mosque requires that all women in visiting groups not enter the main (male) prayer space, rather than asking them individually whether or not they are menstruating.

Ritual purity shapes the lives of Muslim women, determining what pious practices they can carry out when. Access to female religious teachers offers women the chance to learn the intricacies of regulations around purity and defilement without embarrassment. Questions around details of bodily discharge are more easily discussed with other women. Ghina Hammoud, a *shaykhah* in Lebanon, told an interviewer:

> Sometimes the women have questions to do with menstruation, or inter-menstrual or post-natal bleeding, on the issue of blood or menses, and they are shy to ask men: and I have experience in this, apart from the *fiqh* books. I have had menses or post-natal bleeding, or been in a condition of *janabah,* and I can answer them, without shyness, more than a man. Men sometimes get a bit embarrassed.[37]

One of the benefits of the growth in female religious scholars and teachers is that other women can ask them about such personal details without diffidence about debating such details in public (mixed gender) space where they don't belong. Women religious teachers can discuss issues of women's intimate personal and family life, bringing them into the centre of women's teaching

---

'space of disagreement among Muslim jurists,' and her analysis of women's involvement in the process of debate and disagreement within the 'pedagogical space of *da'wa,*' around use of canonical sources (2005:88, 101–106). Also Pemberton 2007:276.

[35] Dale 2016:137.

[36] Maghen 1999:379–82.

[37] Her students agreed with her: "I want to say that it's really nice to listen to a *shaykhah*, because as a woman she feels like I do, she feels for me. A woman's emotions are different to a man's. A woman's composition is not like that of a man. God created each gender with specific composition and feeling. So there are intimate things to do with women that I can only ask a *shaykhah*, I'd be shy to ask a *shaykh*. This is the difference. I feel more comfortable asking her questions, for example, on your menses, on bleeding and childbirth, when to do *salah*, when to stop doing *salah*, the things to do with religion." (Maher 2010; also Minesaki 2012:396)

space.[38] In doing so, they are able to combine their knowledge of religious sources with their embodied understanding of daily life issues for contemporary Muslim women's lives, including intimate details pertaining to religious practice. In both conversation and physical space women are enabled: women's mosques in China commonly offered women space to do their full ablutions there.[39]

A quick response to these concerns is to suggest that ritual purity does not matter, only inner purity. However, a closer reading of the Bible suggests the centrality of purity, including ritual purity. This is worth taking the time to explore, because it is such a central concept for our Muslim friends.

Ritual Purity Concerns in the Bible

There are both areas of overlap and also significant differences[40] between codes of purity in Judaism and Islam. Chapters 11–15 in the book of Leviticus offer the most detailed description of purity rules in the Torah. The first half of chapter 11 deals with clean and unclean foods which the Israelites may or may not eat. The second half of chapter 11 (from verse 24) begins a lengthy discussion of conditions or substances that render the worshipper unclean. They include:

- Corpses (11: also Numbers 11:19–22)
- Childbirth (12)
- Skin eruptions (13)
- Spreading mould in clothing (13) or house walls (14)
- Penis discharge, and sexual intercourse (15)
- Menstruation or other vaginal bleeding (15)[41]

Purity is regained by washing or by offering the stipulated sacrifice, and may also include the lapse of time (unclean until evening or until the 8th day). While Levitical prescriptions may read strangely to western eyes through the lens of a post-enlightenment separation of the physical and spiritual worlds, they map more compellingly onto the worldview of Muslim and other non-western cultures, where issues of ritual purity remain central to daily life and interactions.

In both Judaism and Islam, emissions from the sexual organs are defiling. And the state of purity required to enter a mosque or hold /read the Qur'an may find parallel in passages such as Exodus 19:14–15, where ritual purity is required of

---

[38] Jaschok 2012:43; Le Renard 2012:125.
[39] Jaschok 2012:116.
[40] Gauvain 2005: 359.
[41] DeSilva comments that "Defilement and unholiness separated people from contact with the pure and whole God." So blemished or deformed people could not enter the sanctuary, and blemished or deformed animals could not be offered as a sacrifice to God. DeSilva suggests that defilement or pollution derive from conditions that show individuals' 'unwholeness': this includes skin diseases, bodily discharges and corpses. He cites a quote from Plato's 'Laws': "it is not right for either God or a good person to receive gifts from one who is polluted." (2000:248, 274, 248 note 12).

the community before the encounter with God that yields the Ten Commandments; and Isaiah 6:5–7, where the Prophet's lips must be purified in his vision of God's presence and sending.

Although the laws of clean and unclean animals (Lev 11:1–23: also, Deut 14:1–21) are usually grouped with the other laws of purity, it is notable that, unlike the rest of the ritual purity laws, transgression of these edicts does not include any process for purification. These food laws have to do with maintaining community boundaries, limiting table fellowship with non-Israelites (so Dan 1:8). They ensure that the Israelites will be a people separate from the peoples around them, separated to belong to God (Lev 20:25–6, see also 11:44–46). This is the daily life enacting of separateness or segregation, which is also embodied in (male) circumcision (Gen 17:10–14: 1 Maccabees 1:15).[42]

While eating unclean foods is forbidden in the Old Testament, this does not incur cleansing rituals of washing or sacrifice, suggesting a different dimension of uncleanness. Neither are substances from the alimentary canal (faeces, urine) included in substances that defile. Neither input nor output of food entail ritual purifying.

Gibson adduces archaeological evidence to suggest a preoccupation with purity among Jews in the early first century CE. He points to the unprecedented number of *miqwa'ot* (pools) to enable immersion for ritual purity, which were built in that time in the basements of private dwellings. He also argues that the Bethesda and Siloam Pools were built not to store rainwater for the city, but rather for the ritual purification needs of the tens of thousands of non-residents who would arrive in Jerusalem three times a year for the annual festivals (2009:64–80).

The same concern fills the pages of the New Testament. The Pharisees challenge Jesus and his disciples around questions of purity (Mt 15:2, 23:25ff, Mk 7:1–5, Lk 11:38f). Lepers are 'cleansed' rather than 'healed', reflecting the Torah definitions of uncleanness, and are sent to complete the purification ritual at the temple described in Leviticus (Mt 8:1–4, 10:8, 11:5, Mk 1:40ff, Lk 4:27, 5:12ff, 7:22, 13:11–14). 'Unclean spirits' is a synonym for 'evil spirits' or 'demons' (Mt 10:1, 12:43, Mk 1:23ff, 3:11, 6:7, 7:25, Lk 4:33, 36, 6:18, 9:42, 11:24, Acts 5:16, 8:7). The stories of the demoniac(s), Jairus's daughter and the woman with a flow of blood (Mt 8 & 9, Mk 5 and Lk 8), incorporate a number of categories of ritual uncleanness – unclean spirits, tombs, Gentile territory and pigs, vaginal bleeding and a dead body. So too the story of the Syrophoenician woman (Mt 15:22, Mk 7:24ff) combines together the defilement types of Gentiles, Gentile territory and unclean spirits. The centurion demonstrates his respect for Jesus and Jewish customs by not requiring him to enter the centurion's house (Mt 8:5ff, Lk 7:1ff). Other people who would have been unclean for observant Jews include Samaritans (Lk 10:25ff, John 4), tax

---

[42] Also deSilva 2000:257.

collectors and sinners (Mt 9:10ff, 11:19, Mk 1:15ff, Lk 19:7).[43] And the story of the Good Samaritan draws its tension further through issues of (seeming) corpses and priestly purity requirements (Lk 10:25ff, Lev 21:1– 6). John's Gospel shows the contemporary concern for purity in the description of the large containers of ablution water, which is turned to wine (Jn 2:5ff). Jesus washing the disciples' feet in sacrificial servanthood is a ritual of enacted purity that takes the place of the Communion meal described in the synoptic Gospels. And the discourse on the vine (Jn 15:1ff) talks in terms of us being pruned/cleaned (*kathairo*) through Jesus' word. John's description of the events of the crucifixion reflects Jewish concerns for purity, as Pilate comes out to see the Jewish leaders rather than having them defile themselves on the eve of the Passover festival in coming into see him (Jn 18:28–9, 38; 19:13): and the leaders don't want to leave the corpses hanging on the cross over the Sabbath (Jn 19:31).

Purity rituals are also described. At the beginning of life, the circumcision of John and of Jesus on the eighth day after their birth is a purification ritual, and Jesus' parents offer the required purification offering at the temple (Lk 1:59, 2:21: Lk 2:22–24 – see Lev 12).[44] Paul knows he is likely to find a Jewish worshipping community in Philippi beside the river, which gives easy access for ablutions[45] (Acts 16:13). And in Acts 21:21–26, we see Paul undertaking the rites of purification, and paying for others to do so. The New Testament writers continue to use the language of purity and defilement in describing the Messiah and what He has done. He is holy and undefiled (Heb 7:26); and Peter tells the crowd that God did not let his Holy One experience corruption (Acts 2:27, Ps 16:10). Salvation is described in terms of being sanctified/purified (Titus 2:14, 1 Pet 1:2, 1 Cor 6:11, Heb 9:13–14, 9:22, Lev 17:11, Heb 10:22).[46]

---

[43] DeYoung comments that "Some religious leaders of Jesus' day defined their 'congregation' by who was excluded from membership. There were long lists of those who could not meet the definition. Such lists included women, Samaritans, Gentiles, individuals with criminal records, anyone who was disabled or sick, tax collectors, and those considered 'sinners.' Also, those with certain occupations were not counted as worthy: camel drivers, sailors, herdsmen, weavers, tailors, barbers, butchers, physicians, business people, and many others. The only people who qualified were healthy males of pure Hebrew ancestry who held respectable jobs and followed all the laws of the religion." (2003:16)

[44] Commentators differ as to whether the intriguing 'their' purification in Luke 2:22 refers to Mary with Joseph, or Mary and Jesus. The combination of purity rituals in Lev 12 would suggest the latter reading.

[45] So many mosques also are built adjacent to rivers or canals.

[46] In the Torah, cultic and moral purity were linked. Jesus' response to the Pharisees' questions about purity challenged their man-made additions to the purity code of the Torah. At the same time, he affirmed a focus on purity defined more particularly in terms of moral attitudes and behaviour (Mt 15:10ff, and especially Mk 7:15–19). We see this also in the epistles, describing impurity in terms of moral unrighteousness (Rom 1:24, 6:19, 2 Cor 7:1, Gal 5:19, Eph 4:19, 5:5, Col 3:5, 1 Thes 4:7, Rev 21:27): and purity or cleansing likewise in ethical moral behaviour (2 Cor 6:6, Phil 1:10, 4:8, 1 Tim

There has been a tendency for western Christians, when confronted with ritual purity laws in Islam and other contexts, to discount them as insignificant and rescinded in the New Testament.[47] However, issues of purity and defilement were a major part of consciousness and conversation for the early church. A closer examination of New Testament teaching challenges the easy dismissal of ritual purity laws. The specific purity rules that Jesus countermanded are those rules ensuring separation between Israelites and others – the food laws of Leviticus 11:1–23. These are the regulations that, together with circumcision, were about maintaining the purity of the nation among the surrounding peoples, rather than ritual purity before God. Most significantly, these are the regulations that did not mandate a purification ritual if they were broken, suggesting that while they described substances as unclean for eating, they were not in the same category of defilement as those substances and conditions described in the subsequent text (Lev 11:24–15:33). Mt 15:10ff and Mk 7:14, then, are not to do with ritual purity and defilement as much as they are about food laws that ensure communal separation. We see the same issue in Peter's heavenly vision in Acts 10:9–16: the vision about clean and unclean food is Peter's preparation for his visit to a Gentile house (Acts 10:28), and the subsequent baptism of that household in the Holy Spirit and water, incorporating Gentiles into the nascent community of Christians.

The two most prominent issues that Paul returns to in his epistles are circumcision and food laws/table fellowship, issues that were at the heart of the unity of the new Body of Christ (Rom 14:14ff, 1 Cor 8:1ff, 10:25ff, Col 2:16ff, 1 Tim 4:3). The separation of Jewish people, embodied in circumcision and laws of clean and unclean food, was so deeply graven into Jewish thinking that it had to be dealt with again and again. So, despite Peter's vision, Paul had to challenge him later in Antioch with the essentialness of table fellowship (Gal 2:11ff). It is these purity markers of Jewish separation from Gentiles that have been broken down in Christ at the cross (Eph 2:11ff), initiating 'the Ephesians moment' of reconciliation between the two groups.[48]

4:12, 5:2, 2 Tim 2:21, 1 Pet 2:22).

[47] The description of the Leviticus purity chapters by one commentator is perhaps extreme, but not uncharacteristic of the response of many Bible students encountering Leviticus 11–15: "These chapters are of course very unattractive and in part decidedly repulsive. They are mainly of interest to the anthropologist and sociologist. ... (They are) meaningless and irrelevant..." (Davies 1962:120–121). DeSilva describes contemporary western thinking in his argument that the Christian separation of moral purity from ritual/cultic law is based on the fact that "Christians claimed the Old Testament to be authoritative, yet regarded a large portion of its legislation – the cultic law – to be irrelevant." (2000:255)

[48] Andrew Walls 2002:72–81. DeSilva (2000:296) argues that the concern in the Torah for defilement through disruptions of the physical body is paralleled in the New Testament in its concern for what disrupts relationships within the church as the Body of Christ (2 Cor 12:20–21, 2 Tim 2:21–23 are examples of lists of sins of the physical body and of relationships).

Ritual Purity through Christ Jesus

How, then, are we to understand the rest of the Torah purity code, its prohibitions and its requirements for ritual washing or sacrifice? (And by analogy, ritual purity codes in Islam.) Are they annulled in the New Testament? However, Jesus does not deal in annulment or abrogation of the Old Testament, but rather in fulfilment (Mt 5:17).

In Jesus, we see contagion reversed, and purity fulfilled. As he comes into contact with situations or substances that are defiling, we see that, rather than defilement being contagious, through Jesus, *purity* becomes contagious. He touches lepers and is not defiled, but the lepers are cleansed. He touches dead bodies and does not become unclean; the corpses come back to life. Encountering the holiness of God Incarnate, unclean spirits are cast out, and a bleeding woman is healed. Jesus sits with sinners and is not polluted, but sinners and Gentiles are invited into repentance and a life of faith and holiness. The New Testament is not a denial of ritual purity but a reversal of direction: impurity is not passed on to Jesus, but rather, purity is transmitted from him.[49]

The sacrificial system in the Torah finds its fulfilment in the sacrifice of Christ, once and for all. It has not been annulled but rather, completed. For once the sacrifice of Christ has been made, there is no need or place for any further sacrifice. In the same way the purity code in the Torah finds its fulfilment in Jesus. Entrance into God's community under the old covenant was through (male) circumcision, which was described in terms of purity. Entrance into God's community in the new covenant in Christ is through baptism. Again, a ritual of purity – a ritual of inclusion equally for women and men. In his death, Christ became unclean by being crucified, in order to purify us by his own blood (Heb 13:11–13, Dt 21:22f). So, as we are baptised into the blood of Christ's atoning death (Eph 5:26; Tit 2:14, Heb 1:3, 7–9, 7:26, 9:13–14, 10:19, 1 Pet 1:19, 1 Jn 1:7–9, Rev 7:14), ritual purity, with its requirements of washing and sacrifice, is completed. Once we have been baptised there is no need or place for any further purification ritual in order to approach God in prayer, in the gathering place of His community, or in receiving His Word. The purity requirements have been completely fulfilled – not by our acts of ritual purification, but by what Jesus has done.

Rom 8:1–2 encourages us that there is no condemnation for those who are in Christ Messiah, for the law of the Spirit of life in Jesus sets us free from the law of sin and death that bound us. When we read stories such as those in Mk 5 and Lk 8, dealing with unclean spirits, tombs, pigs, Gentiles, a bleeding woman and a dead body, they tell us of purity and defilement. If the epistle to the Romans tells us how we are set free from condemnation, these narratives tell us about

---

[49] We see a suggestion of holiness as contagious in the Old Testament in Ezekiel 44:19 and 46:20. A parallel may be the way in which the mission of Israel is primarily attractive or centripetal in the Old Testament, but the direction is reversed and the mission of the Church is increasingly outgoing or centrifugal in the New Testament.

how we are set free from defilement. As we hear them, we realise that whatever condition of defilement we are in – whether from what we have done, or from what others have done to us – however impure we feel, we can be absolutely assured that there is no defilement from which Jesus does not wholly purify and set us free.

Implications

Churches today tend to take two different positions on questions of ritual purity.

The Eastern Orthodox churches retain some tenets regarding ritual purity in relation to women. Menstruating women usually do not join in taking the Eucharist.[50] Either women generally or menstruating women in particular do not enter beyond the iconostasis to the inner area behind, where the consecrated Eucharist is contained. These churches continue to hold to a (albeit reduced) code of ritual purity. Women in some contemporary indigenous African and Asian churches also face restrictions on what they can do when menstruating.[51] In contemporary western churches ritual purity is generally excluded, with a focus entirely on moral purity. It is assumed and even taught that ritual pollution is unimportant and irrelevant.

Both positions underrate the presence and action of Jesus Messiah in regard to laws of ritual purity and pollution. Jesus is present and powerful now through the Holy Spirit, as in his incarnation, to reverse the contagious direction of defilement. And it is through the ritual washing of baptism into Jesus that the Christian is completely purified once and for all to participate in every act of piety.

'As a woman in Islam I was always *najas*'

I used to struggle a lot, I was always in doubt: 'Am I still clean to talk to God or not???' As a woman in Islam I was always *najas*, and only with *qosl* (full washing) could I wash away my *najasah* (uncleanness). During women's monthly period, no woman is allowed to pray as they are *najas*. And after that they have to do full *qosl* or otherwise they will be dirty and *najas* for the rest of the month…. You could touch something by accident, so you never know if you are still pure and clean to talk to your God and pray.[52]

How are we to respond to our Muslim friends in discussing concerns of ritual purity and its implications in daily life and pious practices? Suggesting that it is

---

[50] Some Middle Eastern Protestant women follow the same restrictions regarding the Lord's Supper.

[51] Crumbley 2003.

[52] A poignant description by a believer of Muslim background: https://whenwomenspeak.net/article/vol2-no1-april-2018-purity-whole-issue/, p.10.

irrelevant and only inner purity matters, does not address their deeply felt concerns. A deeper exploration of the Bible suggests that we can affirm with them that purity does matter profoundly in approaching God. The Good News is that as we come to Jesus Messiah, His purity is so contagious that we are purified, healed, given new life. In baptism into Jesus, we are so completely purified once and for all that we are always in a state of ritual purity, able to fast, to pray and to read Jesus' cleansing Word. Women need no longer be impure for most of their lives. Rather, they are purified and given absolute freedom to access God at any time and all the time, through the contagious purity of Jesus Messiah.

And this is Good News indeed.

- Ask your Muslim friends about the things that cause daily defilement. What does it prevent them from doing? What do they need to do to enter a state of purity again?
- How much of their time are they in a state of impurity? How much does it differ according to their age/activities?
- Ask them what rules they know around the whole area of purity, defilement and washing.
- Tell them the stories of Mark 5 in terms of Jesus' contagious purity: how do they react?

7. Power: Envy and Blessing

In the town where we are living, as we join in the seventh-day celebration for the new-born baby of our neighbour's relatives, the aunt takes a piece of paper and tears it into the rough shape of a person. She takes a pin and begins piercing the paper doll, "Against the eye of Ahmed; against the eye of Fatima; against the eye of Mariam…" and we hear our own names in the list. She is not ascribing evil intent to us, but rather protection for the baby from involuntary harm.

Walking along the road one day in a Middle Eastern rural town, I pass a woman sitting on the pavement, selling greens from her basket, her baby on her lap. I smile at the child. It's a hot day, and the woman raises the back of her hand to wipe her forehead. It could be just a gesture to wipe off the sweat and dust. But I know that she is using the palm of her hand as a protection to avert any potential evil that might come from me smiling at and admiring/envying her child.

My neighbour knocks on our door one day and asks if he can have one of the incense sticks I sometimes burn (there is often an odour from overflowing sewerage around our building). His baby daughter is ill, and he wants the incense to drive away any evil spirits. I give him the incense, and my husband and I go upstairs with him to their apartment. The little girl is lying there, pale and listless. On the shelf above are bottles of medicine from the pharmacy. A Qur'an is placed on her pillow, and blue beads and amulets are pinned onto the blanket. We read a story from the Gospels of Jesus healing, and pray for the little girl. A couple of days later she is well again, and playing once more with my own young daughter.

The Qur'an warns of the malevolent power of envy:

> Say: "I seek refuge with (Allah), the Lord of the daybreak,
> From the evil of the envier when he envies." (*Al-Falaq* 113:1,5)[1]

The same theme is visited in a number of *hadith*, such as:

> Narrated Ibn 'Abbas: The Prophet used to seek Refuge with Allah for Al-Hasan
> and Al-Husain and say: "Your forefather (i.e., Abraham) used to seek Refuge with
> Allah for Ishmael and Isaac by reciting the following: 'O Allah! I seek Refuge with
> Your Perfect Words from every devil and from poisonous pests and from every
> evil, harmful, envious eye.'"[2]

The daily *salah* prayers also begin with 'taking refuge'. Invoking God's name, it is a protective prayer in the uncertainties of daily life (whether in health, education and employment, communal relationships or wider politics), and especially in the face of surrounding spiritual forces and the impact of envy or the evil eye.

Women carry the primary responsibility for family harmony and health in the extended family in many cultures. When someone is sick, it is women who usually take time out to care for them. They are responsible for their children's success in school, and for household well-being. This is often in situations where the efficacy of health or educational systems can't be assumed, where there is no state social security available, and life can quickly become more precarious through war or natural disasters including floods, famine or earthquakes. The issues that are immediate for women may not be so much the cosmic questions about the meaning of life or the nature of good and evil. Rather, they can be questions about how to prevent their husband taking another wife, or how to ensure their children do well in school, or recover from sickness. How do they access the power needed to provide life's daily needs of food, clothes and shelter, especially in times of emergency or danger? Women in many communities around the world seek power to help negotiate their lives – to become pregnant, to help their children do well, or a husband's business or crop to flourish, when family members are sick. And they look for prophylactic means, whether objects, invocations, or rituals, to avert harm or danger in their lives and the lives of those for whom they are responsible.

The requirements of purity constrain Muslim women from being able to earn merits through pious rituals (*salah* prayer, fasting, reading the Qur'an) for much of their lives. Hence, we may find women more involved in practices that offer

---

[1] See also *al-Baqara* 2:67, *al-Nahl* 16:98, and *al-Nas* 114:1.
[2] al-Bukhari Book 55 #590. Other *hadith* include al-Bukhari Book 71 #634, 635, 636; Book 72 #784, 827: Sahih Muslim Book 001 #0425; Book 024 #5280: Abu-Dawud Book 1 #0036, Book 28 #3875, 3879: Malik's Muwatta Book 49 #49.12.39, Book 50 #50.1.1, 50.2.3, 50.2.4.

other access to spiritual power, to help them negotiate life and fulfil their responsibilities in the challenges life brings.

Many people perceive the world surrounding them as inhabited by visible and invisible forces that affect daily life. Particular individuals, places, objects or times may be seen as imbued with power. Humans feel the need to be able to access positive forces and avert negative or evil forces. People commonly seek to manipulate power through using words (recited or written), magic, objects such as protective charms or amulets, or rituals, in order to negotiate life and its needs. How do our Muslim friends understand the unseen world that surrounds them? We might ask them what objects or places they see as sources of power? What are the forces that they seek protection from, such as the evil eye, or bad spirits, or a curse, or bad luck or failure? What particular times or places are associated with danger or with positive power? And in what ways do people seek to control or manipulate the powers that surround them, to avert evil and attract good forces?

The framework below, including some examples, is useful to help us map people's cosmology, and understand how people see the forces that shape their lives.

		Personal Forces[3]	Impersonal Forces	
Unseen/supernatural	*High/ Cosmic*	Cosmic gods Angels, demons	Fate	**Other-worldly**
	Folk/ Magic[4]	Local gods, ancestors, jinn, ghosts	Amulets, *baraka*, astrological forces, sorcery, evil eye	**This-worldly**
Observable/ empirical	*Natural*	Human relationships	Folk/natural science	

A post-Enlightenment worldview is often characterised by a dualism between material and spiritual, the seen and the unseen worlds – the left-hand column in the table above. Westerners commonly draw a division between the seen and unseen world, the empirical and the supernatural. Most of our daily life is based on interaction with the empirical world. Our understanding of the unseen world focuses on the high or cosmic level, concerned with God, Satan, and questions related to the ultimate purpose of this life, and our destiny in the next. We are largely unaware or agnostic with regard to the middle level, unseen and this-worldly. Living with no conscious experience of the impact of these unseen

---

[3] Adapted from Hiebert et al. 2000:49.
[4] Paul Hiebert describes this unseen, this-worldly dimension helpfully in *The Flaw of the Excluded Middle*, 1994.

powers, westerners may be at a loss to know how to understand people for whom the active presence of such forces is part of daily life.

However, for many other peoples in the world, the division is between the forces of this world (both seen and unseen), and the other-worldly, cosmic forces, which are beyond our power to control or manipulate – the right-hand column. Particularly where so much of life is characterised by uncertainty or precariousness, this-worldly issues require engagement with the 'folk' unseen powers and principalities of this world which must be placated or manipulated, as much as with seen or empirical 'natural' factors. People may seek to manipulate both human relationships and natural science, and also spiritual realities, through rituals or objects of power. This can include 'personal' spiritual beings, such as angels and demons, as well as failure-biased and success-biased 'impersonal' powers.[5]

Failure-biased powers can include sorcery and witchcraft, envy and the evil eye. We often ask 'what' questions about things that happened – was an accident caused by over-worn tyres or a tired driver? What bacteria made someone sick? However, questions about envy or sorcery are usually more 'why' questions, questions of ultimate cause – why did that passing bacteria get inhaled by this child and not another? Why did the tyres blow as the bus was going around that corner? Or why did an oncoming car appear just at that moment?

Failure-biased Forces: Envy and the Evil Eye

The power of envy (or the evil eye) prevails in societies with an understanding of the world as a place of 'limited good' where people have restricted access to resources.[6] If resources are limited, then someone's good fortune (whether beauty, wealth or possessions), means that others will have less.[7] In large societies, individuals or groups can freely compete with one another for limited

---

[5] Douglas 1966:110–113.

[6] George Foster originally developed the theory of the 'image of limited good' in the context of small communal closed system societies who view "their social, economic and natural universes – their total environment – as one in which all of the desirable things in life such as land, wealth, health, friendship and love, manliness and honor, respect and status, power and influence, security and safety, exist in finite quantity and are always in short supply. ... If 'good' exists in limited amounts which cannot be expanded, and if the system is closed, it follows that an individual or a family can improve a position only at the expense of others." Foster 1965:296–8.

[7] This understanding of restricted resources is not limited to small peasant societies. A version of it is known as the 'zero-sum-game' in game theory and in economics. We can recognise the same worldview behind the competitive attitudes in companies and sometimes even Christian organisations, which talk of 'fishing in the same pond' for financial resources or recruits. If there are limited funds or recruits or students, then the gain of 'another' society or college will mean loss for 'ours'.
See further examples in Mark Wood's discussion of limited good mindsets in Euro-American thinking: http://honorshame.com/limited-good/, posted 9/12/2015.

resources. However, in smaller or more communal societies, such open competition is destructive of relationships and devastating to the social fabric. In such a context, where one person's good fortune is understood to mean that others will have less, failure forces can have the social impact of leveling. Sorcery or envy acts against the success of others, so that one person will not prosper at the expense of others. In many societies, young boys may be dressed as girls, with long hair, as a way of tricking and so protecting them from envious or evil spirits that could harm them. Admiring someone's new car or their child can draw attention to it, and so attract the notice of malevolent forces.

Envy is linked to sorcery in countries around the world, among wealthy and poor, highly-educated and illiterate, and its manifestation in the 'evil eye' or 'envious eye' is widespread. The 'evil eye' is an eye that is believed to be capable of harming or even killing living beings by looking at them, whether or not harm is intended by the owner of the eye. Belief in the evil eye has spread around the Mediterranean and beyond. Mediaeval English lists of herbs (and also contemporary Wiccan ones) include herbs for protection against the evil eye, such as anise, or carrying a bag of dried dill over the heart. Different societies have other means of protection: through the area once covered by the Persian Empire, burning a type of herb seed called *espand* or *esfand* on charcoal is seen as protective; and in South Asia people entering a home may be greeted with the acrid smell of fumes of chilli burned for protection. People may also seek safety by invoking the name of God, or reciting Qur'anic verses or having them painted or displayed in a home or on a vehicle. In many places the colour blue (or red in some regions) is believed to offer protection. I have been offered blue beads to wear when I was pregnant, or to pin on the clothes of a newborn child (pregnancy and childhood are seen as times of increased vulnerability to evil forces). Other protective objects include an object in the shape of an eye, or the palm of a hand, known as the *khamsa* (five, from the five fingers). The print of a hand dipped in the blood of a newly killed sheep can be used to safeguard a new car, house or pump.

John Elliott summarises the constellation of beliefs around the evil eye, noting "the remarkable cross-cultural and cross-generational consistency in the ideas and motifs associated with the Evil Eye and its aversion – from 3000 BCE to 600 CE", which has also continued "from the medieval period down to the modern era."[8] These are:

- The eye as active, able to project energy that can harm or destroy whatever its glance strikes.
- The evil eye activated by and conveying envy, miserliness, greed and other related negative emotions.

---

[8] Elliott 2017:157. Elliott's four-volume study demonstrates that practices related to the Evil Eye were widespread in ancient Egypt and Mesopotamia (Vol. 1) and in Greek and Roman society (Vol. 2): referred to in the Bible (Vol. 3). Belief in the evil eye continued to be active in the centuries following the establishment of the early Church (Vol. 4).

- It can be intentionally or unintentionally activated.
- Its victims particularly include children, birthing mothers, attractive youths, and those enjoying success in life, including in the domestic sphere, sport and battle.
- Those who are likely to possess the evil eye include widows, strangers, those with physical impairments or unusual eyes or features around the eyes.
- Defence against the impact of the evil eye can be through words, gestures, rituals and amulets.
- The evil eye is claimed to be responsible for sickness, misfortune, defeat in battle or sport, accidents, property loss and death.[9]

Success-biased Power: *Baraka*

Examples of success-biased powers include luck, and *baraka* (blessing).[10] These forces can also be voluntary or involuntary, recognised by their effects. For example, a saint's tomb may be discovered as a place of power when a healing is associated with it: as the report spreads, more people come for healing. These forces can operate in association with official religious authority – so a religious leader has power to exorcise and heal, or an official religious centre becomes a place of pilgrimage because of its power. Alternatively, they may function independently, such as when unlicensed or uneducated people (including women) can gain followers who testify to their power, a tree or site associated with local spirits becomes known as a source of power, or an unofficial ritual is used to manipulate life events.

Baraka carries the meaning of blessing or power, where the two words are similes. We find the idea of *baraka* in Jewish, Christian and Muslim thought. Parrinder defines *baraka* in Islam as "a mysterious and wonderful power, a blessing from God." Possessed by the saints, "the Prophet Muhammad possessed it in the highest degree. ... *Baraka* is seen in miracles, holy places and people, prayers, blessings and curses."[11]

We can picture *baraka* as something like electricity in how it functions: it is invisible, but still present and powerful. It confers all kinds of benefits when it is accessed. Similarly, electricity gives us light and warmth but if misused or accessed carelessly, it can be deadly. So, people are careful not to bring polluting substances or situations into contact with sources of *baraka*. Sources of *baraka* in Islam can include the Qur'an, the name of God, other invocations, people, objects, amulets, and particular places, times or rituals.

---

[9] Elliott, 2017:159.
[10] Also, the Polynesian concept of *mana.* 'Blessing' and 'luck' are often used interchangeably in English, when people say, "We're lucky," or "We're blessed."
[11] Parrinder and Golden 1973:40. Also Dale 2016:90–97.

Many Muslims around the world interact primarily with the Qur'an as a source of power, rather than seeking to study it for its meaning. *Baraka* can be passed on through words – written or recited. Protective Qur'anic verses are inscribed on vehicles or houses. The power of the Qur'an may be sought for blessing or healing by writing Qur'anic verses (or perhaps the names of the prophets) on paper and submerging the paper in water to drink, or soaking the paper in olive oil, which is then used to anoint an afflicted part of the body.

Blessing comes also from the Qur'an's complete recitation (known as *khitmah*, or 'sealing' the Qur'an). Sometimes I would sit with a group of women meeting together, while each of them took one or more sections of the Qur'an (printed in individual booklets) to quietly recite, until the whole Qur'an had been corporately recited by the group. In the middle stood bottles of water with their lids off, to absorb the power of *baraka* (blessing) from the recitation, and the house in which it took place was also blessed. Reciting particular Qur'anic verses or other invocations two, three, seven or a hundred times, at prescribed times in the day or year would also offer healing, protection, forgiveness or a heavenly reward.[12] The name of God also carries power. This is why after a time of *du'a* prayer with palms held up, it is common to see Muslims make a motion of wiping their faces with the palms of their hands, as they bring the *baraka* from the recited words back onto themselves.

As a physical flow, the healing or protective power of *baraka* can be communicated through contact with a person of power such as a *pir* or *shaykh*, or the shrine of a holy person. A cloth which has touched a sick person may be left at a shrine so that the flow of power may be conveyed through the material back to its owner. Amulets are hung in vehicles or houses, pinned on or sewn into clothes or tucked into someone's wallet. Water from Zamzam[13] is believed to offer extra *baraka*/efficacy to prayers that are said immediately after drinking it. The wafting fumes of incense are not only to perfume the air, but are believed to be protective, driving away evil spirits. Special places (tombs, shrines, the mosque, Mecca) or objects (the Qur'an, amulets, bowls with Qur'anic verses engraved on them) can be seen as sources of power, and special times carry more associations of power (sunrise and sunset, Ramadan and, particularly, the Night of Power in the last week of Ramadan). And rituals, such as going on pilgrimage (*hajj*), may offer particular *baraka*.

How can the Bible help us understand and respond to the forces of envy and of *baraka*, in the communities we encounter?

---

[12] For some examples, see the commonly-used Al-Qahtani حصن المسلم. *Fortress of the Muslim. Invocations from the Qur'an and sunnah* 2006.

[13] The spring at Mecca, reputed to derive from the intervention of God's angel to help Hagar and Ishmael in the desert. It is common for people to come back from Mecca with containers of Zamzam water.

The Bible, Envy and Blessing

An understanding of limited good existed in the cultures in which the Bible was revealed. So, it is no surprise to find that in the Bible there are hints of an understanding of the potent force of envy. A Jewish midrash connects the priestly blessing (Nu 6:24–26) with the evil eye,[14] and other allusions also suggest implicit belief in the power of envy and the evil eye.[15] In the Old Testament we find in Hebrew the expression of the 'evil eye' (*'ayn ra'ah*). It is often linked with being miserly and not willing to share what we have received with others (Deut 15:9, 28:54, 56; Prov 23:6, 28:22). It usually refers more to a person with the attitudes of stinginess, greed and envy, rather than to an independent power. This fits with the emphasis in the Bible on God as having sovereign power, and other forms of power or magic are downplayed or neutralised. However, we may recognise the latent belief in the powers of the evil eye behind the use of the term in relation to envy, avarice and lack of generosity.

The New Testament also uses the term 'evil eye' (*ofthalmos poneros*), again with the connotation of being ungenerous towards others. People are miserly or ungenerous when they don't want to share their resources with others. Nor do they want to see others prosper, because they believe that in a world of limited good, there will be less for them. The phrase 'evil eye' is often translated into English as 'envy', as in Mk 7:22, where it is listed among the evils that come from a human heart and pollute a person.[16] In Mat 20:15, the landowner asks the grumbling labourers, "Is your eye evil because I am good?" (NRSV translates it, "Are you envious because I am generous?").[17] And in Mat 6:22,23 (and Lk 11:34), the evil (sick) eye is contrasted with the healthy or generous eye.

What is the Biblical understanding of blessing? The Bible affirms God's sovereign power, that all power (and blessing) come ultimately from Him. Even if it is mediated through a place or object, it is God's power, given to his people in the context of covenant obedience to him. Like electricity, if it is used well, in a relationship of covenant obedience to God, it is powerful for blessing (Dt 28:1–14). It is given through relationship with God, not because of the intrinsic worth or good deeds of the receiver, or gained through money or using the right ritual or invocations. However, if people seek to use the power like magic, accessing it manipulatively and independent of obedience to God, then it becomes dangerous, and disobedience brings the experience of God's curse (Dt 28:15–

---

[14] "When Israel made the Tabernacle the Holy One (blessed be He), He gave them the blessing first, in order that no evil eye might affect them. Accordingly, it is written: 'The Lord bless thee and keep thee' (Num 6:24), namely, from the evil eye.'" cited in Wazana, 2007:686.

[15] For detailed discussion, see Wazana, and also Elliott, Vol 3:2016.

[16] The list in Romans 1:29ff links envy and covetousness.

[17] For an extended discussion, see Ch.4, "Envy – The Most Grievous of All Evils" in Malina 2001.

68). So, Balaam was unable to use the power God gave him to curse the people of Israel, despite the promised reward (Num 22–24).

We see this pattern at Shiloh, where the Tabernacle was set up, as a special place for God's people to meet with him – but then God abandoned it because of his people's disobedience (Josh 18:1, 1 Sam 1:3: Jer 7:12). The Ark itself, housed for a while at Shiloh, was an object where God's power resided. When the Israelite nation sought to use it as a source of magic to gain victory, they lost it: it was still a conduit of Divine power (both danger and benefit), but could not be used to manipulate God (1 Sam 4–7, 2 Sam 6:12). And even the Temple, blessed by God (2 Chron 5–7:3), would not remain a source of his blessing independent of his people's covenant obedience (Jer 7:1–15, and Ezekiel's poignant vision of God's glory leaving the temple in Ez 10 and 11). If God uses particular places, people or objects, they do not become a magical source of power independent of relationship with Him. A Biblical view of blessing is not a power that can be manipulated, but one that is grounded firmly in the Sovereign Lord as its source.

Blessing is communicated in the Bible through physical touch and through the spoken word. When the name of God is spoken over someone, God's name carries the power of God himself, which is 'laid on' the recipient (Num 6:24–26). When someone speaks a blessing, it cannot be taken back or given away again (Gen 27). It can be passed on also through the laying on of hands (for example, Gen 48:14; Num 27:18). Anointing of kings, prophets and priests also conveys the divine power to them (1 Sam 16:13; 1 Kings 19:15–16; Is 61:1). And it can come through proximity to sacred places (Ex 20:24; Ps 118:26).

The primary content of blessing is fruitfulness and fertility of people and land (Gen 1:28). It includes peace, power and prosperity (Gen 49:25–6), health and wholeness – *shalom/salaam* (Dt 28:1–14). Blessing is given from the one of higher status to lower status: fathers may bless sons, the older blesses the younger (Gen 47:7), and the person who carries God's authority has the power to give blessing (so priests, prophets and, notably, Melchizedek, in Gen 14:19–20). As the writer of the book of Hebrews sums it up: "It is beyond dispute that the inferior is blessed by the superior," (Heb 7:7).

The purpose of blessing in the Bible is not so that the individual may be exalted, but rather that God may be glorified. People are blessed in order to be a blessing – we are meant to be conduits not containers. Blessing gets passed on, and God gets the glory (for example, Gen 12:3, and notably Ps 67). It was when God's community sought to use blessing for their own benefit and building-up, not for the benefit of the nations around them and God's honour, that they encountered judgement.

Eulogeo is the Greek word in the New Testament that most closely carries the meaning of *baraka* in the Old Testament.[18]

---

[18] Words for the state of being blessed, happy, are *asher* (Hebrew) and *makarios* (Greek), as in Ps 1:1; Ps 119:1,2; Matthew 5:3ff.

In the New Testament also, blessing comes from God, through Jesus Christ. It is not a power which can be used separately without allegiance to Jesus. Peter sharply rebukes the magician Simon for wanting to purchase the power of passing on the Holy Spirit to believers (Acts 8:9–24). When some itinerant Jewish exorcists try to use Jesus' name to boost their own power, they are overpowered and beaten by the man they are trying to exorcise (Acts 19:12–20). The New Testament affirms the name of Jesus as the source of Divine power and blessing (Acts 3:6, 4:7–10).

Again, we see blessing communicated through physical touch, particularly through the laying on of hands (Mk 7:32–35, 10:13–16; Acts 6:6, 8:14–17, 9:17, 13:3, 19:6). Blessing is passed on through other physical contact, including Jesus' clothes (Mk 5:25–30), Peter's shadow (Acts 5:15), and other cloths (Acts 19:12), and anointing oil (Mk 6:13; Jam 5:14). By speaking a word, Jesus can heal the centurion's servant and the Syrophoenician woman's daughter (Mat 8:5–13, 15:28). Invoking Jesus' name brings healing, as in the example above (Acts 3:6). The naming of the Trinity brings blessing (2 Cor 12:13). While Jesus Christ is the source of blessing, his followers can also bless others. The proclamation of salvation in Christ is accompanied by the power of Christ (Lk 24:46–49; John 20:21–22; Acts 1:8).

The content of blessing again includes its primary meaning of fruitfulness and abundance. Jesus blesses five loaves which multiply to feed thousands (Lk 9:16), and blesses the bread which becomes the symbol of his body given to bring life to all (Mat 26:26). It is an action so familiar that it brings instant recognition to his Companions at Emmaus (Lk 24:30). Jesus blesses his followers, so that they too can become givers of his blessing (Lk 24:50). That blessing can be used to bring healing, but not to curse or harm others (Lk 6:27–28; Rom 12:14). In the New Testament, blessing in the Messiah also takes on a rich spiritual dimension, recognising its eschatological fulfilment in Christ, in the Kingdom of God. As the apostles bless people, they receive the Holy Spirit. Ephesians 1:3–14 is often taken as a blessing psalm (such as Ps 67), promising us every spiritual blessing in the heavenly realm. The Holy Spirit is the down payment of our future inheritance (also Mat 25:34), and the source of Christ's power and blessing, now indwelling us and enabling us to pass on that blessing to others. Gifts are given not to exalt the individual recipient but to build up the Body of Christ. Fruitfulness includes growing in the fruits of the spirit into increasing Christlikeness.

The promise given to Abraham is fulfilled in Jesus Messiah, so that believers are inheritors of Abraham's blessing (Acts 3:25, Gal 3:8–9). As we receive the blessing of Jesus Messiah, it is for the purpose of blessing the nations, so that God's name will be glorified. To describe ourselves as blessed is to immediately ask the question: "Who are we blessing?"

Blessing, with its promise of fruitfulness and abundance, is the antithesis of limited good. God's blessing is extravagant, for fertility and flourishing, from the first chapter of Genesis. It is demonstrated anew in the life of Jesus the

Messiah – feeding thousands with a few loaves and fishes and with baskets of food left over, telling stories of paying people lavishly for just a few hours' work. These narratives of generosity culminate in an act of costly self-giving that offers life to all. As followers of Jesus Messiah, our lives need to exemplify the same generosity as we seek to bless others.

God's *baraka*/blessing offers protection in a world of envy and fear. And it tells us of a world where envy is robbed of its power, of a world so characterised by self-giving and abundance through Jesus the Messiah, that envy has no place, no need of levelling, for there is no limitation on God's goodness offered freely for all.

My instinct when I met someone with a young child was to compliment their parents, verbally admiring the baby. However, I quickly learned in the Middle East that this was a very anti-social act. If anything adverse happened to the child, I would be held responsible for causing it through my admiration. The Bible doesn't call us to admire: it calls us to bless. Rather than saying nothing, we can ask God's blessing and protection over children or situations. We can invoke God's blessing over people, their families, a new car or home. In doing this, we are actively invoking God's good power for the situation, not just seeking to avert evil. And the blessing and protection of God's name is potent against any kind of evil.

- What are the unseen forces, both personal and impersonal, that your Muslim friends are aware of?
- What objects or places do they see as sources of power? What activities help them to access power?
- In what ways do people seek to control or manipulate the powers that surround them, to avert evil and attract good? What symbols or protective amulets or invocations do you see around you?
- How can you bless the people with whom you are in contact?

8. Reciprocity and Patronage

There is a knock on the door: I open it to find my neighbour's daughter holding a plate containing some of the stuffed vegetables she has just finished preparing for her family. The delicious aroma rises with the steam from the laden plate: I take it with appreciative thanks. Later I will return the plate to her mother, but not empty. Rather, filled with fruit, or a cake I have just made. The exchange will continue as long as our neighbour relationship lasts.

We work hard to get foreign funding for the new school in a poorer region of the country. One fund contributes money for scholarships, so that poorer children might be able to come. A few months later, when it is time to report back to the donors, we ask about the scholarships. The headmistress assures us that they have all been distributed. One has gone to the wealthy Principal's son; the school secretary's child also gets funding; and so does the daughter of another middle-class teacher. The scholarships have not been distributed according to need assessment as we expected, but rather along lines of relationship.

A local colleague is telling a western friend that he doesn't have much spare money for extra expenses. His western friend asks him about his spare flat, and other material assets. "Yes, I own them," the local colleague agrees. "But if our housemaid is struggling with her children's education, that's what I use to pay for them. Or if something happens to my doorman and he needs to go to hospital, that's what I have to draw on to pay his hospital bills. They don't earn much, and they don't have the resources to cope with unexpected crises, so I need the resources for them."

The Qur'an describes God as our Patron:

> Hold fast to Allah [i.e., Have confidence in Allah, and depend on him in all your affairs]. He is your *Maula* (Patron, Lord), what an excellent *Maula* and what an Excellent Helper. *Al-Hajj* 22:78

> Indeed, Allah will not change the condition of a people until they change what is in themselves. And when Allah intends for a people ill, there is no repelling it. And there is not for them besides Him any patron. *Al-Ra'd* 13:11 (Sahih International)[1]

The *hadith* also reflect an understanding of patronage in theology and in and society. For example:

> It is reported on the authority of Abu Huraira that ... (The Prophet said:) "Yes, and pardon us and grant us protection! and have mercy on us. Thou art our patron, so grant us victory over the disbelieving people" (ii. 286). He (the Lord) said: "Yes."[2]

> Abu Tilha, the Companion of Allah's Messenger (may peace be upon him), reported Allah's Messenger (may peace be upon him) having said: Verily, angels do not enter the house in which there is a picture. Busr reported: Zaid fell ill and we went to inquire after his health and (found) that there was hanging at his door a curtain with a picture on it. I said to 'Ubaidullah Khaulani who had been under the patronage of Maimuna, the wife of Allah's Apostle (may peace be upon him): Did not Zaid himself inform us before about (the Holy Prophet's command pertaining to the pictures), whereupon 'Ubaidullah said: Did you not hear when he said: "Except the prints on the cloth"?[3]

Reciprocity

There are two different kinds of primary security on which people depend – material security and relational security. People in the western world generally focus on material security. And even what we call '*social* welfare' is used to refer to financial and other material benefits for people – in other words, *material* welfare. However, in other countries, particularly where there is limited access to material wealth, people's primary dependence is on relational security. By tending to the maintenance of good relationships, security is ensured in times of difficulty.[4] Such relationships are formed and perpetuated through ongoing exchange over time.

In societies around the world, reciprocity is the fundamental principle that undergirds the movement of material and social resources within societies. Reciprocity in giving and receiving is the foundation on which relationships are built and maintained. To be part of a relational network is to participate in the

---

[1] https://corpus.quran.com/translation.jsp?chapter=13&verse=11.
[2] Sahih Muslim, Book #001, *Hadith* #0228.
[3] Sahih Muslim, Book #024, *Hadith* #5252.
[4] See the parable of the Shrewd Steward: Lk 16:1–9.

exchange of gifts, and conversely, to give or receive a gift is to enter into a relationship. Distribution of resources takes place reciprocally along relationship lines. This system of gift exchange is never completely balanced: if both want the relationship to continue, then someone owes and someone is owed.[5] Initiative requires response. And the system is maintained through mutual indebtedness, whether of symbolic, social or economic value. Reciprocity and patronage are key concepts in understanding our relationships with women in Muslim societies.

Reciprocity is particularly important for women in many societies, who carry primary responsibility for maintaining harmony in communal relationships (both human and spiritual). Marcel Mauss in his foundational essay 'The Gift' observes that gift exchange is often linked with rites of passage such as birth, circumcision, menarche, marriage and death:[6] and women are centrally involved at such rites. Hence early rabbinical sources viewed a man preventing his wife from lending kitchen goods to a neighbour or from mourning with a bereaved friend as grounds for divorce, because not being able to give deprived the woman of the social credit she needed for the future.[7]

Exchanging gifts does not constitute a 'paying off' of indebtedness. Rather, accepting a gift implies the commitment to return a gift, in what is a further 'investing into' the relationship. The aim of the exchange is not independence, but rather interdependence.[8] In this exchange, gifts do not have to be equal, either in substance or in amount. Marcel Mauss described systems of exchange in societies as the centre around which social relations, the circulation of goods and the production of meaning all revolved. Gift exchange involved three steps:

- The obligation to give
- The obligation to receive
- The obligation to return

John Barclay in his book *Paul and the Gift*, notes that:

> … the return of the gift represents the desire to reproduce social relations: each party to the gift-relation is in some sense 'produced' by the exchange between them, and social relations can only be maintained or reproduced in the continual motion of exchange. In this sense, the counter-gift is rarely the end of the relationship, replacing an inequality with a stable equilibrium: it is liable to constitute, rather, a form of 'giving-again,' adding to the gift-relationship a continuing forward momentum.[9]

---

[5] Rynkiewich 2011:109.

[6] Mauss 1925/2016:66.

[7] Barclay 2015:25, note 59, quoting S. Schwartz: 'Were the Jews a Mediterranean Society', 2010: p.14, n.26.

[8] Barclay comments that "recipients of gifts *are* under a strong (though non-legal) obligation to make some return for a gift – even if only in gratitude." (2015:18).

[9] Barclay 2015:18.

Local exchange of favours may still continue on a traditional basis of relationships even within societies that are part of the wider global market economy. Participation in local networks involves participation in exchange of favours or gifts and vice versa. These reciprocal relationships allow the flow of goods and resources in a society where status and access to assets are more fixed. The relationship may be between two equals, such as among friends. In such peer relationships, people give and receive the same kind of resources, whether in financial co-operatives, or in swapping plates of food between households. However, in relationships between people in non-equal positions of social power or standing, the exchange may look different.

Hierarchy and Patronage

'Our fingers are not all the same,' says an Egyptian proverb, recognising that people occupy different and uneven positions.

In hierarchical societies, relationship-exchanges are marked by unequal reciprocity. In collectivist hierarchical communities, this exchange of unequal reciprocity takes place through patron–client relationships. The patron offers access to resources such as material goods, protection, influence or employment: economic, political or spiritual benefit. And the client responds with public gratitude, loyalty (even when it is costly, if the patron is out of favour), and sometimes service, gifts, and visits. The relationship may include a spiritual dimension, as between a Sufi leader and their disciple.[10]

The institution of patronage offers access to assets in hierarchical societies. In a patronage relationship we see the mutual exchange of desired goods and services. Healthy relationships are reciprocal relationships. In hierarchical societies reciprocity is still a key measure of relationship, but the elements of exchange may be very different. They do not have to be equal or even in kind. Laila Kamel describes how she drew on these traditional ties to resource a project she had founded among the very poor in Egypt. She cautions against too quick dismissal of patronage ties: "the system of personal networks and kinship ties which had served the poor had also served the rich in feudal Egypt. And yet, here was a system that had survived for centuries but had been left by the wayside because it had been judged 'unprofessional' and 'unsustainable' by western eyes."[11]

The patron is available for assistance when it is needed, and the client does everything in her or his power to enhance the fame and honour of the patron, by telling of the benefit they have received, publicly offering respect and loyalty to the patron, and by providing services when the opportunity arises. So, material gifts or resources can be returned in the form of symbolic capital, as honour. In collectivist hierarchical honour–shame cultures, honour is one of the most prized

---

[10] See Edwards 2013.
[11] Kamel 1994:8.

currencies. Barclay notes that "…the power that is entailed by the possession of honour may be precisely the purpose of the gift-giving."[12]

An important dimension of the patronage system is the role of the intermediary, or broker. DeSilva comments: "Sometimes the most important gift a patron could give was access to (and influence with) another patron who actually had power over the benefit being sought."[13] The patron incurs a debt, and increases her or his own honour through the indebtedness of the client. Brokerage is a highly-valued benefit, where the broker is the *trusted intermediary* who opens the door to a group or individual to whom the client needs access. Hisham Sharabi describes how the distribution of benefits across the patronage system is held together by the use of people as intermediaries to solicit favours on behalf of others. This system:

> … not only socializes the individual into accepting the supremacy of established authority but also trains one in the ways of dealing with it (by securing the) protection and material interests of the individual and the group, including the lowest member of the group … The supplicant, the bestower of favour, and the go-between as well all get something.[14]

The positions of patron, client and broker are flexible and can change in relation to one another according to their needs. We see an example of this in the story in Lk 7:1–10, where the centurion was patron of the local Jewish community, building them a synagogue. But when, as a non-Jew, he needed access to Jesus, seeking healing for his servant, the Jewish leaders in turn were brokers or intermediaries for him to obtain access to Jesus.

Honour, Shame and Gender

Patron–client relationships are marked by reciprocity and mutual faithfulness, and held in place by social sanctions of honour and shame. Malina describes how "The honourable higher-status person, then, like the lower-status person, was expected to live out and live up to that socially ascribed self-image. And this entailed the obligation of serving as patron for clients of lower social strata."[15] The noble patron in turn "evaluates potential beneficiaries not according to the gifts or services they give back, but on the basis of their disposition to feel gratitude, appreciate and remember the gift."[16] Neglecting to return a kindness, forgetting a gift, or repaying favour with insult or injury, were all behaviours to be avoided at all costs by an honourable person who was a client. And while

---

[12] Barclay 2015:19.
[13] deSilva 2000:97.
[14] Sharabi 1988:46, 48.
[15] Malina 2001:101.
[16] See Jesus' evaluation in Lk 18:10-15 of the two men who went up to the temple to pray.

patrons might call clients 'friends', clients would refer to their benefactors as 'patrons', to show their respect and honour. So, both giving, and especially responding with gratitude, were maintained by honour and shame. Patronage relationships can be life-long, and even continue over generations. However, they are (in principle) voluntary, and can be abandoned voluntarily.

In a patronage society, there is no such thing as neutral giving. Distribution of resources flows along established lines of relationship and connection. When we want to know who to give to, we look at the relationships we are already in. Giving a gift or favour to someone may be initiating a relationship of ongoing giving. If we want to get work done, we establish a relationship with the required worker or retailer, and that relationship is expected to continue. A local woman in East Africa regularly worked for a western family. One week she explained that she would be unable to come to work for the next few weeks owing to family commitments. The western family made arrangements to have another local person come to do the work. The following week, the second person was already halfway through the tasks when the adult daughter of the original woman arrived, assuming that she would be given the work that her mother had been doing. Whereas the western family thought about the job in terms of qualifications and capacity to do the work, the local employee expected that the existing work/patronage relationship would naturally be extended to her daughter.

Patronage is a social construct that can displace other conventions, such as gender restrictions. Cohick describes how in New Testament times, "With the practice of public and private benefaction, women gained access to centres of influence and persons of power. As a patron, a woman received public honour; with that came the expectation of privilege and respect. ... Benefaction downplayed the gender of the giver."[17] We see this readily today in countries, even ones with strong social divisions around gender, where women take positions of national leadership, often following family lines. Jesus' followers included women who were his patrons, providing for him out of their resources.[18] Jesus also challenged conventions further by including women in hierarchical relationships such as teacher–disciple.

Western government and mission workers have sometimes introduced structures that disempower local women because they are based on western assumptions of gender roles, ignoring the ways women operate and may be empowered through local structures.[19] Relationships of patronage and reciprocity are fundamental to how women function in most Muslim cultures, as

---

[17] Cohick 2009:323.
[18] Lk 8:2–3.
[19] A parallel example is access to literacy. Street points out a number of examples from Southeast Asia where writing was not used for "religious, judicial or historical purposes", but for notes and letters, recording debts, or courting; and concludes that "the arrival of Islam and Christianity had the effect of reducing the literacy rates, particularly among women, by restricting writing to the male, sacral, and monastic domains" (Street, 1994:101).

those principally responsible to maintain communal relationships. These relationships operate among women, but also across genders, allowing women to occupy roles of influence and leadership in the societies in which they live. This has been evident historically and also currently in Muslim communities and countries.[20]

Abuse/Disequilibrium

Patronage can be abused, and the abuse happens when the relationship of reciprocity is unbalanced. To give when the recipient is unable to respond, giving in order to control, is to establish relationships of paternalism and unhealthy dependency. The client becomes trapped in debt, and is unable to balance the relationship. And to extort exorbitant favours from the client is to build relationships of exploitation, leaving the client in a position of subservience, where the patron does not give in return.[21] A healthy model does not disempower the recipient, but enables both giver and recipient to make significant contributions to the relationship.

Why does patronage matter? There are three important reasons. It helps us understand how the social lines along which many of the societies in which we may become involved, operate. It is a picture of God's relationship with us, important in understanding the biblical teaching on grace. It also provides an important model for our own relationships of discipleship and sharing.

As we enter other cultures, local people become our patrons in the new community. Appreciating patronage as a significant social pattern can help us understand the dynamics and need for different kinds of reciprocity when we are involved in local relationships. This may be relationships where we function as patron (for example, with a house help, students, those with whom we have a relationship in some way, or others who are our beneficiaries – including the beggar we give alms to at the door. Or we may be the client, as in links with our landlady or landlord, or head of our sponsoring organisation or church leader, or those who are senior to us in the NGO or company with whom we are working: the people who give us access to and acceptability in the community which we are entering. Life and daily transactions flow along relational lines. This also makes us appreciate the potential power of women, which can be further amplified by their family connections, their position, their reputation as an honourable woman, or their age.[22]

---

[20] See the discussion on women leaders in Chapter 18.

[21] Chinchen 1995:446–51.

[22] See Chapter 15.

Patronage and Grace

We see reciprocity and patronage operating in the Bible, in the relationships between people. Examples include Abraham and Melchizedek, David and Nabal, Jesus with the women who followed and supported him, and Paul's relationships with the churches he planted.[23]

Understanding patronage in the Bible also gives the context to understanding grace. Grace (*charis*) was a term used first in economic relationships, grounded in giving and receiving benefits, before it ever gained religious meaning. We need to understand how those relationships function in order to understand how people heard and understood grace in New Testament times. *Charis* meant first of all the willing attitude of generosity of the benefactor, and also the attitude of gratitude and loyalty from the recipient. The secondary meaning of *charis* was the actual gift or favour that was the result of the benefactor's attitude.

The covenants between God and his people are agreements along the lines of traditional patronage agreements. Sometimes the obligations on the clients or recipients are laid out, as in the suzerain-vassal covenant in Ex 19:4–6. Others follow the royal grant model, where God as patron gives a favour unconditionally, with his promise to never again destroy the earth by flood (Gen 9:11). This unconditional benefaction is reflected in the New Testament, where God is the Father who makes his sun rise on both evil and good people, and sends rain on the just and unjust (Mat 5:45). This kind of generous endowment to all was seen in Roman times by the patron who publicly endowed a city with a fountain or games or an amphitheatre. But most often elements of both apply: God gives, and his people are expected to respond. Abraham is given God's blessing to have a great name and nation, but he is called to act by leaving his country, kindred and family. David is given an unconditional promise of a throne (family) that would be established forever, but his descendants are expected to obey the covenant obligations or face God's discipline (2 Sam 7).

Similarly, in many of the NT epistles, Paul spends the first chapters describing the gifts and promises that God, our patron, gives us. He then goes on to describe how we, as clients, should respond with gratitude, loyalty and behaviour that is commensurate with honouring our patron God.[24] Paul exhorts the Ephesians: "I therefore beg you to live a life worthy of the calling to which you have been called..." (Eph 4:1ff). And in the letter to Philemon, Paul reminds Philemon of his indebtedness to Paul, and Philemon's own character as a benefactor of the early church. The letter is read in public, invoking the forces of honour and shame to increase the pressure on Philemon to accede to Paul's request to receive back his runaway slave without punishing him.

Going back to the meaning of 'grace'/*charis* we remember that the same word is used for the act and for the response. Seneca identified the three Graces "with

---

[23] Gen 14:18–20; 1 Sam 25:2–35; Lk 8:2–3.
[24] For example, 1 Cor 1:3–10, Gal 1:3–6.

the giving, the receiving, and the returning of the gift."[25] As the Graces perform their dance, the links must be maintained. In a system of honour, grace must be requited by grace, a favour returned with favour, the gift with gratitude. Seneca commented on their dance that "the beauty of the whole is destroyed if the course is anywhere broken." Not to respond to a gift or favour is to break the dance and dis-grace the dance or the relationship.[26]

God as Righteous Patron

We can see God as the Model Patron, who goes beyond earthly models in demonstrating his generosity.

In choosing clients, God chooses the most lowly, not those possessing rank and status. And he gives even to the undeserving, including costly giving to his enemies. As patron, he doesn't wait for those who have affronted his honour to come to him, but takes the initiative in sending Jesus to effect reconciliation. He offers personal patronage (beyond public benefaction) to all who come, without first scrutinising them, even to the point of making them sons and daughters. Jesus is the mediator of God's power, giving his own life to deliver us from sin, death and the power of Satan, in ultimate generosity. And he continues as intermediary in ongoing intercession for us.

As beneficiaries of God's favour, we realise that the gifts given to the Body of Christ are God's gifts for the sake of the Body, so that God is honoured: they are not given to build the power-base of individuals. As recipients, we need to respond generously and fully, for God has given generously and fully to us. Our honourable response should include exuberant thanksgiving, public testimony to what God has done for us in Christ (which is evangelism), doing good works to honour God's name and imitate his generosity, through public loyalty to Christ (even when it is costly), and through wholehearted trust in God's goodness, favour and grace to us.

Discipleship, Mentoring and Patronage

As we look to discipling or mentoring others, the model of patronage offers a way forward. It reminds us that this is not about a neutral passing on of information, but rather a relationship, where both contribute life-on-life sharing. In discipleship we are not offering people a course, but modelling how to live life, in all its dimensions. The quality of the discipleship is directly connected to

---

[25] Barclay 2015:46 – c.f. Mauss above.
[26] We notice the same pattern of mutuality in how 'bless' is used reciprocally in the Bible, where God blesses us with his gifts and favour, and we bless God in public thanksgiving and honouring his name. (e.g., Ps 145). Faith (dependability and trustworthiness) and '*khesed*' (loving compassion, loyalty) in the O.T. are also reciprocal terms that are originally grounded in patronage relationships.

the depth of the relationship.[27] And it is not one way. Paul's writings are rich testimony to the relationship he had with the churches he had planted, where they cared for him physically, and sent him resources. It was not something that he would demand as a wage (unlike some of the travelling teachers), but a voluntary gifting and requiting of favours. The mutuality of the relationship means that both discipler and disciple are honoured. Our relationships of discipling should include reciprocity which is mutually empowering: they need to be 'thick' relationships which operate on multiple lines of exchange. Nik Ripken, asking local believers for what a good 'missionary' looks like, heard them describe 'the one they loved':

> When this missionary's father died, he came to us and asked for our help. We didn't have much, but we gathered an offering of love. We bought him a plane ticket so that he could go home to America and bury his father. This man and his family give everything they have to the poor. They struggle to pay rent and school fees, and put meat on the table. And when he has a great need, what does he do? He doesn't go to the other westerners for money. He comes to us. He comes to the scattered and the poor, he comes to local believers, and he asks for, and gets, our help. Do you want to know why we love him? He needs us. The rest of you have never needed us.[28]

Thick relationships of discipleship in a patronage model allow the new believer to gain their identity through allegiance to the new community of the Messiah, through the discipler who can embody the community's ethos and values. They model what it looks like to be a member of the new community, and they can act as a patron or broker for the newcomer, brokering the new networks and relationships which will offer access to the resources, whether material, social, emotional or informational, that will enable them to survive and ground them in the new community. This can mean making introductions, brokering trust (Acts 9:26–28) and also practical life dimensions, such as providing accommodation if they are thrown out by their families or helping them to find a job, get a car or negotiate a marriage partner.

- How would you describe the relationships in which you function with cross-cultural friends? In what ways are they reciprocal – what is given and what is received? How about relationships where there is a power gradient?
- Have you noticed any links between relationships and gifts or benefits? How have you responded?
- In what relationships do you play the role of a patron? Or client? Or broker?
- Where do you see Muslim women occupying the role of patron, or broker, or client?
- How are we brokers in introducing people to God?

---

[27] Chinchen 1995:446–51.
[28] Ripken 2016.

9. Generous Hospitality

Our friends pick us up and take us to their aunt's house in another suburb for a meal. When we get there, the table is groaning under the variety of dishes that she has spent days cooking. After eating, we sit up on the flat roof together, enjoying the cool breeze and drinking sweet mint tea. Then the hostess offers to show me around her beautifully-kept house. In one of the cabinets is an engraved brass bowl that had belonged to her grandmother. I pause to look and she immediately offers it to me as a gift. I can't take it – it is a precious family possession – so I manage to decline her insistent offering. We finish the tour and soon afterwards return home, reflecting on the costly hospitality that has been extended to us again that evening. It is typical of the hospitality that we experience over more than two decades from people, often strangers, around us in the Middle East.

My daughter and I are gathered in the courtyard of a house in the old part of a ME city with a group of Shi'ite women, looking at boxes and bags and more boxes of clothes. It is a warm summer evening; but the political temperature is even higher. Lebanon has just been invaded, and thousands and thousands of refugees have flooded across borders to seek shelter from the relentless rain of bombs killing and wounding, destroying their houses and livelihoods. And as the world debates and delays on whether to ask for a cease-fire, the country we are living in has opened its doors and resources to those who are pouring in, who have fled with just what they could carry with them. People open their homes; the community opens schools and public buildings for the refugees to stay in. Companies donate food, portable cooking stoves and other resources; restaurants give away hundreds of meals; and people give of their material resources and their time. The Shi'ite women around us range from young students to older women, mothers and daughters and cousins are there. The owner of this house has opened it up, and individuals, companies, shop owners, are donating clothes to be sorted here and distributed. So, we spend the evening working in various rooms around the central open courtyard, sorting the piles into different sizes, into boys' and girls' clothing. 95% of it is brand new, suits that will cheer the hearts of little girls, distract little boys, from the bewilderment of what has happened to them: very little is second-hand. We join them for an evening; but many of the women come over several evenings, or spend time meeting with the refugees and helping them find what they needed from the clothes. Yet again, in what is typical Arab hospitality that reaches across political and geographic barriers, the community is caring for the people at their door in need.

Anna lives in a multicultural area of a large western city:

An evening visit to Ayesha, from Syria, will always involve a vast array of nuts, cakes, biscuits and fruit. Her husband stays for a polite amount of time and then goes, leaving us to eat and talk. Another friend tells me that it makes her happy when guests eat and she feels really bad when they don't. She knows it's a different culture so she understands but still feels bad because she feels she hasn't respected her guest unless they eat. This is the common face of hospitality among my Muslim friends in [this city]. My friends from South Asia are equally welcoming but ask that you give them 24 hours' notice before visiting so they can cook. Visiting equals a meal.[1]

Mona Siddiqui writes of arriving in Cairo for the first time:

After arriving at my pre-arranged accommodation in a relatively poor suburb of the city, I had to wait outside for a while as keys and rooms were being sorted out. I stood there with my new suitcase and new expectations and looked around anxious and curious at the dust, animals and poverty around me. A young woman with a small child was watching me as she squatted near the doorstep of my flat. She stared at me for a while and after some time I saw her get up, find a large piece of cardboard, dust it clean, and place it on the doorstep. She patted on it, beckoning me to sit down and take the weight off my feet. I smiled at her nervously, noting that she had made a special effort for a new guest in the neighbourhood. ... Later on, as I was getting settled in the flat, two young children came up and spoke to me in the local Arabic dialect. I couldn't understand what they were saying and became slightly impatient at their repeated visits and knocking on the door. That evening I discovered that they had been sent by their mother, the same woman, to ask if I needed anything as I was a guest in their midst.[2]

Most people who have lived and worked among Muslims can tell many stories of the rich and often sacrificial hospitality we have received from them.

---

[1] https://whenwomenspeak.net/uncategorized/hospitality-among-the-diaspora/.
[2] Siddiqui 2015:3.

Hospitality is a central virtue in many Muslim cultures. The role of women is pivotal in hospitality. Exploring the place of hospitality further in Islam helps us also to read its place in the Bible, and enables us to understand it as one of the pictures, or redemptive analogies which God gives us for his work through Jesus Messiah, showing God's hospitality to us.

In the Qur'an, *Surah Al-Nur 24:61* encourages sharing meals together:[3]

There is not upon the blind [any] constraint nor upon the lame constraint nor upon the ill constraint nor upon yourselves when you eat from your [own] houses or the houses of your fathers or the houses of your mothers or the houses of your brothers or the houses of your sisters or the houses of your father's brothers or the houses of your father's sisters or the houses of your mother's brothers or the houses of your mother's sisters or [from houses] whose keys you possess or [from the house] of your friend. There is no blame upon you whether you eat together or separately. But when you enter houses, give greetings of peace upon each other – a greeting from Allah, blessed and good. Thus does Allah make clear to you the verses [of ordinance] that you may understand.

The imperative of generous hospitality is also supported in the *hadith:*

Narrated Abu Shuraih Al-Adawi: My ears heard and my eyes saw the Prophet when he spoke, "Anybody who believes in Allah and the Last Day, should serve his neighbor generously, and anybody who believes in Allah and the Last Day should serve his guest generously by giving him his reward." It was asked. "What is his reward, O Allah's Apostle?" He said, "(To be entertained generously) for a day and a night with high quality of food and the guest has the right to be entertained for three days (with ordinary food) and if he stays longer, what he will be provided with will be regarded as *Sadaqa* (a charitable gift). And anybody who believes in Allah and the Last Day should talk what is good or keep quiet (i.e., abstain from all kinds of dirty and evil talks)."[4]

Then he (Muhammad) went to Khadija bint Khuwailid and said, "Cover me! Cover me!" They covered him till his fear was over and after that he told her everything that had happened and said, "I fear that something may happen to me." Khadija replied, "Never! By Allah, Allah will never disgrace you. You keep good relations with your Kith and kin, help the poor and the destitute, serve your guests generously and assist the deserving calamity-afflicted ones."[5]

A South Asian writer, like many Muslims, see the imperative to generosity and hospitality as grounded in Islam:

Our great Prophet [s] teaches us to be generous and how to entertain guests. He wants a Muslim to show gratitude and be kind and happy when receiving guests.

---

[3] https://quran.com/24/61
[4] Al-Bukhari, Book #73, *Hadith* #48.
[5] Al-Bukhari, Book #1, *Hadith* #3.

The Messenger of Allah [s] further guides us by saying: "Whoever believes in Allah and the Last Day should be hospitable with his or her guests." One should respect and welcome his guests, in particular when they are strangers, or have no family or friends in that country.

It may even happen that a guest comes while relatives or friends are being entertained, or other travellers are staying and there is lack of space; or you are unprepared and have few provisions or are even short of money. In any eventuality, guests who come to your home should be made welcome, shown respect and be provided with whatever food and drink are available. One should sit with them in order to make them feel comfortable and happy, and take care to pay great attention to them. Surely, Allah will increase our provision if we welcome our guests and give them food and drink, and will reward us on the Resurrection Day. Allah is All-Generous, who loves the generous ones and dislikes those who are mean.[6]

Cultures throughout the world, especially nomadic cultures, emphasise the importance of costly hospitality to the unexpected guest. Islam, beginning in the context of nomadic desert tribes, has taken up this imperative. Mona Siddiqui comments that, "Islam holds hospitality as a virtue that lies at the very basis of the Islamic ethical system, a concept rooted in the pre-Islamic Bedouin virtues of welcome and generosity in the harsh desert environment."[7] Evelyne Reisacher reminds us that in a region and time "where there were no institutions and no hotels, hospitality was the responsibility of individuals and families. It was considered a sacred virtue, since the survival of strangers in unfamiliar and hostile places depended solely on the protection of generous hosts."[8] Hospitality continues to be honoured in many Muslim cultures, indicated by proverbs expressing its importance, such as:

'Our home is your home.'[9]
'The guest is a guest of God'
'God comes to us in the person of a guest.'

Mallouhi writes on how this may be lived out in the Middle East:

The traditional Arab greeting for a guest entering the home is 'Welcome to the guest of God' and 'The Prophet has visited us.' How we receive guests is very important. An Arabic proverb places importance on honouring the guest: '*Greet us and don't feed us*' (*laqiina wa la ta'meena*). The meaning is that the warmth with which you receive guests is even more important than what you feed them.

[6] Shaikh Abbas Qummi, Safinat al-Bihar, Bab Dhaif, Sunan ibn Maja, vol. 2, Haq al Jiwar (The rights of neighbours), Ikram al-Dhaif (Respecting the Guest). http://ipaki.com/content/html/29/1097.html.
[7] Siddiqui 2016:10–11.
[8] Reisacher, https://fullerstudio.fuller.edu/a-moratorium-on-hospitality/.
[9] This contrasts with the western proverb, '*A man's home is his castle*,' with the image of pulling up the drawbridge against visitors.

Traditionally, a stranger could arrive at your door and expect three days' hospitality before being asked any questions. My in-laws had a *menzul*, a guest house for this purpose.[10]

Bill Musk agrees with the significance of how we welcome people: "The importance of hosting/visiting lies not just in the requirement that it occur, but in the manner in which it is carried out."[11] It is important that in each context we learn how hospitality is expressed, given and received. To be in relationship with people is to give and receive hospitality (and so receive and give honour). Musk continues:

> In the working out of community life, some visits are obligatory. The celebrations at the various rites of passage call for visiting/hosting, but so also do occasions such as the return of a person from a trip or the arrival of new neighbours, or the knowledge that someone has been taken ill. The serving of food and drink is central to such visiting/hosting. ... A refusal to receive visitors is unthinkable, while to fail to make an obligatory visit threatens the fabric of life in an extended family.[12]

Sidiqqui suggests that "'doing hospitality' is not simply about making physical room for others in our homes, but is essentially an attitude to life."[13] It may include having people to our house or going as a guest to the house of others. We honour them through accepting their hospitality to us. Anna notes:

> When I first meet someone I want to continue talking with, I've learned to simply invite myself to their place. More often than not their faces light up... "You want to come to my house? Welcome!" I know that when I go to their home, I am honouring them. In Australia I'd show you honour by inviting you to my house but the opposite is true among my Muslim friends here.... I've learned about a generosity of spirit and heart as I've experienced biblical, Middle Eastern generosity in action.[14]

Living life with an attitude of hospitality can be costly in upending priorities, investing deeply into relationships, and extending or receiving hospitality in ways that make our guest or host comfortable. Inneke suggests that:

> (Hospitality) is about sharing what I have. It is about not looking at the clock and thinking about the work on my desk. ... Hospitality is about praying to be able to really hear what my visitors are saying. It is about having a place in my heart and my head, as much as having a place in my home for people to come and just be. After hosting people, there is an ongoing relationship. Hospitality is connected to

---

[10] Mallouhi 2004:154.
[11] Musk 2004/1995:117. Hence the Egyptian proverb, '*An onion between friends tastes like a roast lamb.*'
[12] Musk 2004:117.
[13] Sidiqqui 2015:18.
[14] https://whenwomenspeak.net/uncategorized/hospitality-among-the-diaspora/

prayer. Whether I pray often or seldom with guests, they become part of my life and my prayer list. It is about sharing from what He has given to me.[15]

An attitude of hospitality can extend to how we encounter one another in reading our religious texts, requiring humility and vulnerability from us. "Hospitality involves openness of heart and spirit as well as of home."[16] Cathy Ross reminds us that "Listening is an important part of honouring the guest. In both hospitality and mission, listening to the other is the beginning of understanding and of entering the other's world."[17]

The actual work of hospitality is disproportionately born by women in countries around the world. In Ramadan they spend long hours cooking to enable families and friends to gather and break their fast together. At feasts and collective celebrations, it is women who do most of the work of preparing and serving the food, playing a central part in enabling the community celebration. In many places, women in a community will gather together, taking turns each week to visit each other. Ahmed Azban describes this custom in one region:

> Often (women) will visit each other during the morning hours when their husbands are at work and the children are in school. A custom has developed that a woman will invite friends to her house one week, with another extending the invitation another week. The hostess prepares special dishes of food and drink and the invited women might bring a dish to share. They relax and talk over many things for hours.[18]

This is part of the essential role women play in maintaining community relationships, through giving and receiving hospitality or other assistance, whether material or otherwise.[19] Paul includes it in the required good deeds of enrolled widows (1 Tim 5:10). Shared meals can be the sign of reconciliation in a relationship that has been broken or strained, replacing words of confession and forgiveness, particularly in cultures that prefer indirect speech.[20] Where caution about purity comes into conflict with the imperative of hospitality, the latter almost always takes precedence.

Ross suggests a missiology of hospitality and relationship as one of four perspectives that women bring to contextual theology (the others are emptiness and hiddenness; comforting, consolation and healing; and sight, embrace and flourishing). "Hospitality is a good metaphor for mission and an appropriate

---

[15] Inneke G.Riddell. https://whenwomenspeak.net/blog/doing-life-together-hospitality-in-se-asia/.

[16] Ann Williams: https://whenwomenspeak.net/blog/the-hospitality-of-god-in-the-context-of-faith-conversations-the-prophets-stories/.

[17] Ross 2011.

[18] Azban 2010:55.

[19] See discussion on Reciprocity in Chapter 8.

[20] https://whenwomenspeak.net/blog/reconciliation-restitution-and-community-in-honour-shame/.

concept for missiology because it implies invitation, warmth, sharing of food, relationship."[21] Rather than large conferences and grand plans, there might be more 'missiology around the kitchen table over a meal', time in nurturing 'relationships, feasting and feeding the stranger, listening to and learning from the other,' offering new perspectives and possibilities to missiology.

However, Ross reminds us that hospitality can also be oppressive of women, who may bear the brunt of long hours of labour so their husbands can offer hospitality.[22] The cultural importance attached to hospitality is demonstrated in how visitors can sometimes find that they have been the recipients of meals that left their hosts without enough food for the rest of the week for their family, in order to offer hospitality and honour to their guests. Esther used hospitality to empower her in negotiating with the king to save her people: but the king's response to Haman reminds us that it wasn't a place of automatic safety (Esther 7:8).

Hospitality as a Redemptive Analogy

The Bible richly abounds in examples of hospitality: any group will quickly cover a board with biblical references on the subject when I ask them for examples. Examples include the parallel passages in Gen 18:1–8 and 19:1–12, on how Abraham and Lot welcome the heavenly visitors. Musk writes: "It is significant that in Gen 18, the meal which Abraham prepared for his otherworldly visitors is described in greater detail than the conversation which ensued between the patriarch and the Lord!"[23] And Mallouhi reflects on how, "Lot was caught between the highest values of his culture, personal honour (in his daughters), and hospitality. He put others before himself and chose the sacred duty of hospitality."[24] (For the Qur'anic references to these incidents, see from *al-Hijr* 15:51 and *al-Dhaiyat* 51:24 [Abraham], and *Hud* 11:78, *al-Hijr* 15:68, *al-Qamar* 54:37 [Lot].) These examples support the Heb 13:12 injunction to offer hospitality to strangers, "for by doing that, some have entertained angels

---

[21] Ross 2011.

[22] Ross quotes Mercy Oduyoye: "Women's experience of domestic hospitality is that of Sarah, a situation in which they work and the men take the credit (Gen 18:1–15). Rebecca's hospitality to the servant of Isaac (Gen 25:15–27) is traditional to Africa. To illustrate the exploitation of women in men's hospitality to men, African women theologians recall Abraham passing Sarah off as his sister, Lot offering his virgin daughters in order to save his male guests (Gen 19:1–8) and the horrible murder of the 'Levite's concubine." (Judg 19:22–30). Oduyoye, Mary, *Introducing African Women's Theology,* 2001:46–7, cited in Ross 2011.

[23] Musk 2004:118. While Abraham offered hospitality, he probably did none of the actual work required: it was a servant who killed and prepared the calf, and obtaining the milk and making curds/cheese and bread are traditionally occupations done by the women.

[24] Mallouhi 2004:155. See also Oduyuye on these passages in the above footnote.

without knowing it." God also provides hospitality, in offering bread, water and rest for the exhausted Elijah.

Jesus Messiah uses the theme of hospitality constantly in his teaching about God, including Luke 11:5–8 (a neighbour who needed bread), Luke 14:7–14 (places of honour); and in his actions, such as Luke 7:36–50 (true hospitality and honour, with the Pharisee and the woman), and Matthew 14:13–31, 15:32–39 (feeding both Jewish and Gentile crowds who were hungry for His Word). His description of God and his kingdom in terms of a woman baking bread (Mat 13:33, Luke 13:21) also suggests an indirect reference back to Sarah, up to her elbows in flour preparing bread to welcome their visitors, where the woman is using the same amount of flour as Sarah (Gen 18:6). Here again, hospitality is not offering 'just enough' food for the visitors, but shown in extravagant generosity: the 'three measures' describe about twenty-two litres of flour – enough bread for a banquet! These teachings and actions of Jesus give substance to his description of our salvation in terms of a great banquet, demonstrating God's hospitality (Mat 22:1–14, Luke 14:15–25).

In the New Testament, sometimes we see Jesus giving hospitality. John's Gospel is book-ended by Jesus inviting disciples to spend the day with him, and Jesus providing barbecued fish and bread for breakfast for the disciples who have been fishing all night (Jn 1:29; 21:9).[25] Sometimes, we see Jesus receiving the hospitality of people, as when he eats at the house of Pharisees (Luke 7:36ff, 14:1ff). Most often, we see Jesus both receiving and giving. He asks the Samaritan woman for water and offers her life-giving water; asks Zacchaeus to entertain Jesus at his home, offering Zacchaeus God's salvation; some of the women who have been healed by Jesus go on to travel with Jesus and his other disciples, providing for them as patrons out of the women's own resources (John 4:7–14: Luke 19:5–9, 8:2–3). We see it clearly in Rev 3:18: Jesus asks us to open the door to him, so that he can come in and share food together with us, calling us into the full experience of God's hospitality.

Understanding hospitality as a picture of the redemption offered to us in Jesus Messiah implicates not just how we read or teach the Bible, but also how we live it. Mallouhi reminds us that:

> For Muslims to feel comfortable with our spirituality they need to feel comfortable with our hospitality. This is more comprehensive than plates of food. Hospitality is not only a custom in our home, but a key into the kingdom of God. The Gospel is the story of God's hospitality in Christ. In both the Old Testament and the New Testament, it is a matter of honour. ... Hospitality is not just serving food; it is a lifestyle. It means offering each person we meet a generous heart. ... It is about making people feel like they are in their own home when they receive our hospitality. ... *'Our house is your house'*. This proverb reminds me that I am not

---

[25] Also Jn 2:1-11, where at the Cana wedding Jesus provides the new wine, referencing Jewish (like Islamic) teaching of heaven as flowing with good wine.

just inviting Muslims into my house, but inviting them to enjoy the blessing of my *home* in Christ in the Father's house. True hospitality is reciprocal.[26]

The imperative to Israel to care for the stranger and alien is grounded in the people's experience as aliens in Egypt (Ex 22:21, Lev 19:34, Deut 10:19). This idea of reciprocity is evident in the Greek word for 'stranger', *xenos*, which can also carry the complementary meaning of 'guest' or 'host.' This lived ambiguity is seen in the role of Jesus on the Road to Emmaus (Lk 24:13-33).[27] In Jesus' teaching on the good Samaritan, the despised outsider becomes the example of how to show love and hospitality to our neighbour, the near insider (Lk 10:30-37). Christine Pohl suggests that "The twin moves of universalizing the neighbour and personalizing the stranger are at the core of hospitality."[28]

Jesus Messiah consistently seeks and receives hospitality from others, in order to offer them God's hospitality. This "intermingling of guest and host roles in the person of Jesus is part of what makes the story of hospitality so compelling for Christians."[29] Jesus asks Zacchaeus for hospitality (Luke 19:1–10), and a Samaritan woman for a drink (John 4:1–42). In accepting their hospitality, he becomes their host, inviting them into all God wants to offer them. In Rev 3:20 he asks the same of us: "I am standing at the door, knocking; if you hear my voice and open the door, I will come in to you and eat with you, and you with me." The story of Mary and Martha (Luke 10:38–32) reminds us that offering hospitality to Jesus Messiah is to listen to his teaching, and is to become his disciple. This reciprocity is expressed well in an Arabic translation of Matthew 9:9–13 (from *The Meaning of the Gospel and Acts in Arabic*): 'Jesus called Matthew and said, "Come and be among those who follow me." …Then Matthew called Jesus and he followed him to his house to receive food and eat with him.' In accepting hospitality, the guest both honours the host, and invites the host reciprocally to come in to God's hospitality.

The food preparation and labour undergirding hospitality are almost always done by women: it is a central part of women's work and women's worlds. Women, then, have a crucial place in the costly hospitality which becomes a redemptive analogy within Islam of God's invitation to us. The picture of motherhood could be seen as the ultimate symbol of hospitality, where the woman shares her own body, blood and breath with the developing foetus, and continues that care throughout life.[30] This image points to the Lord's supper, where we come to receive God's hospitality. As we eat and drink, we remember the cost of this hospitality to Jesus Messiah, and we look forward to joining at God's banquet table.

---

[26] Mallouhi, 2004:153-4.
[27] Ross 2008:4.
[28] Pohl 1999:75.
[29] Pohl 1999:17.
[30] See God and Motherhood, in Chapter 14.

- When have you experienced hospitality from Muslim friends or strangers? What did you notice?
- Who is responsible for the various tasks involved in offering hospitality in your context?
- In Rev 3:20, Jesus is asking us to give him hospitality in order that he might offer us God's hospitality. How can this or other pictures of hospitality in the Bible be pictures for our friends of how God offers hospitality in Jesus?[31]

---

[31] https://whenwomenspeak.net/blog/hospitality-a-redemptive-analogy/.

Part 2

Everyday Life

10. Women's Lives

As we walk through the park in the early evening, groups of people are gathering, anticipating the coming of the New Year. Lebanese families sit together chatting, some young women in hijab, some with their head uncovered. Students from Saudi Arabia group around some picnic chairs, the women in niqab[1] with only their eyes showing. Nearby women from Bangladesh set up for the evening, while their husbands enjoy a game of cricket in the lingering light. I pause to admire clusters of balloons under a rotunda, and a group of teenage girls from Pakistan, all in hijab, come over to chat to me. Some women have grown up in their country of origin and moved here late, with more or less fluency in English. Others have spent nearly all their lives here. Muslim women from around the world are present in this park, all with different experiences of life, family and faith.

My neighbours have invited me to join them at a relative's wedding in an ME city. So, I put on the full-length cover-everything coat over my good dress and cover my head, as they do, to go out on the street and travel together to the wedding hall. We are greeted with a tiny cup of bitter coffee when we arrive, then go to remove our outer wraps and go into the main hall to where the party is being held. The room is beautifully decorated, and packed with people, but there are no men – only beautifully-dressed women. All around me I see revealing, gauzy, sequinned outfits, plunging necklines, tight-fitted dresses, hemlines of every length from floor to high hip, women with long hair flowing, or done up in elaborate hair-do's of sculpted curves and waves, glitter and flower-sprays, rich make-up. And they

---

[1] See Chapter 16.

dance! With no men around, the dancing is sensuous and uninhibited. Young, unmarried women take their turns, while older women sometimes join in, but mostly watch them perform – perhaps keeping an eye out for a potential bride for their brother or son. After a while the bride arrives, in white dress – she does one dance, then sits up on the stage and watches, while the dancing continues, and we are given drinks and a plate of refreshments. Just before midnight word comes that the groom is arriving. We cover up again in our coats and headscarves, and I find it hard to recognise the gorgeous women I have been watching shimmy, undulate and curve for the past few hours, in what has been a total pelvic celebration of womanhood. Then the wedding is nearly over – the groom and his bride dance demurely; a few women of his family join in; and finally they leave, part of a procession of cars driving around the suburb with blaring horns until they arrive at the newly-wed couple's apartment. This evening is part of me learning new ways of womanhood, of celebrating being female.

The first section of this book explored texts and their readings and cultural themes, and how they shape the lives of Muslim women. This next section looks at everyday life realities for women.

The Qur'an notes the single origin and also the differences between men and women, and between nations and tribes. They are equal in being subject to the fundamental measure of piety:[2]

O mankind! We have created you from a male and female, and made you into nations and tribes that you may know one another. Verily the most honourable of you with Allah is that who has at-Taqwa (who is righteous/God-fearing). *Al-Hujarat* 49:13.

However, other verses indicate difference between men and women in how they are treated or their position as witnesses or inheritors, including:

Get two witnesses out of your own men. And if there are not two men (available), then a man and two women, such as you agree for witnesses, so that if one of them (two women) errs, the other can remind her. *Al-Baqarah* 2:282.[3]

In discussing the place of women within Islam, it is helpful to look to the beginning of Islam to see how the new Muslim community, led by Muhammed, affected women and their roles. The time before Islam is described by Muslims as the time of ignorance (*Jahiliya*), a time when people didn't know how to live as God wanted them to. One of the customs was to bury baby girls alive. This is referred to in the Qur'an, *At-Takwir* 81:8-9: "And when the female

---

[2] Further verses cited to support the single origin and fundamental equality of women and men in Islam include *Al-Imran* 3:195, *Al-Nisa* 4:1, 32, 124, *Al-Taubah* 9:71–72, *Al-Nahl* 16:97, *Al-Rum* 30:20. This is discussed more in Chapter 18.
[3] See also *Al-Baqarah* 2:223, *al-Nisa* 4:11, 4:34.

buried alive shall be questioned: For what sin, was she killed?", and *An-Nahl* 16:58–9:

> And when the news of a female is brought to any of them, his face becomes dark, and he is filled with inward grief! He hides himself from the people because of the evil of that whereof he has been informed. Shall he keep her with dishonour or bury her in the earth? Certainly, evil is their decision.

As Islam grew, it provided more regulations for its followers, which included Muhammad prohibiting this burial of live baby girls. Al-Bukhari records it in his *hadith*:

> Narrated Al-Mughira: The Prophet said, "Allah has forbidden you (1) to be undutiful to your mothers, (2) to withhold (what you should give), or (3) demand (what you do not deserve), and (4) to bury your daughters alive. And Allah has disliked that, (A) you talk too much about others, (B) ask too many questions (in religion), or (C) waste your property."[4]

Overall, Haifaa Jawad sees Islam as opening up possibilities, as:

> ...women, under the leadership of Muhammad, enjoyed full freedom to develop their individuality and personality and to take part in shaping their own society. Moreover, women took advantage of the liberty offered to them: they participated effectively in public life; took part in prayers at the mosque together with the men; acted as *imams* for women (and sometimes for both sexes in their household); joined their colleagues in military expeditions; granted protection in war and asylum to fugitives; devoted themselves to the study of theology, the Qur'an and the traditions; travelled widely, and moved freely and mixed with men with self-respect and dignity.[5]

Leila Ahmed is more reserved about the impact of Islam on women, within marriage and in the community:

> ... the situation of women seems to have varied among the different communities of Arabia. Moreover, although Jahilia marriage practices do not necessarily indicate the greater power of women or the absence of misogyny, they do correlate with women's enjoying greater sexual autonomy than they were allowed under Islam. They also correlate with women's being active participants, even leaders, in a wide range of community activities, including warfare and religion. Their autonomy and participation were curtailed with the establishment of Islam, its

---

[4] Al-Bukhari Book #73, *Hadith* #6. See also Book #41, *Hadith* 591, and Book #92, *Hadith* #395.

[5] Jawad 1998:14. See also Stowasser 1994:15; Gerner 1984.

institution of patrilineal, patriarchal marriage as solely legitimate, and the social transformation that ensued.[6]

In the early Muslim community, we see active women around Muhammad taking responsibility, involved in the various wars, arguing with other members of the community, and even challenging Muhammad.[7] Was such lively community engagement in fact a remnant of the earlier freedom of women, or rather an emancipatory innovation from Muhammad? Leila Ahmed suggests that by permitting some practices and prohibiting others, "Islam fundamentally reformulated the nexus of sexuality and power between men and women."[8] She describes the lives of two of Muhammad's wives, Khadija and Aisha, as embodying the changes brought by Islam.

> ... (Khadija's) economic independence; her marriage overture, apparently without a male guardian to act as intermediary; her marriage to a man many years younger than herself; and her monogamous marriage all reflect Jahilia rather than Islamic practice. ... (Aisha, in contrast) was born to Muslim parents, married Muhammad when she was nine or ten, and soon thereafter, along with her co-wives, began to observe the new customs of veiling and seclusion."

This impact on women was reflected by Muhammad's great-granddaughter Sukaina, who said that she was merrier than her sister Fatima, because she was named after her pre-Islamic great-grandmother, but Fatima was named after her Islamic grandmother.[9]

Islam outlawed practices such as female infanticide, and the Qur'an gave women rights to their own bride price (*An-Nisa'* 4:4), and of inheritance and owning property (although inheritance was slanted towards the males [*An-Nisa'* 4:7, 11–12]). At the same time, Islam seems to have reinforced shifting patterns of marriage and inheritance towards a male-centric system of authority and descent.[10] And other traditional female roles of religious leadership in pre-Islamic times,[11] including the activity of the diviner-prophetesses (*kahinat*), were also now prohibited in the new Muslim community (*Al-Baqarah* 2:102, *Al-Naml* 27:65) and *hadith*.[12]

---

[6] Ahmed, Leila 1992:42. See also Mernissi 1975:34–37 and Engineer 1992:34–5; and Küng's more positive assessment in Küng 2004, 2007:157.
[7] Some of these women are described in Chapter 12.
[8] Ahmed 1992:45.
[9] Ahmed 1992:42, 43, 60.
[10] See Chapter 13.
[11] Clarke 2007:351. See also Ahmed 1992:58–60.
[12] For some examples, see http://www.muslimguide.se/Prophet_Muhammad/All-Hadith/R_S/vil/hadeeth/riyad/17/chap303.htm.

People in Places and Times

Muslims have a deep fundamental sense of family embeddedness, of belonging to the worldwide Muslim community or '*ummah*'. The word '*ummah*' is linked with the Arabic word for 'mother'. Within that worldwide community, each person is shaped by family, ethnic, sectarian, regional and national loyalties, which tell different stories of who they are and how they can behave.

Religious texts and cultural themes are realised in different ways in everyday life. Rather than relying on textbooks, in each encounter we need to ask: Who is this woman? What is her experience, and what influences have shaped her life to this point? Below, are brief descriptions of eight different Muslim women. Have you encountered women like these? How might you describe some of your Muslim friends? What are some of the influences and possibilities that you see in their lives, textual, cultural, and social?

Zaynab is a daughter in a polygamous Beduin household in the western Egyptian desert. Beduin society shapes what is seen as an acceptable lifestyle for a woman. That model links with the Beduin groups across the wider Middle Eastern region more strongly than it does with rhetoric from the Egyptian government around urban educated women, and it is different again from what is advocated by religious teachers from the Gulf preaching on the internet channels that come through the concrete walls of Zaynab's home.

Ebtisam is a serious, hard-working young woman, whose face is illuminated by warmth when she smiles. She has a couple of brothers, and helps her mother with home duties. Ebtisam is an English teacher in a secondary school. After leaving university, she took further classes in English and teacher-training in a foreign institute in the city to develop her expertise. Ebtisam attends classes at a mosque, and has memorised the whole Qur'an, and how to recite it. When not at school, she teaches girls at the mosque, helps women to memorise the Qur'an, attends some of the twice-weekly lectures to women, and also acts as a translator when the *shaykhah* meets with foreigners.

Amina has grown up in urban Australia: her parents are from Pakistan. Her parents' relationship grew increasingly abusive after they emigrated to the west, and her mother eventually separated from her husband. That decision cut her mother off from the wider Pakistani community, and her only friends are a couple of other women in a similar situation. Amina's uncles in Pakistan help support her mother, and it is their advice and money from Pakistan which determines what school Amina can go to in her Australian city. Some of her peers wear hijab like she does; others don't. They are all struggling between the conservative expectations of their parents' generation, and what they see around them in the wider western society. At the same time, they are feeling under increasing western media pressure against their Muslim identity and dress.

Fatima is from a Shi'ite family in a majority Sunni country. She attends the Shi'ite mosque and spends time with her extended family and other young women from the Shi'ite community. At the main Shi'ite mosque nearby she encounters people from Iran and across the Muslim world. However, she knows that her Sunni schoolmates see her as heretical, not a real Muslim. The current national government is dominated by another minority sect, so it gives more space to minority religious groups. If the majority Sunni group came to power, Fatima's community would face more restrictions and possibly violence, as do other Shi'ite communities across the Muslim world.

Eman grew up and went to university in a large ME city: she then went on to do her doctorate in TESL in a foreign university. Married with two children, her family of origin is well-off and well-connected, as is the family she married into. She lectures now at university, and continues to travel regularly and attend international conferences. She doesn't observe Muslim practices (fasting, prayer) with much rigour. At a recent conference, she was talking with friends about a couple of their colleagues who had recently died, through different causes. "Someone must have put the evil eye on them!" Eman exclaimed, and the others agreed.

Ina is an Indonesian Muslim from Java. Her maternal grandfather, and his forefathers before him, ran an Islamic boarding school, and there are many generations of Islamic religious teachers in her family. She was brought up following this 'purist' form of Islam, which rejects superstitious beliefs and practices. Her father was from a family which, while Muslim, still holds traditional Javanese beliefs about supernatural powers. When her father was dying, Ina discovered that he had supernatural powers which he wanted to hand down to one of his children. Since none of his children were interested, he passed the powers on to Ina's cousin as an 'inheritance.' Ina feels somewhat proud that her father had this amazing power, but is conflicted, because she knows it is not 'right' to believe in things other than God.

Lamia is Kurdish, and grew up also speaking Farsi. Married young, she has lots of initiative, and wanted to work outside the home, but her husband forbade her. When things got difficult, she and her husband sought asylum in the west, with their young daughter. Travel was difficult and dangerous: when they made it, they were imprisoned in a detention camp for several years. Now in the community, they are struggling to manage with minimal resources. Their friends are other people they got to know in the detention camp. Lamia is using all her initiative to manage getting schooling and resources needed for her daughter and the two sons since born to them. She has been to the local mosque just a few times, seeking local networks to help survive.

Fadiyah sits in the small circle of girls on the upper balcony of the mosque, where a young woman is teaching about the practice of Islam. Fadiyah's attention is divided between listening to the young woman teaching, and thinking about going to the shopping centre of town after class with her friends to look at clothes. Fadiyah is sixteen, born into a middle-class family in a suburb near the mosque. Now in secondary school, she attends some of the mosque classes for girls about Islam, and their summer programme. She would like to go on to university and study engineering when she finishes school. However, her family expect to arrange her engagement soon, so that she will be married when she is about eighteen.

All these women are Muslim, but they come from very different situations with different challenges and family expectations. As you read these stories, what are the issues and challenges faced by each of these women? What is celebrated, and what is circumscribed? How might Jesus meet them? What stories of women in the Bible might you tell to them?

Texts and cultural themes are realised in different ways for different people according to their circumstances, home and family, and life events. The communities into which people are born play an important part in forming how someone perceives themselves, others and the world. In many countries, national ID cards specify the individual's name and sectarian affiliation as well as occupation and nationality. Even without an ID card, a person's name, clothing, jewellery and the area in which they live suggest clues of the community to which they belong. These belongings shape everyday interactions, from degree of friendship through to job openings or romantic possibilities and finally, place of burial.

The tensions between belongings can open up different possibilities for behaviour.[13] Muslim women give allegiance to their families and communities, to the *ummah,* and to God. Obedience to family (and husband) is frequently expressed in terms of obedience to God: however, where there is a conflict, obedience to God is the higher allegiance. As women grow in textual understanding of Islam, this can give them room to manoeuvre and even to challenge family traditions and pressure through invoking the requirements of Islam.[14] In learning about their rights and responsibilities as Muslim women, rather than solely as members of extended families or ethnic groupings, women find a stronger position from which to negotiate life issues including marriage or divorce. Even requirements of strict segregation in some countries can open up opportunities for women, where teaching institutions require female staff, and women midwives and women doctors are wanted.

In the first section of this book, we looked at big themes, at texts and their interpretations, at cultural tropes. In this second section of the book, we explore more of the daily details of women's lives: how the textual and cultural themes of the first section play out in the everyday lives of Muslim women in areas such as family, marriage and motherhood, and life cycles. We will also look at clothing, education and the place of women in society.

As we meet Muslim women, you may find questions such as those in Appendix 1 are helpful in getting to know them as individuals in their particular contexts. In addition, each chapter in this book has suggested questions. In a gendered society, women can talk with women; men reading this book may need to ask the questions to other men (or it may be possible to have some of these discussions with women among your professional colleagues). But the most important thing is spending time with your friend, drinking tea, sharing sorrows and joys, and, if possible, meeting one another's families, and praying for them. Our first action as we meet with women or men, whatever their circumstances,

---

[13] Dale, 2018.
[14] Afshar, Aitken & Franks 2005:278; Minganti 2012:384.

is to sit down with them and listen to their stories. From listening, we can share our own lives. That includes celebrating joys and also sharing our own pain; as we do so, our friends may weep with us and share their suffering. I sat with an Arab friend some years ago, and the Palestinian poem of exile and lament that we were reading together drew my own tears of grief at recently leaving a country I loved. My tears elicited tears from my friend, and she told me of the sorrows in her own life.

This sharing allows us to seek God together – God who is not outside our suffering. In the book of Job, God describes Job as speaking rightly of him.[15] Job's 'right speaking' (not the pious truisms and theologies of Job's friends about God) included pouring out his pain, even arguing with God, constantly returning to address his plaint to God, in a faith in God so robust that he could not express his suffering outside it. The psalms of bitterness, lament and even cursing give voice to our deepest suffering and most raw emotions. Not against God, they evoke his presence in our darkest times. Stories of women in the Bible tell of God's faithfulness to women in precarious situations of danger, bereavement, childlessness and exile: of God who appears to and answers the tears and prayers, spoken or unspoken, of women such as Hagar and Hannah, whose story is evoked by Elizabeth's story and whose song gives words to Mary's song. The restoration of Job is marked by his daughters being honoured, named (in contrast to their brothers), and given an inheritance along with their brothers.[16] As we listen to and honour the stories of Muslim women, we join the Bible which names women and tells their stories, as part of the greater story of God's action in the world through history (and her-story).

- Describe a Muslim woman that you know. What communities does she belong to? What are the different allegiances shaping her life and the possibilities for her?
- What are the implications for how she behaves and what she does, and what she hopes for?
- Are some of these communal expectations different or in conflict with one another? If so, how does she resolve them?
- As you listen to your friend's story, what does it evoke of your own story?

---

[15] Job 42:7–8.
[16] Job 42:13–15.

11. Family

Out for a walk within the allowed restrictions of the Covid-19 lockdown, I meet and chat with a young Middle Eastern Muslim mother, walking with her two young children. We talk about the plan for easing restrictions. She is worried. "Even when we get to the last step, they're still limiting gatherings to fifty people," she tells me. Our family doesn't know when we can get together again: we're more than fifty people." The western government officials are working with a very different understanding of what 'family' means.

The Qur'an affirms the importance of kinship relations. *Al-Nisa* ('The Women') begins:

O mankind! Be dutiful to your Lord, Who created you from a single person,[1] and from it created its spouse, and from them both He created many men and women: and fear Allah through Whom you demand (your mutual rights), and (do not cut the relations of) the wombs (kinship). Surely Allah is Even an All-Watcher over you. *Al-Nisa 4:1.*

And the *hadith* reinforce it:

---

[1] This word is *'nafs'* (soul) and it is feminine in grammatical form. See Wadud's (1999) discussion of this verse.

Narrated Jubair bin Mut'im: That he heard the Prophet saying, "The person who severs the bond of kinship will not enter Paradise."[2]

Our family is the first group to which we belong, and that shapes our identity. Family is the beginning of wider circles of allegiance – ethnic, regional and national, and faith. For example, someone might be from a particular extended family, Sunni, belonging to a Sufi order, of Bengali ethnicity and Indian nationality. Or identify as Shi'ite, with their family roots in a certain village, and be of Lebanese nationality. Or belong to a particular Sunni Beduin tribe which crosses national borders in their nomadic herding and family networks, but has 'Iraq' as country listed on their state identity card. Some of these belongings or allegiances may, at times, be in tension with one another. And the strength of our allegiance to any one of the different groups to which we belong is often greater when we feel that the group is under threat.[3] Family relationships and allegiances spread out in extending circles of loyalty, summed up in the proverb: '*I against my brother; I and my brother against my cousin; I and my brothers and cousins against the world.*'

Western societies tend to be more individual. In individualistic societies, the interests and needs of the individual are more important than that of the group. There is a focus on individual action and decisions, on initiative and self-sufficiency. Nonconformity is not seen as negative. The ties between individuals are loose, and people can move easily in and out of groups as needed. People are expected to look after themselves and their immediate family. Moving along the spectrum to more highly collectivist or group-oriented cultures, people's behaviour and motivation can look quite different. These include societies with strong class or caste systems. In collectivist cultures people remain part of the group into which they are born for life, and act together rather than independently. Decisions are made cooperatively, on the basis of what is best for the group rather than for individuals. People are integrated into strong cohesive groups, which offer protection to their members in exchange for unquestioning loyalty. Group boundaries are clearly defined.

Hofstede suggests a number of characteristics of collectivist societies:

1. People are brought up in extended families, and are seldom alone, day or night.
2. Children think in terms of 'we' rather than 'I'.
3. Friendships are predetermined by family lines or loyalties.
4. Maintaining harmony is an important virtue, in the context of continuous face-to-face social contact.

---

[2] Al-Bukhari Book #73, *Hadith* #13.
[3] Amin Maalouf comments in his insightful book, *On Identity,* that "People often see themselves in terms of whichever one of their allegiances is most under attack." (2000:22, also 13).

5. 'No' is almost never used. 'Yes' can have a range of meanings, from merely 'Yes, I can hear you,' right through to 'Yes, I agree with you and will act.'
6. People look to the opinion of the group rather than their own opinion.
7. Group loyalty means that resources are shared.
8. Family rituals and celebrations are very important.
9. People are comfortable with silence.
10. Collectivist societies are shame cultures. People belonging to a group, when a member of that group has broken social rules, will all feel ashamed. Shame is social, constructed between people, whereas guilt is individual.[4]

The communities to which we belong form how we see ourselves, others and the world; and this is greater in more collectivist cultures. In strongly group-based societies, the family rather than the individual is the primary unit of the community. Interdependence is valued rather than independence: the mature individual is the one who successfully functions within and contributes to a web of multiple relationships. Allegiance and group membership follows family lines of loyalty. Most Muslim societies are strongly collectivist societies, where group opinion is more important than that of the individual, and the (extended) family is the fundamental social unit. Mallouhi describes:

> ... the social structure and culture of Muslims in which a person is always in relation with, and connected to, one other social unit, usually a group. Western emphasis on self-concerned individualism appears deviant and detrimental to a society where one's duty is to do what is in the best interests of the group. ... (They) do not expect to live as individuals taking responsibility for their own affairs. Life is lived in the community of family and friends, and they all help each other in the business of everyday life.[5]

The group offers belonging and protection to the individual, in return for absolute loyalty. And the group, rather than the individual, is responsible for maintaining correct behaviour. Because the individual is representative of the group to which they belong, responsibility for individual behaviour rests with the group, to ensure that its members behave in a way that is moral and not deviant. This control is often enforced through the social mechanism of shame, particularly for women: they are warned against individual behaviour (for example, wearing a skirt that is too short) that could bring shame on their families. When necessary, more severe sanctions are invoked. Being cast out of one's family means being cast out of everything that defines who you are, and

---

[4] Hofstede 2005:86–92. He also suggests that the most important values in a collectivist society are:
- filial piety (obeying, respecting and honouring one's parents)
- chastity in women
- patriotism (pp.80-81).
[5] Mallouhi 2004:133–5.

cut off from the social networks and connections to negotiate all of life. Mallouhi comments:

> ... the extended family views its members as resources, not independent agents. The family takes responsibility for the behaviour of its members, supports them materially, and can be counted on to come to members' aid when needed. The family must be able to count on its individuals to give it supreme loyalty, for only then can it be a viable unit, guaranteeing to fulfil its legal and social obligations.[6]

Conversely, a group may be punished or sanctioned for the behaviour of an individual within it, as part of trying to persuade the group to bring the individual into line. This can apply to families, and also nations. Nationally, a number of Muslim countries brought in sanctions against Danish products after the publication of the Danish cartoons about Muhammad. On a family level, if someone has done something shameful, their parents will lose respect and honour in the community, and it can mean that no one will be willing to marry their siblings.

The difference between collectivist family-based cultures and more individualistic ones has implications on how we perceive and relate to one another. Dhami and Sheikh note how: "One of the most striking features of Muslim society is the importance attached to the family. The family unit is regarded as the cornerstone of a healthy and balanced society. The different plane of emphasis from that found in individual-centred cultures is, for many, remarkable."[7] Muslims may be surprised at the degree of freedom given to individuals to behave how they like in the west, independent of their family and the wider community. It is not uncommon for writers from Muslim societies, with an emphasis on and concern for family, to position Islam over and against what is perceived as the degeneration of family and family values in the 'Christian' west. Muslims from countries characterised by commonality in ethnic and religious identity can perceive a post-religious, post-modern western world as 'Christian', and so conclude that Christianity equals immorality. Sayyid Qutb, ideologue of the Muslim Brotherhood, commented that: "The family system and the relationship between the sexes determine the whole character of a society and whether it is backward or civilised, Jahili or Islamic."[8]

Collectivist societies are often patriarchal, where authority is conferred through gender and age. Younger people and females defer to the authority and wishes of older people and males. Relationship with significant males carries power. The mother-in-law and sisters-in-law may exercise authority over a new bride. Where relationship is defined by bloodlines, the mother–son relationship is likely to be much stronger than the husband–wife relationship. For example,

---

[6] Mallouhi 2004:141–2.
[7] Dhami and Sheikh 2000: 352–56.
[8] http://www.missionislam.com/family/index.htm. See also Maududi's extended discussions on this theme in his book *Purdah and the Status of Women in Islam* (1981).

senior women in many Middle Eastern, African and Central Asian societies have considerable influence in tribal affairs. In Southeast Asia, a number of the societies are matrilineal, where women generally have more power and independence in society.

'Blood can never turn to water,' says an Arab proverb, showing the strength of family (and also that blood bonds are much stronger than legal ones in defining family – hence the weaker position of wives and daughters-in-law). This can shape patterns of marriage and authority. In many societies, marriage is also along family lines (endogamous),[9] where the preferred spouse is your cousin. When women are embedded in the family and honour of their husband, marrying within the extended family may be seen to offer more security. That embedding can come with physical constraints. There is a saying in the Middle East that 'Women move three times: from the womb to their father's house, from their father's house to their husband's house, and from their husband's house to the grave.' The Pashtun proverb is starker: *'Women: the home or the grave.'*[10]

One of the key ways for a woman to gain respect and honour is to marry and have children (especially a boy in patriarchal cultures, but a girl may be celebrated more in some Southeast Asian cultures). While some Muslim communities give preference to sons, there are *hadith* which promote good treatment of daughters:.

> Whosoever has a daughter and he does not bury her alive, does not insult her, and does not favor his son over her, God will enter him into Paradise."[11]

> Narrated Abu Sa'id al-Khudri: The Prophet (PBUH) said: "If anyone cares for three daughters, disciplines them, marries them, and does good to them, he will go to Paradise.[12]

While women's household duties and responsibilities may vary according to context, women manage kinship networks everywhere.

A few weeks ago, I was with a Syrian family who had migrated to the west – an older woman with her daughter and son-in-law, and their small children. Like most Syrian families, they had suffered the death of close family members in the conflict. I knew the small town they had come from. But now their house there was demolished and the fruit trees that they had lovingly tended over the years were razed. As I talked with the older woman, her tears came and went, flowing freely as we talked of family and home. So much had been destroyed: not just physical buildings and trees, but family memories – links to past recollections together with the prospect of building new memories with extended family and

---

[9] At different times in the OT history of Israel, there was a strong preference to marry within the tribe or nation, and not to marry foreign women. At other times, exogamous relationships were more common.

[10] See Chapter 16.

[11] Musnad Ibn Hanbal, No. 1957.

[12] Book #41, *Hadith* #5128, Sunan Abu Dawud.

familiar spaces, for the new generation. Her story was that of so many women and men today, in a world where unprecedented numbers of people have been forced from their homes, both refugees and internally-displaced people. Around the world, 25–30% of displaced families are female-headed households. Among some refugee groups, those numbers rise to 40–50%. These include many women who have seen their husbands or sons killed, or lost their children in their desperate flight. They have experienced bereavement, rape, torture, and seeing family members beheaded in front of them. As refugees, they continue to fear violence and harassment. Many young girls among them are forced into early marriage, as the family fear for their safety and honour.

What does this mean for us when we enter another culture? If we enter a family-based, collectivist culture, we do not enter as one person among a collection of other individuals. Rather, we step into a society of groups – families, clans, and tribes, where to belong means to belong to a particular in-group. Respect is given, not so much on the basis of individual achievement, but according to the recognised group(s) with which we are connected. Single women entering a Muslim culture may find respect according to who they are linked with. This relationship can be with the family of a local landlord or employer, but it is helpful to have a sponsor (local or expatriate) to make the connection. Lila Abu-Lughod was surprised at her father's insistence on accompanying her when she first arrived in Egypt to do anthropological research, and was making links with the Beduin community. She reflects,:

> What I had not considered was that respectability was reckoned not just in terms of behaviour in interpersonal interactions but also in the relationship to the larger social world. … Any girl valued by her family … would not be left unprotected to travel alone at the mercy of anyone who wished to take advantage of her. By accompanying me, my father hoped to lay any such suspicions to rest.[13]

To the extent that we become adopted into a family, we become protected, part of that network of relationships. At the same time, the belonging and protection can carry obligations. We are expected to behave in a way that conforms to group social norms and brings honour, and have relationships which do not contravene the social networks of the particular group that adopts us. Interpersonal behaviour and obligations are then based on the perception of common bonds, whether through mutual acquaintances or shared ethnicity, so that we perceive each other as members of the same in-group. Conversely, people with whom we have no connection have no claim on us.[14]

Understanding how collectivist cultures function may help us as we read the Bible. One of the characteristics of the English language is that there is no

---

[13] Abu-Lughod 1986:11–12.
[14] However, patronage relationships can form bonds that go across extended family and in-group linkings.

distinction made between 'you' singular and 'you' plural. A consequence of this is that we tend to read 'you' in the Bible as though it is addressed to individuals whereas, in fact, many of the occurrences are to 'you' plural – the whole community. People from collectivist cultures may find it easier to engage with being addressed and asked to respond communally rather than solely as individuals. Similarly, it is important that if we get to know individual people, we try to do so as part of their extended family by building relationships with and becoming known and trusted by the group to which they belong.

The Bible strongly affirms the value and sanctity of family as created by God, including the lines of the extended family beyond just the nuclear family unit. The emphasis on family is not just something we can endorse as a social value. It is also a picture of what we are called to become through what Jesus has done – becoming part of God's family, God's own children, in relationship to our Heavenly Father. We see afresh how radical this new family status and relationship is, beyond that of created beings in relation to the Creator, even beyond being obedient servants or slaves of God.[15] The very strength of family in collectivist society can make it a redemptive picture of what God is calling us into. To be a Muslim is to be part of the *Ummah*, the international community of Muslims everywhere. Likewise, the New Testament calls us to remind one another that we are part of God's worldwide family of believers. This means that as people give allegiance to Jesus Messiah, they are becoming part of a much greater family of mutual belonging all around the world. Being members of that family, we are committed to care for and be strengthened by one another even beyond our blood or ethnic family loyalties.[16] The analogy goes even beyond that of family, to the intimacy of being one body, the body of Jesus Messiah in the world. This metaphor of how we live out our redemption in Jesus also means that we cannot exist independently as individuals or individual churches. Rather, we must all depend on one another so that the family, the body of Jesus Messiah, may be complete with all its members and equipped[17] for all that God calls us to.

While the Bible affirms family as a powerful analogy of our redemption in Jesus, it also challenges and redefines family structures. As children of God, our first loyalty is to our heavenly Father, and to Jesus who calls us into His family, beyond our primary family relationships. This is seen vividly when Jesus' mother and brothers call him to leave his teaching, and Jesus turns to the crowd and tells them, "Whoever does the will of God is my brother and sister and mother."[18] Even Mary's special status as the mother of Jesus, so honoured also in the Qur'an, does not exceed the primary requirement of attentiveness and

---

[15] John 1:12–13. Also, John 8:21–36; Heb 2:11–13; 3:5–6. Contrast with the Islamic saying that "God took us from being slaves of men to slaves of God."
[16] 1 Peter 5:9.
[17] Eph 3:15f; 1 Cor 12.
[18] Mark 3:21, 31–35: also recounted in Matt 12:46ff and Luke 8:19ff.

obedience to God's Word in Jesus.[19] Allegiance to Jesus, as the one who calls us into the new family of God, has priority over earthly family allegiances.[20] We see the significance of giving priority to Jesus and Jesus' family, particularly in contexts where allegiance to Jesus leads to people being rejected from their own birth families. Practically, it can mean that those of us who remain within our own families are called to give costly priority to providing space, time and bonds of family loyalty and mutual assistance to others who have lost their families, for the sake of Jesus.

The Torah commandment to 'love your neighbour as yourself',[21] was written in a context when the neighbour would most likely have been part of your in-group, probably part of the extended family who would naturally live in proximity to one another.[22] However, in the story of the good Samaritan, Jesus pictures a member of the Jews' ethnic enemies caring for a Jew as though he was part of his own in-group, and asks us to follow his example and do the same in a radical change to treating everyone we meet as members of our own extended family and in-group.[23]

The family codes[24] in the New Testament show the importance of family structure for the emerging Jesus community, but at the same time they challenge traditional family hierarchies of power and importance. Authority at that time was conferred by maleness, age and free (non-slave) status. However, the New Testament household codes ask for *mutual* lines of submission and accountability. Those who are accounted higher in the hierarchy have correspondingly more responsibility for how they behave towards others. And everyone is given equal significance before God, with equal right of access to God. In the Gospels, family members who were considered less important at that time, including women and small children, become models of discipleship.[25]

In a collectivist and often patriarchal society encountering the community of Jesus Messiah, what might be the place of women? Lewis looks at the early church and the church in other non-western nations, to see why women are so attracted to the person of and faith in Jesus Messiah. They were drawn by the

---

[19] Luke 11:27–28.
[20] Matt 10:37f; Luke 14:26f; also, Luke 9:61.
[21] Luke 10:27, Lev 19:18.
[22] Note that the Torah also contains plenty of injunctions to care for the stranger living among us, as well as the widow and orphan – all people who have lost their immediate natural 'in-group' connections.
[23] It is possible that this parable fundamentally underlies the idea of universal human rights, challenging the natural human tendency to tribalism and to privileging the rights and needs of our own community over outsiders.
[24] Eph 5:22–6:9; Col 3:18–4:1: also 1 Pet 2:13–3:7. Shi-Min Lu's "Women's Role in New Testament Household Codes" offers further discussion of the context and implications of these passages.
https://www.cbeinternational.org/resource/audio/womens-role-new-testament-household-codes-dialogue-confucian-filial-piety.
[25] Gal 3:28; Matt 18:1–5; Luke 7:36–50.

requirements of Christian men to treat their wives well, and the equal requirement of fidelity from both partners. In the new community in Christ, women were known by their own names (not only as the wife or mother of someone else), encouraged to attend Christian worship meetings, and received the possibility of education and medical treatment (from women). Often, women had greater interest in the spiritual world, too. Women (whether mothers or wives, servants or nurses) were gateways of the Good News to unbelieving families. They began teaching and sharing with their neighbours; many of these 'Bible women' became itinerant evangelists, pastors and teachers. Their role became particularly important when the church was under pressure; women tended to be drawn less into western leadership structures, where entry to training was restricted by seminary places, and those trained became easily visible targets in times of persecution.[26]

- When you think of family, who do you think of? Nuclear or extended?
- What are the lines of mutual responsibility and obligation?
- Ask some of your Muslim friends. How do your answers compare?
- What local groups are you identified with or part of? How does that affect how people view you?

---

[26] Lewis 2004:145. Also, Stark 1997.

12. Role Models

As the main teacher in the mosque programme, Amira is a role model of what it looks like to be a pious Muslim woman, for the women she teaches. She gives them her expertise in how to memorise and correctly recite the Qur'an, and how the authoritative commentaries interpret it. In return, her students sometimes give her token material gifts, or invite her to a meal where she comes and teaches more informally, answering questions from her hostess and other women the hostess has invited from her family or friends. Some of the young women may help her at home with domestic duties or with her children. Also, they repay her by publicly acknowledging and honouring her as a good model and teacher.

"Today we will see the way we can arrive to conformity with the Prophet (PBUH) (*Al-Nisa* 4:69). Sayidna Ibn Omar did what the Prophet did. One day the Prophet was walking along a path and stopped for a little while in one place and then continued. Ibn Omar came along there and stood in the same place and then continued on the path. See this love! … Ibn Omar loved him and followed him in all details." (From a mosque teacher, to the women assembled for her lecture.)

The Qur'an and *hadith* both refer to Muhammad as the primary role model for all Muslims:

Indeed in the Messenger of Allah you have a good example to follow. *Al-Ahzab* 33:21.

Muhammad said, "So fear Allah and have patience. And I am the best Salaf (predecessor) for you."[1]

Barlas says of this *hadith*, "Today we'd say, 'I'm the best model for you.'"[2]

Role models give tangible form to community values. Living out the approved ways of being, they are the embodied *telos* of a communal liturgy of how to move in the world. Role models make possibilities real and give them flesh. We discover who we want to be by finding role models – people who embody what we value by how they live, dress, walk or talk. Girard proposes that all our desires are mimetic, borrowed through other people. Our desire for a given object (or *telos*) is always provoked by the desire of another desiring the same end. Through our desire we are drawn to the model who is the mediator, and who becomes the focus of our desires.[3]

Muslims look to Muhammad as the ultimate ideal role model, embodying a life lived in proper submission to God in all its details. The practice of Orthodox Islam is a detailed codification of behaviour firmly grounded in the example and precepts of Muhammad, in minute detail. However, women referred to in the Qur'an, and in the history of the early Muslim community, also offer powerful role models. These women can play a significant role in determining what Muslim women can and cannot do, including dress, daily life, and the role they play in the family and society. Texts, history and community combine to offer possibilities or prohibitions for Muslim women in their lives. In this chapter we look briefly at the women mentioned in the Qur'an and *hadith*: you will find many of these women cited as examples in Muslim lectures, sermons, and books for women in Muslim bookshops. We also note possible models in contemporary communities.

A number of the women referred to in the Qur'an are also mentioned in the Bible.

- Adam & his wife (*Al-Baqarah* 2:30–39, *Al-A'raf* 7:11–27, *Al-Hijr* 15:26–43, *Ta-Ha* 20:115–124, *Sad* 38:71-85). In the Qur'anic account Satan tempts Adam directly, not through Eve (*Ta-Ha* 20:120f).
- The wives of Noah and Lot (*Hud* 11:81, *Al-Ankabut* 29:32–3; *Al-Tahrim* 66:10). In *Al-Tahrim* 10–12, these two women are examples of warning.[4] They are contrasted with Pharaoh's wife and Maryam, mother of 'Isa (Jesus), who are models to be emulated.
- The wives of Abraham. There is more detail given to Sarah (*Hud* 11:69–72; *Al-Dhariyat* 51:24–30). Her role with Abraham is paralleled to that of Khadijah who was her husband Muhammad's first follower and

---

[1] Saheeh Muslim: no. 2450. http://www.mideastweb.org/Middle-East-Encyclopedia/salafi.htm.

[2] Barlas and Finn 2019:7.

[3] Alison 1996; Girard 1996; McDonald 2003.

[4] Stowasser comments on this chapter, "The main theme of Sura 66 is female rebellion in a prophet's household and its punishment." (1994:39).

supporter.[5] Perhaps surprisingly, there is little about Hagar: the only reference is indirect (*Ibrahim* 14:37). However, Hagar becomes increasingly important in Islamic tradition as 'mother of the Arabs'.[6]

- The Aziz's[7] wife (*Yusuf* 12:22–53), named in the traditions as Zulaykha. The account of her love for Yusuf and attempted seduction is recounted in detail in the Qur'an. Some traditions tell of her continued love for Yusuf even when she was old and widowed, and that Yusuf prayed to God and her youth was restored, and she finally married him. Hence, she takes her place as a repentant and, ultimately, rewarded role model.
- The women who were part of the story of Moses: his mother and sister (*Al-Qasas* 28:7–13, 20:40), Pharaoh's wife (*Al-Qasas* 9), and Moses' wife (*Al-Qasas* 23–27).[8] Wadud[9] notes that in *Al-Qasas* 7, Moses' mother is described as being given inspiration (*wahy*) like the prophets.
- The Queen of Sheba (*Al-Namal* 27:23–44), named in the *hadith* as Bilquis.
- The wife of Zakariya (Zechariah) and mother of Yahya (John the Baptist) (*Al-Imran* 3:40).
- Maryam, described as the mother of 'Isa (*Al-Imran* 3:35–51; *Al-Nisa'* 4:156, 171; *Al-Ma'idah* 5:17, 75, 78, 116; *Maryam* 19:16–34; *Al-Anbiya'* 21:91, 101; *Al-Tahrim* 66:12). We find the name of Maryam also as Aaron's sister (*Maryam* 19:28), and linked with Moses (*Al-Mu'minun* 23:50). While various women are alluded to in the Qur'an, only Maryam (Arabic form of Mary), the mother of 'Isa (Jesus),[10] is given her own name.

There are also a number of references to Muhammad's wives in the Qur'an.[11] Many of the rules around behaviour for Muslim women today derive from verses in the Qur'an connected to Muhammad's wives, and their relationship with him. These allusions occur in *Al-Nur* 24, *Al-Ahzab* 33 and *Al-Tahrim* 66, and all of them are said to derive from the revelations that occurred in the later period when Muhammad was resident in Medina.

---

[5] Especially emphasised in Sara's story "is the fact that [she] was the first to believe in her husband's mission, together with his cousin, or nephew, Lot. In this manner, the story of Sara and Abraham is now mainly presented as a pragmatic antecedent to the history of Khadija and Muhammad, since it was Muhammad's wife, Khadija, who first believed in the Prophet's mission together with his first cousin, later also son-in-law, Ali ibn Abi Talib." Stowasser 1994:46.

[6] For example: *Hagar: The Princess, the Mother of the Arabs; and Ishmael, the Father of Twelve Princes*, by Chheenah 2012.

[7] Potiphar in the biblical account of Joseph.

[8] In the Bible, it was Pharaoh's daughter who adopted Moses. There is no mention of the Hebrew midwives (notably named in Exodus) in the Qur'anic account.

[9] Wadud 1999: 38–9.

[10] There has been a lot of debate about how the name 'Jesus'/'Iesus' acquired the Qur'anic form of "Isa'. The most common view is that it is derived from a Syriac translation of his name.

[11] See Chapter 13 for more discussion of Muhammad's wives. Also, Stowasser 1994.

Al-Nur 24:4–26 refers to when the camp moved on without Muhammad's young wife Aisha, and she was picked up by a young soldier who caught up with the army with her on his camel. This revelation is said to have been given to Muhammad a month later, to resolve his uncertainties around the incident and the ensuing gossip.

Al-Ahzab 33:6 gives rise to the description of Muhammad's wives as 'Mothers of the Believers.' With this special status came the command that they could not marry again after Muhammad's death (*Al-Ahzab* 33:53). Remarriage, whether due to widowhood or divorce, was widespread at the time.

Al-Ahzab 33:28–29 reflects a major crisis between Muhammad and his wives. There are a number of different accounts about the nature of this crisis. Some point to the wives' desire for more possessions, or quarrelling over food. Others link it to arguments between Aisha and Hafsa, or to Muhammad having sexual relations with his Coptic concubine Maryam on a day allowed to Hafsa. He is said to have secluded himself from his wives for a month before these verses were revealed, offering them a clear choice between God and Prophet, and the world and its adornment. All of them, starting with Aisha, chose the former.

Al-Ahzab 33:32 designates Muhammad's wives as not like other women – hence their unique title of Mothers of the Believers, and the injunction not to remarry. In this passage (*Al-Ahzab* 33:30-34) they are described as doubly punished or doubly rewarded for their deeds. They are to stay in their houses, and recite or recall God's verses. However, these women, and the stipulations for their lives, have become normative for Muslim women in many parts of the world today.

Al-Ahzab 33:36–38 gives Muhammad freedom to take as his wife Zaynab who, at the time, was married to Zayd, the freed slave and adopted son of Muhammad. *Al-Ahzab* 33:50–51 extends the account of Muhammad's special marital privileges. He can marry who he wants without restrictions, and can also leave them for a while and receive them again later.

Al-Ahzab 33:53, 55 are the beginning of the requirement of seclusion for Muhammad's wives. Again, there are different accounts of the reason for this revelation. Many accounts derive it from guests who lingered too long after the feast for Muhammad's wedding to Zaynab. Others suggest it came when the hand of one of Muhammad's wives accidentally touched another man's hand. And these verses are followed by *Al-Ahzab* 33:59, with the ordinance of complete covering for women. (This was followed by the later revelation of *Al-Nur* 24:30–31, on veiling – just after the declaration of Aisha's innocence.)

Al-Tahrim 66:1–5 again has different incidents suggested as the stimulus for this revelation. Some link it to the incident with Maryam the Coptic concubine: others to some of the wives (either Hafsa and Aisha, or Aisha, Sawda and Safiyya) plotting to stop Muhammad spending more time with a wife who offered him honey drinks. And as noted above, *Al-Tahrim* 10 follows with a warning about the penalty for disobedient wives.

How the Qur'an describes women, and its accounts of the interactions between Muhammad and his wives, shapes the possibilities and prohibitions guiding the behaviour of Muslim women today. Books describing the women in Muhammad's family focus especially on their exemplary generosity to the poor. Specific traditions about them are used to decide details of jurisprudence and daily practice. *Hadith* about Aisha and Umm Salamah which present them as guides and teachers are used to challenge the *hadith* that describes women as lacking intelligence and piety. Some contemporary writers argue for reform in the practice and interpretation of Islamic law on the basis of Muhammad's wives, who provide:

> ... a new model of womanhood in Islam, for it is now well known that several of his wives challenged male supremacy and, as widows, took an active interest in public and political affairs. Several, such as 'Aisha, Umm Salama, and Umm Habiba, were renowned for their 'intellectual qualities,' and 'Aisha is said to have been one of the principal sources of 2,210 *hadith*.[12]

Muhammad's Female Companions

Zaynab al-Ghazali (1917–2005) was one of the most influential Muslim women in Egypt in the last century. As a young woman, Zaynab had joined the Egyptian Feminist Union organised by Huda al-Sharawi, a pioneering woman activist in Egypt. Zaynab recounts how her father used to ask her, "Will you be like al-Sharawi, or will you follow the example of Nasibah Ka'b?" and she would respond, "I will be like Nasibah."[13] She left al-Sharawi to found her own Islamic women's network, the Muslim Women's Association (MWA). Through the MWA, its teaching and social work, and al-Ghazali's link with the Muslim Brotherhood, she inspired thousands.

The traditions describe Muhammad's Companions, who continued to be influential in shaping the thinking of the Muslim community (particularly the *Maliki* school of jurisprudence). Among them we also hear of the female Companions (*Sahabiyat*). Many of them were immediately involved in battle, both in succouring the wounded and in direct fighting. Fatima Mernissi describes them as "actively involved in the Prophet's preaching, battles and debates."[14] They include martyrs, poets and warriors. Below are listed some of the prominent female Companions whose stories are told as examples and role models for Muslim women today.

Summayah bint Khabat was a freed slave, and one of the first seven to swear allegiance to Muhammad. Without powerful connections, her family were

---

[12] Anouar 2002:86.
[13] One of the early woman Companions of Muhammad.
[14] Mernissi 1996:98–9.

among those who bore the brunt of early Muslim persecution, and Summayah was killed by Abu Jahl, becoming the first martyr in Islam.

Asma' bint Abu Bakr was the paternal older sister of Aisha. When her father, Abu Bakr, fled with Muhammad from Mecca to Medina, they hid in a cave for a while, and she took provisions to them. When they prepared to go to Medina, she packed food into a leather bag. Lacking anything with which to tie up the bag, she tore her belt, or girdle, in two and used one part to tie it. For this reason, she is known as 'The Lady of the Two Girdles' (*Dhat al-Nataqin*).

Um Haram bint Malhan was a woman who lived on the outskirts of Medina, and Muhammad often stopped to rest at her house. Later in Uthman's caliphate, she joined a naval force to Cyprus. There, she fell off a mule and broke her neck and died, and a mosque marks where she is buried in Cyprus.[15]

Al-Khansa Tamadur bint Amr ibn Shareed was a poet. Her first long poem was a eulogy to her brother after his death. Before the Battle of Qadisiyah, she exhorted her sons to fight courageously, which they did until they were all martyred.

Sayfiyah bint 'Abdul-Muttalib, Muhammad's paternal aunt, killed a man in the Battle of the Trench, and was also active in the Battle of Uhud. When Muhammad died, she eulogised him in poetry.

Nasibah bint Ka'b Maziniyah al-Ansariyah is often cited as someone who took an active role in a number of the battles of the early Muslim community. In the battle of Uhud she took water to the fighters, but when she got there and saw the Muslims losing, she took sword, bow and arrows from escaping fighters, and fought beside Muhammad, protecting him. He described her: "Whenever I turned left or right on the day of the battle of Uhud, I always saw her fighting in my defence."[16] She sustained twelve wounds from the fighting, including a wound on her neck that remained with her. She also participated in a number of other battles, including the Battles of Khaybar and of Hunain.

Umm Waraqah bint Abdullah bin Harith Ansariah, was a wealthy widow, known to spend her time in prayer, meditation and reciting the Qur'an. When she asked Muhammad what to do about observing prayer in her household when there was no man to lead it, Muhammad told her that she could lead the prayer in her house. Hence, she is cited to show that women can lead prayer in a mixed congregation of women and men. Umm Waraqah wanted to die on the battlefield for Islam, but Muhammad told her to stay at home and she would gain martyrdom. She had told her two slaves that they would be free after her death, so they conspired to kill her in her sleep and escape. They were found, tried and put to death.[17]

---

[15] Her grave is on the shore of the Larnaca Salt Lake, near Larnaca, and is marked by the Hala Sultan Tekke, also known as the Mosque of Umm Haram.

[16] 'Ali Qutb 2007:186.

[17] This *hadith,* generally cited as support for a woman leading men and women in prayer, is found in Appendix 2. Al-Qadarawi comments on this: "It is reported by Imam

These women and others played an influential part in the fledgling Muslim community. Their stories tell of women of character and initiative, showing faithfulness and devotion to Muhammad, stoicism in facing bereavement of sons in Muslim battles, and active participation in battles themselves. Their examples continue to be significant in shaping the lives of Muslim women today. Other chapters refer to significant women in Muslim history.[18] These women can also act as role models, dependent on how accessible their stories may be to Muslim women in their own contexts. The more immediate the women or their stories are, the more powerful their example.

Contemporary Muslim Women Role Models

Layla grew up in a family where women weren't highly educated. So, when she left high school early, her only options were housework or manual labouring in the field. In the local mosque women's programme, she met women who were tertiary-educated, many of them working in offices or schools as well as teaching other young women in the mosque. With encouragement from the female shaykhah at the mosque, Layla learned the Qur'an and became a teacher for younger girls. At the same time, she went back to school and graduated and went on to university. Now she has the respected title of 'teacher' in her community.

Our learning is primarily social and imitative. The people we know or know of offer possibilities and narratives of who we can be. People make possibilities real, give them flesh. They are role models in our communities of how to live and what we might become. As role models, they give tangible form to the valued stories, the honoured ways of being in the community. Women can discover who they want to be by finding role models who embody what they value in how they live, dress, walk, work and talk. Through embodying particular ways of behaving – ways of speech, deportment and dress, and also professional possibilities – women provide powerful role models for other women in their daily lives.

In our first community – our family – both fathers and mothers can be influential in shaping the possibilities to which we aspire. Some women describe fathers who encouraged or taught them, creating space for them in the wider community. Examples include Nazira Zayn-al-din (Lebanon), Zaynab al-

---

Ahmad, Abu Dawud, and others on the authority of Umm Waraqah, who said that the Prophet (peace and blessings be upon him) appointed a muezzin for her, and ordered her to lead the members of her household (who included both men and women) in prayer." http://www.islamopediaonline.org/fatwa/dr-yusuf-al-qaradawi-comments-females-leading-co-gender-friday-prayers-and-women-leading-other. However, for an opposite reading of this *hadith*, see
http://www.newislamicdirections.com/nid/articles/female_prayer_leadership_revisited.
[18] See Chapters 4, 13, 17, 18.

Ghazzali (Egypt), Huda al-Habashi (Syria) and Malala Yousafzai (Pakistan). However, the first dominant role model for women is, most frequently, their mother. Huda al-Habashi, Syrian *shaykhah*, while looking back to her father as a strong influence for her in role modelling piety and providing opportunities for study, described her mother as her main influence. At a time when most girls were illiterate, her mother was celebrated in the village as one of two girls who had learned to read. In her own generation, Huda became one of only four or five girls in her school to memorise the whole Qur'an. Huda's daughter went on to break new ground in their conservative community by going abroad to study.[19] The female role models in the family offered a trajectory for women pursuing scholarship that took them beyond the communal norms.

Families are the primary place to find role models. Alternate role models can also be found in wider groups, particularly if they are affiliated communities. For a woman from a traditionally conservative middle-class family, the female teacher affiliated with the mosque – dressing and behaving publicly according to the community expectations of female modesty – may offer more radical possibilities for roles that are not in opposition to, but are grounded in and growing beyond the domestic sphere. However, women members of parliament or even government ministers in the country may not provide women with available roles if they come from a different sectarian community or class.

Cross-cultural workers may also offer role models, especially if their lives are characterised by recognisable patterns of piety. They can also help introduce women to the examples of others who are culturally near to them: inside or near role models are powerfully reproducible.

Paul encourages us to "pattern your lives after mine, and learn from those who follow our example", as he himself follows the example of Christ (Phil 3:17; 1 Cor11:1). Stories of women in the Bible can offer powerful models of courage and initiative. They include wives, women who led, warriors, wise women and working women (such as Deborah, Ruth, Esther, Huldah; Mary Magdalene, Priscilla, Phoebe, and Lydia). Mary, mother of Jesus looked back to Hannah in her song (Lk 1:46–55: 1 Sam 2:1–10), and also to Hannah's example of giving up her son to God's call. The Bible also tells of God acting to answer the prayers of women in situations of powerlessness or desperation (Hagar, Tamar, Hannah).[20] It tells of how God takes up the stories of individuals as part of his greater story of redemption, reminding us that our own life narratives are part of an immensely greater narrative. We realise both how minor and, at the same time, how significant our own lives and stories become.

---

[19] Dale 2016:106.

[20] The Bible also tells terrible stories of women who are abused. Long before the #MeToo movement, the Bible recorded that this abuse was happening and told the stories of the women, even including their names sometimes. It refused to pretend that it was alright, or to ignore or hide the stories, even when leaders and kings were involved.

- Choose one of the women from the list of women in the Qur'an who are also mentioned in the Bible. Compare and contrast with the biblical account. How is she described in the Qur'an? What is emphasised? What are the lessons taught? Why might she be included?
- What do we know of the women who followed Jesus, and of women in the early church? What similarities or differences do you note with the women around Muhammad? In what way are these women role models for the Christian community today? For you?
- Who are the role models to whom your Muslim friends look as examples for their lives, past or present? Whose behaviour do they cite as an example for them to follow? What do you notice about their role models? What values do they embody? What possibilities do they open up for those who seek to imitate them?

13. Marriage

There is a knock on the door. When I open it, a woman is standing there, a stranger. "Do you have a daughter of marriageable age?" she questions. "I'm asking for my nephew." I know what the steps are to follow: she and other woman relatives of the prospective bridegroom will come for a visit and evaluate my daughter for deportment, physical beauty and strength as she serves them refreshments. At the same time, they will be making enquiries with our neighbours and other family connections, to find out if our family is respectable, or has any peculiarities in behaviour, less desirable connections or family members. If all that goes well, the prospective bridegroom will come with his family to meet her. This time, she will be modestly covered with only her face showing – he will be largely dependent on his female relatives for more description. Then the formal legal ceremony will follow, with only the men of the family involved: the bride's father or guardian, the bridegroom, the shaykh of the mosque. Sometime after all that will be the wedding party, following which the couple will move in together. For now, I explain that my daughter is fifteen years, and we want her to finish her education before thinking of marriage – I hope my visitor will be able to find another suitable candidate for her nephew.

I have just come from a conversation with my neighbour, who has had a worse argument than usual with her husband. The mark where he struck her still shows on her face. As I prepare lunch with my local friend, I ask her, "What do you do if a man raises his hand against his wife?" She is silent for so long that I think she hasn't heard me, and I'm about to repeat the question when she asks me, "Is that not acceptable in your country?" It is my turn to be silent, wondering about what was happening behind the apparently amicable interactions in her marriage, and others I witness.[1]

I am exploring proverbs of the country I am living in. Whenever I ask about marriage, people chuckle and tell me, 'Marriage is like a watermelon, that has to be cut and tasted to know its value.'

In other words, you can't know for sure how it will go until you get into it! How true – for both 'love' and 'arranged' marriages.

What does the Qur'an have to say? There are a number of verses dealing with marriage, as guidance for the newly-formed Muslim community, especially in *Al-Baqarah* 2 and *Al-Nisa'* 4. Relevant verses include: *Al-Baqarah* 2: 222, 223, 235; *Al-Nisa'* 4:3,4,20–21, 24–25, 34–5, *Al-Ma'idah* 5:5; *Al-Nur* 24:32; *Al-Rum* 30:20–21; *Al-Shura* 42:11, 49–50.

Polygamy (and concubinage) is permitted within Islam: *Al-Nisa'* 4:3, 24–5, 129; *Al-Mu'minun* 23:1–7; *Al-Ahzab* 33:30. The actual practice of polygamy is seen in some cultures more than others, and is also dependant on the husband's wealth to support more than one wife. Many take the second part of *Al-Nisa' 4:3* as an injunction to monogamy, for who can be completely impartial among his wives? (also *al-Nisa* 4:129)

> And if you fear that you will not deal justly with the orphan girls, then marry those that please you of [other] women, two or three or four. But if you fear that you will not be just, then [marry only] one or [the slaves] that your right hand possesses. That is more suitable that you may not incline [to injustice].

An oft-quoted *hadith* describes marriage as 'half of religion.'[2] Marriage in Islam is contractual, establishing (or strengthening) a relationship between two extended families. While 'love' marriages may be accepted in some areas, many communities prefer to have marriages arranged, where the different factors (family class and connections, wealth, education, beauty or whiteness of skin) are carefully matched between the prospective couple. If the arrangement is done with care for the interests of the couple, such marriages often work well. Because of the uncertainty of marriage described in the proverb, cousin marriage is often preferred. The genetic risks are generally known, but still offset by the positive of marrying your child into a known family. Also common are reciprocal arrangements, where a brother and a sister will marry the sister and brother in another family: or two sisters will marry two brothers, thus strengthening the

---

[1] The issue of domestic violence in the west is gaining increasing attention now, including across conservative religious communities.

[2] Anas ibn Malik reported: The Messenger of Allah (peace and blessings be upon him), said, "Whoever Allah provides with a righteous wife, Allah has assisted him in half of his religion. Let him fear Allah regarding the second half." Source: al-Mu'jam al-Awsaṭ 992. Grade: *Sahih* (authentic) according to Al-Suyuti.
https://abuaminaelias.com/dailyhadithonline/2013/04/16/nikah-half-deen/

interfamily links and making the marriage ties harder to break. The focus on marriage can mean that women may consent to be a second or third or even fourth wife rather than remaining unmarried.

Pre-Islamic Marriage

Changing patterns of marriage and understandings of divorce and adultery, and the example of Muhammad and his wives, formed the context for what is written in the Qur'an and *hadith* on marriage.

The sixth and seventh centuries were a time of transition in Arab kinship systems. In the earlier patterns of descent, women and their children remained within the woman's extended family, in a matrilineal system. As Mernissi describes it:

> ...women's sexuality wasn't bound by the concept of legitimacy. Children belonged to their mother's tribe. Women had sexual freedom to enter into and break off relationships with more than one man, either simultaneously or successively. The woman could either reserve herself to one man at one time, on a more or less temporary basis, as in a *mut'a*[3] marriage, or she could be visited by many husbands at different times, whenever their nomadic tribe or trade caravan came through the woman's town or camping ground. The husband would come and go; the main unit was the mother and child within an entourage of kinfolk.[4]

Leila Ahmed relates how divorce and remarriage at the time were apparently common for men and women, and *either* could initiate it:

> The women in the Jahilia, or some of them, divorced men, and their [manner of] divorce was that if they lived in a tent they turned it round, so that if the door had faced east, it now faced west ... and when the man saw this, he knew that she had divorced him and did not go to her."[5]

Hind, wife of Abu Sufyan, was a woman from Mecca at the time of Muhammad who led the other Meccan women in taking an oath of allegiance to Islam.[6] Leila Ahmed's description of Hind's oath of fealty to Muhammad offers further evidence of greater sexual freedom for women before the time of Muhammad:

---

[3] *Mut'a* (also described by Bukhari: Book #62, *Hadith*#13) is a marriage of pleasure, or temporary marriage, where a man or woman can agree to live together for 3 nights. They can extend it if they wish and part when they wish. Still practiced by Shi'a and some Sunni Muslims, Smith instances it as the last type of matrilineal marriage, because it doesn't give the man an heir.

[4] Mernissi 1975:37.

[5] Ahmed (1992:44), quoting *Kitab al-Aghani;* also, Engineer 1992: 27.

[6] This oath-giving by women is described in the Qur'an, *al-Mumtahanah* 60:12. *Al-Mumtahanah'* means 'she that is being examined'.

Muhammad led, and Hind responded.
"You shall have but one God."
    "We grant you that."
"You shall not steal."
    "Abu Sufyan is a stingy man; I only stole provisions from him."
"That is not theft. You will not commit adultery."
    "Does a free woman commit adultery?"
"You will not kill your children [by infanticide]."
    "Have you left us any children that you did not kill at the battle of Badr?"[7]

Hind's question, "Does a free woman commit adultery?" suggests that sexual relationships engaged in by a free woman were not described as adultery.[8]

Mernissi points to echoes remaining in the Arabic language today of this matrilineal system of marriage and descent. *Rahim* (womb) is a common Arabic kinship word, together with *batn* (stomach, womb) as the technical term for a clan or sub-tribe, and *umm* (mother) as the origin of Umma (Muslim community).

She summarises matrilineal and patrilineal marriage characteristics in this table:[9]

	Matrilineal Trend	**Patrilineal Trend**
Kinship rule	Child belonged to the mother's group	Child belonged to the father's group
Paternity rule	Physical paternity unimportant: the genitor does not have rights over his offspring	Physical paternity important because the genitor must be the social father
Sexual freedom of the woman	Extended, her chastity has no social function	Limited, her chastity is a prerequisite for the establishment of the child's legitimacy
Status of the woman	Depends on her tribe for protection and food	Depends on her husband for protection and food
Geographical setting of marriage	Uxorilocal[10]	Virilocal[11]

Robertson Smith[12] called these two kinds of marriage *sadica* (matrilineal) marriage, and *ba'al* (patrilineal, or dominion) marriage. The terms describe the relationship between husband and wife. In *sadica* marriage, where the woman was being visited from time to time by a man, she was called his *sadica* (friend).

---

[7] Ibn Sa 'd, 8:4, cited in Ahmed 1992:57–8.
[8] Ahmed 1992:44.
[9] Mernissi 1975:34.
[10] Or 'matrilocal', where the couple resides with or near the wife's parents.
[11] Or 'patrilocal', where the couple lives with or near the husband's parents.
[12] Smith 1885/2014:75–6.

In the other marriage type, the word *ba'al* indicates that the husband is the wife's 'lord' or 'owner': he has authority over her and he alone has right of divorce. Smith argues that effectively, Islam speeded up the transition from matriliny to patriliny by enforcing the patriliny model, and condemning matriliny as *zina* (adultery). His view is supported by one of the *hadith* in Al-Bukhari, which lists Aisha's description of four types of marriage in the Jahiliyah:

- As today: a man betroths his ward or daughter to another man, who assigns her a dowry and marries her.
- A man tells his wife to ask for intercourse with another man, and the husband then doesn't touch her until it's clear that she's pregnant from the other man. (The aim of this model of marriage is to have a child.)
- Less than ten men visit the same woman and have intercourse with her. If she becomes pregnant, after the birth she calls all the men and names one of them as father, who then is responsible for that child.
- Many men frequent a woman and she accepts them all. She has a sign at her door. If she becomes pregnant, when the child is born it is attached to the man whom it most resembles:

"When Muhammad came ... he destroyed all the types of marriage of the Jahiliyah except that which people practice today," concluded Aisha.[13]

While there is evidence for polyandry (multiple husbands) in the time of Muhammad, both Hekmat and Mernissi argue that polygamy (multiple wives) was *not* widespread, especially in the major cities of Arabia.[14] A *hadith* records that Muhammad himself opposed it as harmful to women when his daughter Fatima was involved, refusing to let her husband Ali take a second wife.

Muhammad and His Wives

As supreme example for all Muslims, Muhammad's relations with his wives continue to set an important precedent for marital relationships today. The Qur'an legitimised polygamy of up to four wives: however, Muhammad was given a special exemption to have more (*Al-Ahzab* 33:50–52). The *hadith* provide rich details about Muhammad's wives, and parts of the Qur'an reflect their interactions with Muhammad. The following description of Muhammad's wives also includes the other women in his family: his concubines, and also the daughters who were his only surviving offspring. Famous because of their relationship with Muhammad, some of his wives became influential in shaping the new Muslim community, particularly as transmitters of *hadith*. Although

---

[13] Ahmed (1992, p.44 and 254) cites this tradition from *The Translation of the Meanings of Sahih al-Bukhari*, 9 vols., trans. Muhammad M. Khan (Medina: Dar al-fikr, 1981), 7:44

[14] Mernissi 1975:140, 141. Hekmat 1997.

none of his wives (after Khadijah) bore Muhammad any children, they are
honoured by the sobriquet 'Mothers of the Believers' (*Al-Ahzab* 33:3). As
such, they are regarded as exemplary models for Muslim women today (*Al-
Ahzab* 33:32, 50, 53), and books on these women can be found in almost
every Islamic bookshop.

Here are Muhammad's wives in the order in which he married them.

1. Khadijah

Muhammad's first wife was his employer, Khadijah bint Khuwaylid. Khadijah
initiated the marriage when she was forty and Muhammad was twenty-five.
Khadijah bore him two sons (who both died young) and four daughters. And it
was to her arms that Muhammad fled when he had his first visions of Gabriel,
and she comforted and encouraged him. Mernissi comments: "This is the way
Islam began, in the arms of a loving woman."[15] Muhammad remained
monogamous for the twenty-five years of his marriage to Khadijah. Khadijah
died in the same year (619AD) as Muhammad's powerful uncle Abu Talib,
leaving Muhammad bereft of two of his main protectors.

In the years after Khadijah's death, he took a total of ten more wives. All of
them, apart from Aisha, his child-bride, had been married before. After mourning
Khadijah, Muhammad asked Khawlah bint Hakeem about who he should marry,
and she suggested two names.

2. Sawda

Sawda, a Muslim widow, was one of the names proposed to Muhammad, and he
married her. She was described as dark, slow and fat, and sometimes comic. One
tradition describes Muhammad as sombre one day, until Sawda told him, "You
prostrated so long yesterday (with his wives prostrating in prayer behind him) I
thought my nose would bleed!" and Muhammad laughed. When she thought that
Muhammad might divorce her, Sawda surrendered her marital rights in order to
remain among his wives as one of the Mothers of the Believers.

3. Aisha

Aisha was the other name suggested as a wife. She was the daughter of Abu
Bakr, who was one of Muhammad's followers. The marriage took place when
Aisha was six, the marriage was consummated when Aisha was nine, and she
came to live with Muhammad where he was living with Sawda, along the eastern
wall of the mosque at Medina.

The relationship was put under strain in an incident when the young Aisha
was travelling with Muhammad in an army caravan. When they stopped to rest,
she was left behind when the caravan set off again: she had gone to relieve
herself, and stayed to search for a necklace she lost, and her curtained carrier

[15] Mernissi 1992:103.

(*hawdaj*) was loaded onto the camel, without realising that the young woman wasn't in it. Safwan ibn al-Mu'attal al-Sulami, a soldier following the army, found her and led her on his camel to rejoin the caravan, but the incident aroused immediate gossip. When Aisha heard about it, she asked to return to her parents' house, and wept there for days. Muhammad came to visit and asked her if she was innocent, or if not, to confess her sin to God. Aisha asserted that God would vindicate her innocence, and Muhammad received a revelation from God vindicating her (*Al-Nur* 24:11–21).

Many stories are told of Muhammad's special love for Aisha, as well as of her feistiness. On one occasion, when Muhammad had received the verse *Al-Ahzab* 33:51, she commented to Muhammad, "I feel that your Lord hastens in fulfilling your wishes and desires!"[16] Despite Muhammad's fondness, the *hadith* also record a time when he struck Aisha.[17]

Widowed at eighteen, Aisha died at sixty-six. Known as Muhammad's favourite wife, and the transmitter of many *hadith*, she remains an influential figure in Sunni Islam. Her father Abu Bakr became the first caliph after Muhammad.

Muhammad's marital relationship with her as a nine-year-old is the basis for some conservative Muslim communities today allowing marriage to girls as young as nine.

4. Hafsa

Muhammad married Hafsa, who had been widowed in the battle of Badr, three months after his marriage to Aisha. It was a fiery relationship at times. At one point he divorced, and then remarried her. Hafsa was the keeper of a copy of the Qur'an, which suggests that she may have been literate. Her father, 'Umar ibn al-Khattab (also hot-tempered), was a close follower of Muhammad, and became the second caliph (known for some of his harsh rulings to women).

An-Nisa' 4:3: 'Marry other women as may be agreeable to you, two or three or four' is said to have been revealed soon after this marriage, after the battle of Uhud, when many Muslim women were widowed.

5. Zaynab bint Khuzaymah

Zaynab was one of the women widowed in the battle of Uhud. Muhammad married her and she came to live near Hafsa and Aisha: however, she died just eight months after her marriage to Muhammad, at age thirty.

---

[16] Sahih al-Bukhari, Volume 6, Book 60, Number 311.
[17] Sahih Muslim (Book #004, *Hadith* #2127).

6. Umm Salamah (Hind bint Abu Umayyah)

Umm Salamah and her husband (both Muhammad's cousins) were among the first converts to Islam, and first emigrants to Abyssinia.[18] When they returned, her husband was one of the first group to go to Medina; however, Umm Salamah's brothers prevented her going with her husband, and also took her son away. She wept until she was allowed to go with her son to Medina (accompanied for protection by Uthman, although he was not yet Muslim). Her husband died after leading Muslim troops in battle at Badr and Uhud, where he was wounded. After a waiting period, Umm Salamah married Muhammad. She was among the Companions who could give legal verdicts. She died at age eighty-four, the last of Muhammad's wives.

Known as a wise woman, she advised Muhammad to persuade his men through his own example, when his men were rebelling against the truce of Hudaybiyah.[19] Some cite this incident to show that Muhammad let women give him counsel, and therefore must have trusted their intellect and devoutness.

7. Zaynab bint Jahsh

Muhammad married Zaynab to Zayd, his freed slave and adopted son. Zaynab, of noble birth, was not pleased to be married to a freed slave, and their married life wasn't peaceful. Coming to visit Zayd one day, Muhammad entered the house and saw Zaynab. Zayd divorced her so that Muhammad could marry her. However, Muhammad was aware that he would be criticised for marrying his adopted son's wife. Then Muhammad received revelation that an adopted son did not have the same position as a real son, and also that God had given Zaynab to him, so he married her (*Al-Ahzab* 33:4–5, 37, 40, 54). Hence Zaynab claimed that she was the only wife where God had organised the marriage. She died aged fifty-three years. The Qur'anic verses linked to this incident are cited as the basis for the Muslim prohibition on adoption.

8. Juwayriyah bint al-Harith

The daughter of the chief of the Banu Mustalaq tribe, Juwayriyah was known for her great beauty. Her husband was killed in battle with Muslims, and Juwayriyah (then twenty years old) was given as a slave to Thabit, one of the Muslims. She came to Muhammad to discuss her ransom agreement with Thabit, pleading her position and lack of ransom money with Muhammad, who proposed marriage with himself instead. Aisha describes how attractive she was: "No one saw her except he became captivated by her. ... As soon as I saw her, I disliked her entering Muhammad's place, for I knew that he would see what I saw in her." After her marriage to Muhammad all her fellow-tribespeople were freed, so that

---

[18] Modern-day Ethiopia, where some of the early Muslims went for refuge from persecution in Mecca.
[19] Al-Bukhari, Book #50, *Ahadith* #891.

Aisha commented: "I know of no other woman who brought greater blessing to her people than Juwayriyah."[20] She died aged sixty-five years.

9. Safiyyah bint Huyay ibn Akhtab

Safiyyah was a seventeen-year-old daughter of the chief of the Jewish tribe of Banu Nadheer. Her father had been killed by Muslims after the Battle of Banu Quraydhah, and her husband was killed in the battle of Khaybar (see *al-Hashr* 59:2-5). Because of her beauty, a number of Companions wanted Safiyyah. Muhammad offered her marriage, freedom as a dowry and Islam. He married her on his return journey to Medina. Aisha and some of the other wives were jealous of her beauty. Zaynab refused to lend 'that Jewish woman' a camel on a journey when hers was ill, so Muhammad ignored Zaynab for two to three months. Safiyyah was about sixty when she died.

10. Umm Habibah Ramlah bint Abi Sufyan

Umm Habibah was the sister of Yazid and of Mu'awiyah (the fifth caliph). She was married to 'Ubaydullah who had converted from Christianity to Islam. While in Abyssinia he returned to Christianity, and is said to have died of drinking. Muhammad heard of Umm Habibah's penury, and offered to marry her. When her father (an enemy of the Muslims) visited her as an envoy of the Quraysh after they reneged on the treaty of Hudaybiyah, she rolled up Muhammad's mat and wouldn't let her father sit on it, telling him, "You are a polytheist." Her action is cited to encourage Muslim women in allegiance to Islam even before family. Umm Habibah is ranked third after Aisha and Umm Salama for her knowledge of *Hadith* and eloquence. She was about seventy when she died.

11. Maymuna bint Harith al-Hilaliah

Of the Banu Halal tribe, Maymuna was the half-sister of Zaynab bint Khuzaymah (who had died soon after her marriage to Muhammad), sister-in-law of Abu Bakr (first caliph), and aunt of Khalid bin Walid.[21] Married and separated, she had married again and was widowed very early. She offered herself to Muhammad[22] when he visited Mecca to perform the pilgrimage rituals (*'Umrah*[23]) seven years after the Muslim community had emigrated from Mecca to Medina (*Hijrah*[24]). She was twenty-six at the time, and the last woman Muhammad married. When

---

[20] 'Ali Qutb 2007:137, 141.

[21] He led the Muslim forces to victory in Syria and beyond after Muhammad's death.

[22] This is linked to *al-Ahzab* 33:50.

[23] Minor pilgrimage to Mecca.

[24] The immigration of the Muslim community under Muhammad's leadership from Mecca to Medina, where an Islamic polity was established.

Muhammad became sick before he died, he was in her apartment, and asked to spend the last days in Aisha's apartment. Maymuna died aged about eighty.

Muhammad's Concubines

As well as his wives, Muhammad also had concubines. Maryam, a Coptic concubine from Upper Egypt, is the most well known. She was beautiful and curly-haired, and the wives were jealous of her. Hafsah is said to have found Muhammad with Maryam, and exclaimed, outraged: "on my day, during my turn, and in my bed!" Muhammad offered to stop seeing Maryam, and *Al-Tahrim* 66:1–5 was revealed, telling Muhammad not to ban what God has ordained for him. Maryam gave birth to a son, Ibrahim, who died at eighteen months.

Rayhana bint Zayd ibn Amr was a member of the Banu Qurayza (a Jewish tribe who, including her husband, were slaughtered by Muslims). She refused to accept Islam and marry Muhammad, and so was sent to the harem as a concubine.

Women Who Refused to Be His Wife

Asma bint al-Numan, Mulayka bint Kaaba, and Fatima bint Abd Duhhak are among the women who either refused to be among his wives, or were divorced before consummation.

Some ask why Muhammad had so many wives, when Muslim men are only allowed four concurrently (*Al-Nisa'* 4:3). One common answer is that it was out of compassion, as most of them (apart from Aisha) were widows, either of Muslims or taken captive as booty. This is inadequate to explain all his alliances or interventions. Others cite his extraordinary vigour, visiting each wife on their nightly roster, as a further demonstration of his unique prophetic role. It might be interesting to ask your Muslim friends what they think. Whatever the reason, it is perhaps surprising that the alliances produced so few children. The only offspring recorded were from Khadijah and Maryam the Coptic concubine, and only Khadijah's daughters lived to adulthood.

The Qur'anic verses and *hadith* which relate to Muhammad's wives suggest a polygamous household which was often beset with wifely rivalry and jealousies. It is the texts and rulings derived from the quarrels and complexities of those relationships which continue to shape the lives of women and what they can and cannot do, in the Muslim world today.[25]

---

[25] Geraldine Brooks describes her struggle as an unaccompanied female journalist, to get accommodation in a hotel in Saudi. Looking towards Mecca at the early morning call of the *muezzin*, she reflects that "The reason for my sleepless night lay in that desert town. I couldn't check myself into a Saudi hotel room in the 1990s because thirteen hundred years earlier a Meccan named Muhammad had trouble with his wives" 1995:3.

Muhammad's Daughters

Muhammad had four daughters through Khadijah. Three of them died during his lifetime: Zaynab, Ruqayya and Umm Kulthum. Zaynab married Abu al-as ibn Rabee, her maternal cousin, who eventually accepted Islam. She died five years after the small Muslim community emigrated to Medina. Ruqayya, and Umm Kulthum were initially married to their paternal cousins Utbah and Utaybah, sons of Abu Lahab. However, when Abu Lahab became the Prophet's most bitter adversary (he was cursed in the Qur'an: *Al-Masad* 111), they left their husbands. Uthman (later the third caliph) married Ruqayya, and they joined the community's emigration to Abyssinia, and later to Medina. After Ruqayya's death, Muhammad offered Umm Kulthum to Uthman. So, he was (consecutively) married to two of Muhammad's daughters. Schimmel comments, "Since a simultaneous marriage to sisters is forbidden, he married the one after the early death of the other, and this is why he carries the sobriquet *dhu' n-nurain,* 'the owner of the two lights.'"[26]

Fatima, Muhammad's other daughter, was of frail health, usually attributed to the deprivation she went through as a ten-year-old, during the boycott of the early Muslim community.[27] She married Ali ibn Talib, who became the fourth caliph. Ali, Muhammad's nephew, was not wealthy; Muhammad told him to sell his sword in the market and use that money as a dowry. The couple were poor: it is recorded that their house was furnished with a bed, a pillow filled with dry palm fronds, a plate, a glass, a leather water bag and a grinding stone for flour. Fatima worked hard, and was often weary with her poor health. At one point Fatima asked Muhammad if she could have one of the slaves taken in battle, but Muhammad told her that he would give her something better, and taught her prayers to recite.[28] Fatima is described as having a very close relationship with Muhammad, who was fond of her. When Ali was contemplating taking a second wife after Fatima, Muhammad refused to allow him, exclaiming:

> I will not allow 'Ali Ibn Talib, and I repeat, I will not allow 'Ali to marry another woman except under the condition that he divorce my daughter. She is a part of me and what harms her harms me.[29]

Fatima and Ali had two sons, Hasan and Husain, and two daughters, Zaynab and Umm Kulthum. Fatima died about six months after Muhammad. As the only surviving daughter, and the only one whose offspring are recorded, Fatima is the

---

[26] Schimmel 2003:29.

[27] The rest of the Quraysh declared a boycott against the Ban Hashim and Ban al-Muttalib clans, and they were forced to live in the Shi'b (valley of) Abi Talib. It is recorded as a time of harsh privation for two or three years, until the boycott was lifted.

[28] *Subhanallah* (Glory be to Allah) thirty-three times, *Alhamdulillah* (All praise to Allah) thirty-three times, and *Allah-u-Akbar* (Allah is the greatest) thirty-three times.

[29] Al-Buhkari, Al-Sahih, p.453, X-67, B., cited in Hekmat 1997:109.

foremother of Muhammad's descendants. So she occupies an exemplary position, particularly among Shi'ite[30] communities today.

As the new religious community grew, battles were fought around tribal alliances and hostilities. The stories of Muhammad's wives and daughters give a picture of the early Muslim community as part of a society where women were often married and also widowed young: after Khadijah, apart from Aisha, Muhammad's wives had all been widows.

The women in Muhammad's family, his wives and daughters, occupied a significant role in determining the leadership of the young Muslim community after Muhammad's death. Of the first four caliphs, known as the 'Rightly-Guided,' the first two were fathers of Muhammad's wives, and the other two were married to Muhammad's daughters. The fifth, Mu'awiya, was the brother of one of Muhammad's wives.

While the names of many of the women around Muhammad are often cited, Aisha and Fatima, in particular, stand out as influential examples both to the early community and communities today. But they inspire two different communities – Sunni and Shi'a – so much so that the way these two women are described can indicate the identity of the speaker or writer. While Aisha, in particular, is the source of many *hadith* in Sunni collections, Shi'ites have different authoritative sources, and reject Aisha because of her opposition to Ali as the fourth caliph, when she led the army in battle against him.

The Mothers of the Believers had a preeminent place among the new community, particularly Aisha. They were able to retain some flexibility in stipulating marriage conditions for some generations, predominantly for aristocratic women.[31] Ahmed describes this "community of independent, celibate women" (Muhammad had decreed that no man should marry his widows) who received the highest pensions in the state after his death, some of whom commanded prestige and authority, and "occupied a prominent place at the material and spiritual centre of Islam at this moment of its consolidation and expansion."

Muslim Law and Marriage Patterns Today

Marriage practices vary widely around the Muslim world, between and even within different cultural groups. There is always the legal/religious ceremony, and usually the wedding feast; in some countries there may also be a civil contract. Consummation usually happens after the wedding feast: the latter may include men and women together, or in separate celebrations. The contractual nature of marriage means that in some contexts, women are able to set prenuptial agreements that give them access to education or financial security, or

---

[30] Shi'ite look to leadership of the Muslim community through descent from Muhammad, rather than the Sunni understanding of election by the community.
[31] Ahmed 1992:75ff.

monogamy or equal right to divorce. This possibility depends on the local laws, and the power of the woman or her family. Feldman & Williams comment that: "In patrilocal peasant households, males dominate, sons are preferred to daughters, and women's behaviour is highly circumscribed since family honour is prescribed by female virtue."[32] In many Southeast Asian communities, women have much higher status and freedom. There are also *urfi* marriages, where a written agreement is signed by mutual consent in the presence of two witnesses. These can often be agreements between two students or young people, who wish to enter into a relationship of intimacy, while keeping it secret from parents.

The place of women, patterns of marriage, polygamy and divorce, are affected by community patterns of family and gender, local and state regimes, class and ethnicity, history (including colonisation and war), resources, and social movements. Changing from place to place, this remains an area of ongoing reform and contestation, where state policies are fought out on women's bodies.[33] The rulings of the various schools of Islamic law have different regulations for particular situations, which may advantage or disadvantage women. Groups such as Sisters in Islam in Malaysia have worked to improve the lives and experiences of women, within the framework of Islam and existing *Shariah* court laws.

Female-headed households exist everywhere, such as when women are widowed. They are more evident in countries where a large part of the male population has emigrated for work, or among refugee populations. Bride kidnappings can still occur among formerly nomadic peoples, such as Turkmen, Kyrgyz and Kazakh communities.[34] Muhammad's example of marrying Aisha is used to validate child marriage in some conservative Muslim communities.[35] Increasing women's education has been shown to have the most significant impact in reducing child marriage and empowering women.

Under Muslim law, the *mahr* (brideprice) is agreed on between the two families, and paid by the groom to the bride, either in full at the time of marriage, or an amount is agreed to be paid to the wife in case of divorce. It can be paid in money or in gold jewellery. The Muslim husband is responsible for maintaining his wife and children; the wife is not obligated to share her wealth or earnings. This is given as one reason that the inheritance of men is twice that of women. Inheritance is based towards agnates (male relatives on the father's side). In cultures with a dowry system, gifts flow from the bride's family to the groom, and the *mahr* may be fixed or nominal.

---

[32] Feldman & Williams 2007:81.
[33] Feldman & Williams 2007:82.
[34] Bowring 2005:417.
[35] We should note that child marriage still occurs in some parts of the west. Syrett 2016, also https://theconversation.com/child-marriage-is-still-legal-in-the-us-88846. As of December 2017, in some US states girls, could legally marry as young as age 13 years if they have parental consent.

Other Regulations

Within the early Muslim community there were tensions about the place of women and relationships between husbands and wives. Some of those tensions related to differences between the Meccan and Medinan communities and marital patterns. Umar ibn al-Khattab complained that "we, the people of Quraysh, used to have the upper hand over our wives, but when we came among the Ansar [helpers], we found that their women had the upper hand over their men, so our women also started learning the ways of the Ansari women."[36] Umar himself (second caliph) was reputed to be harsh with his wives, and sought to keep women in their homes and out of the mosque. He instituted segregated prayer, and advocated a male imam to lead prayer for women as well as men (in contrast with Muhammad's endorsement of Umm Waraqa leading prayer for her household, and Aisha and Umm Salamah acting as imams to lead other women in prayer). In another *hadith* attributed to him, he comments: "When the Prophet was alive we were cautious when speaking and dealing with our women in fear that a revelation would come [from God] concerning our behavior. But when the Prophet died, we were able to speak and deal with them [more freely]."[37]

The Qur'an set down regulations around divorce: *Al-Baqarah* 2:226–241; *Al-Nisa'* 4:19–21, 35, 130; *Al-Ahzab* 33:49; *Al-Mujadilah* 58:2–4; *Al-Talaq* 65:1–7. There is also a strong *hadith* against divorce:

> Narrated Muharib: The Prophet (peace be upon him) said: "Allah did not make anything lawful more abominable to Him than divorce."[38]

Generally, Islamic law permits a man to divorce his wife by saying "I divorce you" three times. A woman may get a *khul* divorce, where she pays money, or relinquishes her right to her *mahr* (brideprice). Before the age of seven, women have custody of children; beyond that age the father has custody rights.[39]

Qur'anic verses on adultery include *Al-Nisa'* 4:15–16, 25; *Al-Nur* 24:2–13. The Qur'an requires four witnesses to the act of adultery, and most schools of Islam require four men. However, al-Jaqziyya (d.1350) agreed that the word of eight women would be sufficient; others have suggested two women and three men. Qur'anic injunctions are further modified by *hadith* recounting Muhammad's responses as the new Muslim community brought different cases to him for direction, and this includes the penalty of stoning for adultery that is practised in some communities.[40]

---

[36] Cited by Ahmed, pp.52–3.

[37] El Fadl 2001:223.

[38] Al-Bukhari, Book #12, *Hadith* #2172: also, Abu Dawud, Book #12, *Hadith* #2173. See also the *hadith* cited above about Muhammad's daughter Fatima, containing an implicit acknowledgement that polygamy can be harmful to women.

[39] These laws may be modified by national laws in different ways according to the country.

[40] See Appendix 2 for the *hadith* on adultery and stoning.

A number of well-known *hadith* deal with husband–wife relationships.[41] The commonly-cited *hadith* about the majority of hell's inhabitants being women links it directly to wives being ungrateful to their husbands. There are also *hadith* on a wife's refusal to sleep with her husband; a husband's rights over his wife, and how a woman's access to Paradise depends on her husband being pleased with her.

The Bible records polygamous marriages, including multiple wives and concubines. It describes the sometimes-murderous tensions between the sons of David's different wives. However, both Jesus' teaching and Paul's requirements of leaders in the church show monogamous marriage as God's intended ideal, from the time of creation (Mt 19:1–12; 1 Tim 3:2, 12). The Bible goes further in endorsing singleness as an honourable alternative, both through the example of Jesus himself, and also Paul. While creation points towards marriage, our heavenly destiny is singleness (Gen 2:18-25; Mt 22:30). Marriage is described in the Bible as a sacrament. In other words, it is not just a contract entered into between two people (or families or communities), but rather an act where God is involved, where the husband and wife become 'one flesh'. Both sides have mutual responsibilities towards each other (and to any children who are born). In the Christian marriage service, both the husband and wife are involved and both are honoured.

- What are the patterns of marriage in the community where you are?
- What is the place of the Islamic ceremony and of the public celebration? Who is involved in each? Are there any other associated rituals? (Civil service? Engagement party?)
- What Qur'anic verses or hadith are most often cited? What proverbs do people use to describe marriage?
- Do a search in the hadith. What do they say about marriage? What historical incidents are they linked to?

---

[41] See Appendix 2.

14. Mothers

It is Mother's Day. The school is hung with banners. For weeks, students have been preparing plays and poems to recite in honour of their mothers and other significant women in their lives. My experience of quiet family gatherings in the west (amid a wave of frenetic commercialism in the shops) has not prepared me for the very public celebration of 'Mother's Day' in the Middle East. Public institutions, including religious places of worship, have gatherings where people recite speeches to mothers, buildings are decorated with celebratory posters and pennants, and people give gifts or cards of appreciation to any woman who stands in a nurturing role to them. Mother's Day is celebrated in many parts of the Muslim world. Women are celebrated, and gifts are given in acknowledgement of encouraging female relationships, whether to mothers, women teachers or mentor-friends.

Narrated 'A'ishah: The person who has the greatest right over the woman is her husband, and the person who has the greatest right over the man is his mother.[1]

The Qur'an emphasises the need to honour mothers, in *Al-Ahqaf* 46:15:[2]

And we have enjoined on man to be dutiful and kind to his parents. His mother bears him with hardship. And she brings him forth with hardship and the bearing of him, and the weaning of him is thirty months, till when he attains full strength and reaches forty years, he says: 'My Lord! Grant me the power and ability that I

[1] Al-Hakim in al-Mustadrak: 'Al-Bazar' (1986:85-6). Quoted in Schleifer.
[2] Also, *Al-Nisa'* 4:1; *Al-Isra'* 17:23–24; *Luqman* 31:14.

may be grateful for Your Favour which You have bestowed upon me and upon my parents, and that I may do righteous good deeds, such as please You, and make my offspring good. Truly I have turned to You in repentance, and truly, I am one of the Muslims.

The *hadith* echo the same theme:

Narrated Abu Huraira: A man came to Allah's Apostle and said, "O Allah's Apostle! Who is more entitled to be treated with the best companionship by me?" The Prophet said, "Your mother." The man said. "Who is next?" The Prophet said, "Your mother." The man further said, "Who is next?" The Prophet said, "Your mother." The man asked for the fourth time, "Who is next?" The Prophet said, "Your father."[3]

A man once consulted the Prophet Muhammad about taking part in a military campaign. The Prophet asked the man if his mother was still living. When told that she was alive, the Prophet said: "(Then) stay with her, for Paradise is at her feet."[4]

While 'Mother's Day' began in the west, it is a tradition which taps deeply into existing cults and celebrations of motherhood in different cultures. In Muslim cultures, mothers are deeply revered; mothers and motherhood are celebrated in proverbs, poetry, songs, folk tales and religious texts. A Turkish neighbour tells me of the proverb, '*Rivers stop flowing when a mother calls.*' Ghannam's description of the "central role of the mother in raising children, managing the household, and producing and reproducing families, communities, and nations," is true in many parts of the Muslim world.[5] Mothers carry primary responsibility for the success, health and well-being of their children. An Egyptian woman described to me her work in rearing and marrying off her children as '*risalitna*' (our mission, or vocation) – the same term that is used to describe Muhammad's vocation as Prophet. Motherhood is seen as the sacred mission given to Muslim women, to bring up the family, ensure their '*salaam,*' their health, well-being, success in study and life. A woman's first place of responsibility is family and home, and it is here that she is primarily judged on her success, before any involvement in other spheres of life. Here, women seek God's blessing and power in this life, to fulfil their practical duties of care for their families.

Even in affairs of state, mothers can play a powerful role behind the scenes. In some of the Gulf states, mothers of the sheikhs can influence decisions that are made. In Syria some years ago, Hafez al-Asaad, then president, had been sick

---

[3] Al-Bukhari Book #73, Hadith #2.

[4] al-Tirmidhi. While this *hadith* is widely quoted, it is not rated as a strong *hadith:* some commentators consider it weak or even fabricated. http://authentichadiths.blogspot.com.au/2012/03/authenticity-on-hadith-paradise-is.html.

[5] Ghannam 2005: 508.

in hospital. His younger brother, who had authority over the elite Presidential Guard in the army, brought his troops to surround the palace, to force his older brother to hand over power to him. What could Hafez al-Asaad do, himself still weak, to resist the coup? He took his mother with him and went down to speak to his younger brother. His brother withdrew, and the coup was averted. At that moment, Hafez's mother had more impact on the future of the country than the best army troops and tanks. The elevated position given to mothers in Islam is sometimes instanced to show how women are honoured within Islam. However, this offers no place to the childless woman: women receive honour in relation to their offspring, not in their own right.[6]

In Islamic law, if a woman breastfeeds a child, it establishes a biological relationship between them, which includes the same marriage prohibition as in birth relationships (the suckled child could not marry another child of the woman who has breastfed her/him). The Qur'an spells out these relationships:

> Forbidden to you (for marriage) are: your mothers, your daughters, your sisters … your foster mothers who gave you suck, your foster milk suckling sisters, … (*Al-Nisa'* 4:23).

And the *hadith* confirm it:

> Narrated 'Aisha: (the wife of the Prophet) that while Allah's Apostle was with her, she heard a voice of a man asking permission to enter the house of Hafsa. 'Aisha added: I said, "O Allah's Apostle! This man is asking permission to enter your house." The Prophet said, "I think he is so-and-so," naming the foster-uncle of Hafsa. 'Aisha said, "If so-and-so," naming her foster uncle, "were living, could he enter upon me?" The Prophet said, "Yes, for foster suckling relations make all those things unlawful which are unlawful through corresponding birth (blood) relations."[7]

Within Islam, suckling kinship is as strong and legally binding as kinship by blood or marriage (and more powerful than adoption, which is not legal within Islam, but does occur).[8] And it is a kinship relationship that can only be conferred through women. The number of feedings required to establish the relationship varies according to different legal schools: it may be five or ten, and the child should generally be under two years of age. This would mean that a male child who had been suckled would be within the woman's *mahram* (close male relatives). But that relationship doesn't include maintenance or inheritance rights.[9]

---

[6] In the Qur'an, apart from Mariam, mother of 'Isa, no women are named: they are known only by the names of the men whose wives or mothers they are.

[7] Al-Bukhari, Book #62, *Hadith* #36.

[8] See El Guindi 2020.

[9] Mattson 2005:2.

As primary caregivers to young children in the home, women occupy a key role as purveyors of faith to the next generation. While Muslim law expects that children will follow the faith of their father, in fact the mother may be more influential. Dwi Handayani, looking at children of mixed (Muslim–Christian) parentage, found that about two thirds of them followed the faith of their mother.[10] Rebecca Lewis notes that when men come to faith in Jesus Messiah, those men who continue on in their faith and are able to lead others are most often those with believing mothers, or sometimes believing wives.[11]

The Place of Maryam

Given the importance of mothers, it is not surprising that Maryam (Mary), mother of the Messiah is given a preeminent role in the Qur'an. The only woman identified by name, her name is also given to one of the Qur'anic surahs, chapter 19,[12] and all the other chapters that carry individual names are names of prophets. And Maryam is included in the list of prophets (*Al-Anbiya* [Prophets] 21:48–91). This, together with the fact that God's angels spoke to her to tell her of the coming birth, has given her the status in Islam almost of a prophet.[13] Those who support her prophetic role point to *Al-Imran* 3:42–43, where she is described as chosen above all women. Some in the more literalist school gave Maryam an exalted position, along with Sara and the mother of Moses, as *muhaddathat* (spoken to by angels). Those who disagree with Maryam having this status point to *Yusuf* 12:109 and *Al-Nahl* 16:43, which suggest that prophets are men, and cite also the requirement of physical purity, which would be broken at menstruation. Some see her as a man, since "among women are some who are perfect and knowledgeable and who attain the standard of men – they are in a real sense man."[14] The mystic Ibn al-'Arabi (1165–1240) describes Maryam as the second Adam, in generating Jesus.[15] (Intriguingly, he taught that Adam was really the first female, for Eve was born from his inside.) However she is categorised, Maryam, mother of Isa, is highly regarded by Muslims. Many Muslim women's circles take *Maryam* 19 as a favourite recitation to bring blessing; some women may even pray through her, as a saint. I have seen pictures of Maryam stuck up on the house walls of Muslim friends, and some Muslims may join the popular Orthodox fast and feast of the Virgin.

---

[10] Handayani 2018.

[11] Lewis 2004.

[12] Most of the other personal names used as titles for Qur'anic surahs are names of prophets (*Yunus* 10, *Hud* 11, *Yusuf* 12, *Ibrahim* 14, *Muhammad* 47, *Nuh* 71). Jardim points out that the titles of *Surah*s 3 (*Imran* – Mary's family), 4 (Women), 58 (the woman who disputes) and 60 (the woman to be examined) also represent female figures; *surah*s 3, 19, 58 and 60 all give women speaking roles (2014:155).

[13] The medieval Zahirite school accorded her prophetic status. Stowasser 1994:67–82.

[14] Stowasser 1994:78. Also Smith & Haddad 1989; Clarke 2007.

[15] Rahman 1966/1979:146.

The Qur'an tells of the Messiah's birth, in *Maryam* 19. God tells Zakariyya of the coming birth of his son. Here, Zakariyya's dumbness is for only three days, and as a sign rather than a response to disbelief. God sent his spirit to Maryam (understood to be the angel Gabriel, who mediates Maryam's conception by breathing in her shirt), and her virginal conception is a sign and mercy from God (*Maryam* 19:20, 3:47). The newborn child speaks to Maryam, weary after childbirth, to tell her of God's provision of water and dates, and again to name himself Prophet, vindicating his mother by implication of the accusations of sexual impropriety.[16] We see an exhausted woman who receives food and water; a maligned woman who is publicly vindicated. (This account of the child speaking from the cradle may derive from an early Arabic apocryphal fable from second century Egypt, the 'Gospel of the Infancy of Jesus Christ' [Injil-il Tufuliyyah].[17])

In both Islam and Christianity, Maryam's importance comes as mother of the Messiah, seemingly validating the concept of motherhood as the supreme role for woman. It is thus ironic that she receives this role while still unmarried, via virgin birth (which subverts the idea of the marriage relationship as the ultimate purpose for all women). And it also means that she attains motherhood from the position of ultimate shame, as an unmarried mother. In the Qur'an, it is through the miracle of her son speaking from the cradle that she is vindicated (*Maryam* 19:27–33). In the Gospel, it is Joseph's willingness to give her his name and protection in marriage that saves her from public disgrace, with its associated risk of death by stoning (Matt 1:18–25). But her example challenges women to be willing to go beyond cultural norms and even suffer family and public shame in order to obey what God calls us to. And where we find the cultural focus on Maryam being honoured as the Messiah's mother, we also see Jesus challenging it, making clear that it is primarily a relationship of obedience to God through the Messiah and discipleship within the community of faith, which bring women honour, rather than maternity – even of the Messiah! (Luke 11:27–8; Matt 12:46–50, Luke 8:19–21.) Of course, such obedience may include (for women as for men) godly relationships with spouse and children, but it finds its relational source and focus in the Messiah.

Looking at the Islamic understanding of the significance of breastfeeding for maternity, how do we comprehend the place of breastfeeding, both in how it is practised in our community, and in faith? The mystery of God's incarnation in Jesus extends to his birth from Mary's womb, and his nourishment as a toddler. Numerous pictures and sculptures have been inspired by the concept of Mary breastfeeding Jesus. In the vulnerability of God become human in Jesus, the

---

[16] *Maryam* 19:1–34, also *Al-Imran* 3:46–47.

[17] The fable includes this passage: "… Jesus spoke when he was in the cradle, and said to his mother: 'Mary, I am Jesus the Son of God, the Word, which thou didst bring forth according to the declaration of the angel Gabriel, and My Father hath sent me for the salvation of the world.'"

feeding of humanity by faith on the shed blood and broken body of Jesus was preceded by Jesus feeding on humanity, as he received the nourishment of breastmilk.

God and Motherhood

Barlas argues against the description of Islam as a theological patriarchy, because the Qur'an rejects designations of God as a father.[18] She describes patriarchy as "father-rule and/or a politics of male privilege based in theories of sexual differentiation."[19] How, then, do we understand the 'Father' language in the Judeo-Christian tradition? Does it reflect an understanding of God based in a politics of male privilege? The temptation of this reading can be accentuated by English grammar, where we have both the Father and Jesus referred to by male pronouns, and also the Spirit (in Hebrew a female pronoun and in Greek, neuter). These are grammatical terms, not about the essential being of God –yet they can shape our attitudes. What does the Bible really say about God's nature?

Genesis 1:27 tells us how "God created humans to be like himself; he made men and women." So, God is not reflected primarily in the male, but by both male and female: God is not one gender or without gender, but beyond – bigger than gender. The Bible invites us to call God 'Father', not just Lord – a relationship of parental intimacy that goes beyond slave–master obedience. The Bible is also replete with *maternal* images of God.

In Deut 32:11, God is described as a mother eagle, and in 32:18 as giving birth. The Psalms compare God to a woman (123:2–3) and a mother (131:2). Isaiah also uses rich imagery likening God to a woman in labour (42:14), a nursing mother (49:15) and a comforting mother (66:13). Hosea also describes God as a mother, both nurturing (11:3–4) and as a mother bear (13:8). In a number of contexts, the biblical writers use the imagery of sheltering under the shadow of God's wings. This is a maternal image of God as the female bird who offers shelter to her chickens from danger. Examples include Ruth 2:12, Psalms 17:8, 57:1, 91:4; and in the New Testament, Matt 23:37 and Luke 13:34. So God who is Father is also pictured in maternal images, as nurturing, protective mother, or filled with maternal fury (Hosea 13:8).

There are also two non-maternal female images of God: the woman carefully sweeping her house to find what is lost (Luke 14:8–10), and a woman baking bread (Matt 13:33, Luke 13:20-21).

The creative Spirit of God, as we noted above, is always referred to with the female pronoun in the Hebrew Old Testament. It is the Spirit who comes bringing creation out of chaos (Gen 1:2); gives creativity and skill in craft to create furnishings of beauty and colour (Ex 35:30-35); ecstasy (1 Sam 10:6, 10),

---

[18] Barlas 2002:96–98. The verses she cites include *Al-Nisa* 4:171; *Al-Ma'idah* 5:18; *Al-Taubah* 9:30.
[19] Barlas 2002:93.

new life (Ez 37). And in the New Testament, it is the Spirit of God who births us (John 3:3–8). As with the same metaphor cited in the Old Testament above, it would be hard to get a more female, maternal image of God!

The divine Word of God became incarnate, taking on flesh, as Jesus of Nazareth, Son of God. Julian of Norwich, an early English theologian, describes Jesus in maternal terms as mother as well as brother and Saviour. She links Jesus to the divine Wisdom, and she argues for Jesus as like our mother through four successive premises.

1. Jesus Christ is the ground of our being, and then took on our being as he became incarnate in Mary's womb.
2. He brings each of us to birth through the great travail and suffering of his death on the cross, and counts that suffering and cost all joy for the privilege of giving us life, new birth in him.
3. Jesus feeds us with his own body and blood. As the mother places her new-born child on the breast, Jesus leads us into his breast through his open side.
4. As a child grows, the mother allows the child she loves to be disciplined when needed so that it can grow in virtue and grace. So too Jesus in his love for us. It is only when we fall that we can both know our own limits, and more fully know the marvellous love of our Maker for us.[20]

We find God's maternal care deeply within the Trinity.

A colleague working in a Muslim community in Central Asia was talking to people about God's unconditional love for them. They told her bluntly, "If you want to tell us of unconditional love, don't talk to us of fathers – our fathers are mostly drunk or absent or abusive. If you want to speak of unconditional love, tell us of maternal love."

On the other side, we often talk about those who have had negative experiences of their fathers, needing to find healing in encountering God as the true Father – the ideal that our best father models can only try to reflect. Yet it is also true that many of us need to find the image of the true Mother in God, in a way that goes beyond the often-damaged images of motherhood we encountered in our own families.

As we encounter the love and reverence given to mothers in many Muslim cultures (and as we see the influence they wield), we may be able to point more adequately to the fullness of God as the one who loves, births and nourishes us, by drawing on the rich female as well as male images of God that we encounter in the Bible. We have to go beyond grammatical gender to know God as the one who fully embodies the loving parent, from which every mother and father must take their example.

- Ask your Muslim friends for some of the proverbs they know about mothers.

---

[20] Julian of Norwich, 2015:130–133 (ch.60,61).

- What responsibilities do mothers have, at different times in their life and the life of their children?
- What is their influence?
- How is a man's relationship with his mother described? And with his wife?

15. Life Cycles, Life Rituals

The room is full of women, with men also joining in on the edge of all the activity. In the centre the new baby, just a week old, is carefully wrapped and laid in the large decorated sieve. The women ululate loudly and one of them bangs a brass mortar and pestle noisily, so that the baby will grow up brave even in the face of threatening sounds. The new mother carefully steps seven times across the incense burner, as the smoke wafts through the room, as protection against the evil eye. The grandmother takes the sieve, shaking it horizontally, telling the baby to be obedient to the family. And then it is carried through the house, with one of the group scattering salt or rice as they process round the area, for protection or prosperity. Afterwards the extended family and guests sit together, enjoying candy and nuts together with the *mughat*[1] drink, given to help the new mother in breastfeeding, and served to all those who attend. This is the Egyptian seven-day celebration after a baby's birth, to name the baby, keep away the evil eye, and make sure the child grows up brave and obedient.

Life Cycles

Over the course of a woman's life cycle, her position and influence in her family and in the community can change substantially. Muslim women can often be portrayed in popular media as powerless, under the authority of their father or

---

[1] From the root of the glossostemon bruguieri plant.

husband. At some times in their lives, women are relatively powerless; at other times they exercise considerable influence within the extended family and beyond. In more matriarchal societies, such as those in Southeast Asia, patterns of influence and authority may look different again. And structures of patronage can confer authority and power almost regardless of gender. Women's position in the family varies with the country and also their education, family background, and their stage of life.

When girls reach puberty and grow towards marriageable age, they may face more restrictions, designed to protect their and the family's reputation. A young newly-married wife, especially if she is living with her husband's family, can come primarily under the authority of her mother- and sisters-in-law. When I was working in adult literacy training classes in a Middle Eastern country, the government focused most of its attention and advertising on women between fifteen and thirty-five years. However, these were the years when a young woman was most required for domestic duties, with the often arduous responsibilities of cooking and cleaning for the extended family, quite apart from childcare. And these were the years when women typically had the least freedom to go out. Spending too much time out of home was seen as immodest and inappropriately free behaviour, risking her reputation (in a context where gossip was as socially deadly as the plague).

For husband we could also read, "husband and his female relatives". Patriarchal societies are not defined by authority residing in the males so much as authority coming through the males, including to their blood relatives. Spatial restrictions on movement do not necessarily reflect social position. Authority and age are also linked.[2] So the mother and sometimes sisters of a man may exercise considerable authority in the extended family. Abudi comments:

> A woman's life cycle in the patrilocally extended family is such that the deprivation and hardship she may experience as a young bride are eventually superseded by the control and authority she will have over her own daughters-in-law. The powerful post-menopausal matriarch is thus the other side of the coin of this form of patriarchy.[3]

Time and childbearing can radically change a woman's position in the extended family and society. When a woman has children, especially sons, in many Middle Eastern and Central Asian families, her status increases. When a woman's son grows up, his mother becomes more powerful, often exercising a major influence over the family decisions that are made. Kraus too describes the major role played by some women, mothers or grandmothers of the ruling sheikhs, in running tribal affairs in the Emirates.[4] The government officials of

---

[2] Suad Joseph 2000.
[3] Abudi 2011:44 citing Kandiyoti 1988:32.
[4] Kraus 2008:30.

the Middle Eastern country I described above could have done better aiming their literacy campaign at the older women, the mothers or mothers-in-law, who exercised considerable power over whether the young women could come out and attend literacy classes or not. The older woman, post-menopausal, is also free of many of the factors that restrict ritual purity. This opens the way for increased religious observance, which also confers authority.

Below are some of the life stages that women may go through, and the rituals that mark the different phases.[5]

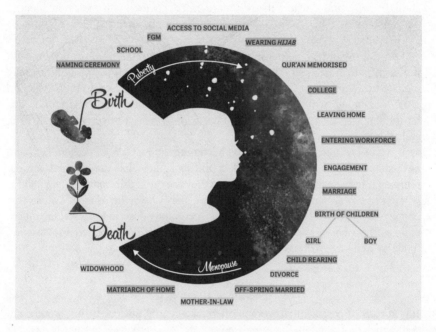

Rites of Passage

Rites of passage (also called *rites of transformation*) are rituals that recognise transitions in the life cycle, and help ensure safe passage for the individual and their community at times of crisis or risk, such as at birth, puberty, marriage and death. The ritual is a ceremony that helps the individual and family successfully negotiate life changes, and mark the difference in the individual's social position and relationships. Arnold van Gennep[6] first developed the term, suggesting that it can involve three phases.

---

[5] © When Women Speak, January 2019.
[6] van Gennep et. Al. 1961.

i) *Separation*, showing that the person is detached from their earlier status. It can sometimes involve a physical 'cutting away', like cutting hair, or circumcision.

ii) *Liminality*, where the individual is between two states, having left one but not yet joined the other. It can sometimes involve a time of unconsciousness (sometimes drug-induced), outside the normal space. Baptism in Christianity symbolises the unconsciousness of death before rising to new life, as well as a rite of purification.

iii) *Incorporation*, where the person re-enters society with their new identity or status. This may be marked by symbols such as new clothes, or exchanging rings in marriage.

Every community has rites of passage. Some communities observe them with formal rituals more than others. Rites of passage in Muslim communities may include times such as at birth (for example, the seven-day ceremony described at the beginning of this chapter), at circumcision, when the whole Qur'an has been memorised, when a girl puts on the *hijab* (often at puberty), at marriage, and at death.

Rites of passage involve someone becoming a new class of person, having a new status in society. Rituals reflect the attributes that are desired for the individual in their fresh stage of life: and they are often different for men and for women. As rituals develop or are adapted, they show the kind of values that people want to hold on to. In the seven-day ceremony described above, the model child will be brave and obedient.[7] Taking up the *hijab* in puberty focuses on modesty as a key attribute for a woman.

The Place of Women

It is at rites of passage that women often take central place. Muslim women are sometimes described as 'marginalised' in society. Perhaps it is truer to say that we find them presiding at the 'margins', the doorways or boundaries of life transitions (somewhat like Janus, Roman god of transitions, who is often pictured with two heads as he looks to the past and forward into the future). Muslim women use the symbols and rituals that invoke divine blessing to help family members negotiate the often-dangerous crossings from one life stage to another.

What are some of the roles that women play in rites of passage? At birth, women are in attendance, when even fathers may not be present, and women

---

[7] For example, the coming-of-age birthday in the west, whether 18th or 21st, may emphasise independence and making decisions for oneself (getting the keys to the car, legally able to drink alcohol). Other rites of passage, for example, those including teenage circumcision, may celebrate courage and enduring pain without flinching. Baptism includes symbols of new life and purity, while the Jewish Bar Mitzvah focuses on participating in Jewish religious law and community.

organise the naming ceremony. At male circumcision, women can be the ones who are celebrating, with dancing, music and sweets.[8] Girls are often encouraged to put on the *hijab* at around puberty, and a special ceremony may be held to mark it. When someone has memorised the Qur'an (again, often around the age of puberty), a party is held to honour them, whether in their home or the mosque. I attended a celebration where women had booked out a restaurant hall to honour the women in the women's mosque programme who had memorised the Qur'an, and only women could attend. In earlier times, the party would have been held in the private women's quarters in their homes.

While men (the groom and the father of the bride) sign the official marriage certificate in the mosque, it is women in the family who are usually the ones involved in negotiating and deciding which girl is an appropriate bride for their son or nephew or brother. In one Middle Eastern city I sometimes had women ask me if I had a daughter of marriageable age or a suitable expatriate friend for their nephew or son. Where women dress in conservatively-covering clothes, women in the family can often visit a prospective bride to get an idea of her beauty and physical build before the potential groom is allowed to meet her. In earlier times, young women were assessed and marriages planned at the communal bath houses. Now it can happen at the women's gathering to celebrate a wedding, when the young women dance, and the older women watch them and talk together. At the consummation of marriage, it is the mother of the bride who may visit the couple next morning. Mothers are more often the ones accountable for children succeeding in school. At times of sickness, women take responsibility to care for family members. In some communities, women may read the Qur'an over people who are sick or possessed, for their healing.[9]

At death, women wash the bodies of women who have died. Mahmood records how a popular woman teacher in a working-class area in Cairo was authorised as someone who could teach others because she "'knew her religion' – she had often helped to prepare dead bodies for a proper burial."[10] Traditionally men, not women, go with the body to be buried. However, women, like men, gather together to mourn and to seek blessing for the dead through recitation of the Qur'an. Roushdy-Hammady records Turkish immigrant women, responsible for physical and spiritual needs of the sick, learning the Qur'an in order to be able to read aloud at a patient's bedside and also during funerary rituals.[11] In the Caucasus, the female *mullah* has the role of reciting Qur'anic verses in Arabic at

---

[8] Doumato 2000:193.
[9] Doumato 2000:13. During Anglican and Catholic church services in Jordan and Syria I also witnessed older women coming forward or men bringing a sick child to have the Gospel read over them (literally, holding it above them while it was read aloud).
[10] Mahmood 2005:92.
[11] Roushdy-Hammady 2007:124. Also, Doumato, 2000:137.

funerals, as well as singing laments.[12] In wearing black, women embody community grief at times of bereavement.

Sarah Mullins suggests that:

> … we could say that religious power and authority resides both with the Muslim imams and with the women. While the power and authority of the Muslim imam is community-based and exercised through established authority in the mosque, women will engage in rituals and superstitious practices quietly within the family context.[13]

Rites of passage are most often described in the context of popular or informal religion. However, they intersect also with the official domain of religion. Women leaders may rework indigenous rituals to make them into "rituals acceptable to Islam."[14] The absence of women from leadership in more 'official' faith rituals does not necessarily imply lack of power or influence in home and in society. Life cycle rituals reinforce cultural values and traditions, especially at times of pressure or persecution. These are times when women gather together, and it gives them a primary role of authority and influence in family and community well-being. In this place of maintaining family well-being, it is often women who are the conservers of family traditions and faith practices. As with norms of daily behaviour and dress, ways of marking celebration or grief – passages of life – are shaped within family customs and local traditions and norms. Women's central place in life passage rituals gives them a crucial role in shaping how families and communities go through times of transition or crisis.

Rites of Solidarity

Rites of passage (also called rites of transformation) mark people's transition from one stage of life to another. Another kind of ritual, known as *rites of solidarity* or *rites of intensification*, are about community welfare rather than the individual, and are designed to reinforce communal values and social identity. Based around calendar times, they may be weekly (Friday prayer and the *khutbah* mosque sermon, Sunday worship services), seasonal (football or other national games) or yearly (Ramadan, *Eid al-Fitr*, *Eid al-Adha,* and the *Hajj:* Christmas or Easter). Other examples include Qur'an recitation, *dhikr* gatherings and celebrations commemorating the birth date of Muhammad or local saints.

There are also *rituals of renewal,* which are sometimes subsumed under rites of solidarity. These are performed at times of crisis, and are designed to revive or renew the environment or broken social relationships. Examples include the

---

[12] Pfluger-Schindlbeck 2007:233.
[13] Mullins 2006:81.
[14] van Doorn-Harder 2006:29

istisqa prayers for rain, and the *zar* ceremony[15] in the Horn of Africa and adjacent parts of the Middle East. Eleanor Doumato suggests that women involved in *zar* rituals were often those most restricted by physical segregation, and that, "Women could find relief and enhanced self-esteem in the Zar ritual, because there they could express themselves in ways otherwise not open to them or acceptable in the larger society."[16]

In *rites of intensification*, it is often men who occupy the place of leadership in faith rituals that take place in more 'official' religious times and spaces. However, the gender separation between rites of passage and of intensification is not clear-cut. Most commonly, both women and men have parallel roles in rituals. If women are present at birth, it is a man (usually the father) who recites the *adhan* call to prayer in the ear of the newborn. The groom and the bride's father sign the official papers for a marriage, while the women may be more involved in the choice of bride, and the wedding celebration. When women and men pray *salah* or *dhikr* prayer in separate groups, a man leads the men, and a woman can lead the women in prayer. In China in some regions, the *Hui* Muslims have separate mosques for women and for men. It is usually women in the community who do the cooking for the shared meal which is an essential part of many official celebrations and rites of passage. In Ramadan, in particular, women work long hours cooking to enable the family and communal celebrations of the month. In different parts of the Muslim world women may be allowed to recite the Qur'an publicly, or at funerals or gravesides. In some countries both women and men share in monthly meetings around a meal and making donations into a common fund but in many places it is more often women who are involved. In times of persecution, it may be women who maintain official rites, out of public sight or surveillance. Mother will whisper secrets of group identity to daughter, and continue proscribed religious practices in the home away from state supervision. Under seventy years of Soviet rule, Tajik women continued practices of prayer and fasting, and in women's group rituals in village communities "a female learned in religious matters would lead others in prayers or in problem-solving ceremonies."[17]

Around the Muslim world, women are commonly involved in vowing rituals, and in making pilgrimages to shrines and tombs to gain blessing, seek healing or fertility, through the power or intercessions of the holy person buried there. Doumato comments that, "In vowing rituals women can try to bargain with God or a saint and to come away with hope."[18] Rehana Ghadially mentions pregnancy and vows related to family finances, problems or illness, as frequent causes for

---

[15] Boddy 1989: https://en.qantara.de/content/the-egyptian-zar-ritual, https://anthropology.ua.edu/blogs/primatereligion/2014/03/19/zar-spirit-possession-and-its-bias-towards-women/
[16] Doumato 2000: 177, 183.
[17] Tadjbakhsh 1998.
[18] Doumato 2000:128.

Shia women's ritual meal trays.[19] Many women visit shrines seeking fertility or healing. Some tombs and shrines belong to female saints, and both women and men visit them to receive blessing. Gathering with other women can provide social interaction and a chance to connect with wider community events and information. It can give access to social and material resources. This is more significant in strongly gendered societies, where a woman's primary companions may be the women in her husband's family. Doumato describes these gatherings as creating "bonds of obligation among those who participate, and those bonds are forged into networks of women's communities."[20]

Another activity to gain blessing involves reciting the '*B'ism Allah*' (In the Name of God the Compassionate the Merciful) 1000 x 1000 plus 100 times. Women will sit together with a pile of dried beans in front of each of them, moving one bean for each repetition, to mark the number.[21] Other women's gatherings include assemblies as diverse as Shi'ite mourning ceremonies in Pakistan,[22] Ismaili ritual meal trays, and regional pilgrimages in India;[23] and Bori cult rituals in Hausaland.[24] In North Africa and the Gulf, the *zar* ceremony functions to help women possessed by the *Zar* (a non-malevolent spirit) to ascertain and meet the spirit's demands in order to gain relief from the symptoms of possession. The ceremony may extend over a number of gatherings, and often includes food, the sacrifice of an animal, music and dancing until the dancers become ecstatic.[25] Religious rites can offer God's blessing/power for women, enabling them to fulfil their responsibilities for household well-being and harmony. Women's gatherings may serve to reinforce or challenge community norms.[26] Ghadially comments on how, among Bohra Ismaili rituals in India:

> ...ritual observances facilitate both the maintenance and reproduction of the community as a social and religious unit over time. Due to their domestic role, women are the socializers of the next generation of Bohras. Children and young girls often accompany women at religious gatherings and this instils in them an awareness of the traditions and practices of the community. By bringing them

---

[19] Ghadially 2003.

[20] Doumato 2000:128.

[21] D'Souza records a similar practice among Shia women in South India, where the women track the number of times they call on Ali for help, with the prayer beads. They then use seeds to mark a hundred and a thousand repetitions. 2004:191.

[22] D'Souza 2004:116ff; Hegland 2003.

[23] Ghadially 2003:309–322.

[24] Cooper 1998:21–37.

[25] Doumato pp.170–184; Boddy 1989.

[26] Jaschok suggests that female Chinese Muslim teachers, because they were more restricted, sometimes brought a conservative view to women's religious education that resisted more modernising approaches.
Jaschok and Shui 2000:116.

together, Hajari and other women's ceremonies reinforce a distinct Bohra identity and make community cohesion possible.[27]

Some Muslim women are challenging male monopoly of official religious space, by leading rites such as mixed prayer or giving the Friday *khutba* sermon. In 2005, Amina Wadud led a group of 80–100 women and men in community prayers in New York.[28] Over a decade earlier she had given a Friday *khutba* sermon in Cape Town, South Africa. While these incursions are happening primarily in western contexts, there are women in Muslim countries who privately endorse them and point to supporting *hadith*.[29]

As with rites of passage, looking at the rituals and symbols in rites of solidarity helps us learn what characteristics are valued by the group as part of their communal social identity. Friday prayers highlight group religious unity, and also gender separation. Ramadan break-fast meals, like western Christmas, emphasise family meal-sharing. Unlike Christmas, Ramadan also evokes the importance of discipline through communal fasting. People meeting around recitation of the Qur'an invoke the belief in the blessing or power conferred on people and place through its recitation. *Dhikr* gatherings may celebrate a sense of ecstatic union with the divine that goes beyond set words and actions. Celebrating the birth date of a saint affirms their local links, together with the power they possessed that can be accessed by their followers.[30]

Rituals in Discipleship

Rituals around rites of passage are an important part of discipleship. This is partly because they symbolise and thus help evoke the ideal attributes of the individual in their new status or identity. Hiebert describes rites of transformation as:

> … like remodelling houses. We must tear down parts of the old to give rise to the new. We must move through chaos to reach a better order. … Without living rituals,

---

[27] Ghadially 2003.

[28] The call to prayer was given by Suheyla Al-Attar, and the gathering took place in a building belonging to the Episcopal Cathedral of St. John the Divine in New York, after three mosques had refused to host it, and a gallery withdrew its offer following a bomb threat.

[29] A Middle Eastern *shaykhah* quoted me the *hadith* from Abu Dawud which records Muhammad giving Umm Waraqah permission to lead the people of her household in prayer. However, those who oppose female leadership of mixed prayer argue that she only led the females in her household or, alternatively, that the permission was given to her as an isolated case. See Chapter 12 & Appendix 2.

[30] Sporting finals in many communities focus on team loyalty, the valorisation of athletic prowess and national or regional pride. Many churches have initiated daily prayer together online during Covid-19, as way of affirming shared faith and communal belonging through prayer.

we have no appropriate ways to affirm our deepest beliefs, feelings, and morals, which lead to new lives in a new community and the world.[31]

Many in the west have grown up wary of rituals, viewing them as meaningless and formulaic. However, in much of the world important decisions and transitions are marked by rituals that are performative (in the way that a marriage ceremony actually changes the legal and social status of a couple). Rather than rejecting rituals, we can seek to ensure that the rituals and symbols are relevant and meaningful in what they express and enact.

Enacted rituals and symbols allow meaning and values to be taken up at every level of our being – physically, intellectually and emotionally. Ronald Grimes suggests that rituals go beyond intellectual assent, in being able to drive meaning "deeply into the bone".[32] Rites of passage can enable both the individuals and their community to recognise and give expression to the transformation that is happening in significant transitions at every part of life.

In both the Old Testament and Islam, circumcision carries the meaning of purity, and belonging to the community. Both these meanings are included in baptism. And baptism also takes up the theme of death and new life, and men and women being made members of the new community, equally. One of the reasons that Christian weddings have such an evangelistic impact may be how they honour the woman together with the man. Rituals around death link to beliefs about the nature of the afterlife and how we enter it.

Whether women and men meet separately or together, we need to consider what part they play in the community and gatherings, the meaning carried by the symbols and rituals, and what this expresses about the nature of the community. Rites of solidarity are an important part of forming new communities, grounding communal values into the lives and hearts of its members and gatherings.

In Kazakhstan a group of Uighur Christian women, of different ages and from different churches, started a tea group. Like the traditional women's tea groups, they included a money exchange. However, when it caused relational problems for people who couldn't pay back, they dropped the exchange. Anne Jansen describes how the group continued their meetings:

> When there was a decision to be made, everyone had her say. The final decision rested with the more mature (not necessarily the oldest). These teas were six-hour parties where we ate, sang, danced, told stories and testimonies, read from the Bible, prayed and ate some more.[33]

As a new community of faith emerges, rites of passage and of solidarity around sacred scriptures, shared prayer and other pious activities will be part of their gatherings. Like rites of passage, they can become an important part of

---

[31] Hiebert 2008:324.
[32] Cited in Moon 2017:92.
[33] Jansen 2000:192.

discipleship both of the community and of its individual members. We can explore existing religious rites of intensification within the community or near neighbours, and the part they play in community formation. Importantly, we need to ask what communal values we want to affirm, and what rites and symbols will express this. Symbols and rituals may communicate different things in different cultural contexts. The characteristics that are valued as evidence of personal and communal maturity may also look different in other cultural contexts.[34] Communities living in diaspora settings away from their home country and culture will choose different rites of passage and symbols to keep and let go. Similarly, gatherings of followers of the Messiah that are coming into existence in new contexts will work out what rites of solidarity that will best express and build their faith as a new community, will look like.

- What rituals or rites of passage can you identify in your own life?
- Ask a Muslim friend about the different stages in a woman's life (girlhood, teenage years, marriage, young children, when her children are grown and married, …). Who does she have her closest relationships with at each stage? How much influence or power does she have in the family and society, at the different stages?
- Ask your friend what happens at special times of transition from one life stage to another, such as birth, circumcision, puberty, marriage, or death. What do people do? What roles do women have?
- As rites mark the transition for a person into a new stage of life, you can ask what kind of person is being formed. What characteristics are endorsed within the rite?

---

[34] Hibbert & Hibbert 2016:243–256.

16. Modesty and the Veil

During a family holiday, I am sitting on a beach in Cyprus in a one-piece swimming costume. As I look to my right along the beach, there are British and European tourists, many of the women wearing only the bottom piece of bikinis. On my left sits a Saudi tourist, all clothed in black, with only her eyes showing. Am I being modest or not? I wonder, bewildered. How can concepts of appropriate clothing and 'modesty' be so disparate in different cultures and contexts?

"The *hijab* is an emblem," the *shaykhah* tells the group of Muslim girls listening intently as they sit in front of her. "It signifies that I belong to the school of Islam. A flag symbolises the state, and this *hijab* symbolises Islam. So, take care of it and beware not to taint it. … No one can inflict an insult on a flag because it is a symbol and an identity."[1]

A veiled woman is one of the most common images of Islam today. But there is a wide variety in types of veiling, and also what it signifies. In religiously or ethnically mixed societies, the veil can mean that Muslim women are the most visible representatives of their community and so also the most vulnerable. However, the veil is commonly claimed as a protection for women.

---

[1] Meltzer & Nix 2012.

The Qur'an

The Qur'an sets guidelines for modesty for both men and women, with more extensive directions for women:

> Tell the believing men to lower their gaze and protect their private parts. That is purer for them. Surely Allah is all-acquainted with what they do. And tell the believing women to lower their gaze and protect their private parts, and not to show off their adornments except that which is apparent, and to draw their veils all over *Juyubihinna* (breasts) and not to reveal their adornments except to their husbands, or their fathers, or their husband's fathers, or their sons, or their husband's sons, or their brothers or their brother's sons, or their sister's sons or their women or the slaves whom their right hands possess, or old male servants who lack vigour, or small children who have no sense of feminine sex. And let them not stamp their feet so as to reveal what they hide of their adornment. And all of you beg Allah to forgive you all, O believers, that you may be successful. *Al-Nur* 24:30–31

The requirements can be modified for older women:

> And as for women past childbearing who do not expect wedlock, it is no sin on them if they discard their clothing in such a way as not to show their adornment. But to refrain is better for them. And Allah is all-hearer, all-knower. *Al-Nur 24:60.*

Recommendations for Muhammad's wives include staying in their houses and not displaying themselves, of being screened and cloaked from others (*Al-Ahzab 33:32–33; 53–55, 59*). Even though they are 'not like other women' (33:32), these injunctions have often been more widely cited as applicable to all Muslim women.

Qur'anic injunctions for modesty are taken up in a variety of ways in different Muslim communities. Modesty is expressed in clothing, and also behaviour and voice. It can be linked with fashion, piety, or community honour.

Veiling: Styles and Significance

While Islam is associated with the image of veiled women, the veil isn't uniform; it can take different shapes, and also have different meanings. Customs and regulations around veiling can differ according to history and geography, class, age and ethnicity. What is consistent is that clothing is not neutral. What we wear sends signals both about us, and the groups with which we identify. Clothes, jewellery, and how the head veil is tied all say something about the individual's ethnic, economic and sectarian background; the community they come from. Their communal affiliations affect how they relate to people from other communities.

Modes of covering range from veils that cover the face (including the *burkah* and *niqab*) to the *chador* and *hijab* that cover hair and neck, through to a scarf that can show some of the hair, or no covering at all.[2] Regional culture and fashion choices also affect the shape of how the full face-covering or *hijab* may be worn. Even more conservative dress, including full-length coats and skirts, are characterised by careful choices of lapel cut, material, buttons and belts, that are linked to different degrees of fashion or age. And the more conservative and all-encompassing the outer clothing, such as the black *abaya* or full-length coat, the greater the variety of dress that may be worn under it. Outward conformity to public rules of modesty can cover everything from long skirt and conservative undergarments[3] to designer wear tight jeans or short skirts. Living in a conservative suburb in a Middle Eastern city, I followed my neighbours' example and kept the encompassing prayer over-skirt and long top hanging beside the front door, so they could be donned quickly to follow the rules of covering if a stranger was at the door.

There are different meanings attached to veiling. In conservative social contexts, through wearing the veil women are able participate in public life, while preserving their modesty and chastity, and signalling their piety. Or the veil may be worn as a symbol of resistance to western influence. Dress and veil can also signal position in the hierarchy of seniority, where devoutness as well as age give people higher rank. Conservative dress and, particularly, the veil, or even the face-covering *niqab,* show women as more devout. Women will talk about being 'ready' or not yet ready, to take on the next stage of conservative veiling. Sometimes a life-crisis or, more frequently, something such as making the pilgrimage to Mecca, will cause a woman to start wearing the veil. Often, puberty is a time when girls are encouraged to put on the veil and adopt more conservative modes of dress. In some communities, this can happen in a ceremony, attended by other women, of putting on the veil.[4] Wearing more conservative dress can be a way of women seeking to protect themselves if they are walking in public or need to take public transport, where there is more chance of encountering male harassment. Or conservative clothing and veil might also signal more pious allegiance for women of marriageable age. It can be linked with middle-class aspirations for women attending tertiary institutions who come from rural or working-class backgrounds. At different times and places state governments have forbidden or enforced the veil.[5] Just a small piece of cloth, it is loaded with meaning.

---

[2] For women making the pilgrimage to Mecca, at the confluence of sacred time and space, face-covering is forbidden. Hair is covered, but not the face. This follows Maliki and Hanafi schools. Some Shafi'i and Hanbali scholars advocate women covering their face and hands, also.

[3] I was told that this was important in case someone was in an accident while out, and had to go to hospital.

[4] Meltzer and Nix 2012.

[5] For example, the veil has been forbidden by the Shah in Iran, Ataturk in Turkey, and the contemporary French government. It is currently enforced in Iran, Saudi, and under the Taliban in Afghanistan.

The early 20th century saw women in many Muslim societies move from conservative garb to unveiling. Then the 1970s and 1980s saw the reverse trend, returning to covering clothes, including veiling. In some ways, this reflects the choices of third-wave feminism.[6] Many young Muslim women adopted the veil that their mothers and grandmothers had removed, wearing it as a statement of piety, resistance, identity, or even a fashion statement.

Islamic clothing is becoming more of a fashion trend, particularly in Indonesia and western Muslim communities. 'Modest Fashion' is a $200 billion-a-year business, and Muslims have become mediators of style from streetwear to haute couture to sportswear. Muslim fashion bloggers are attracting thousands of followers in countries around the world. While Muslim modest wear appears at fashion weeks in New York, Torino and Paris, local designers are entering the global market, creating deeper understandings for how Muslims and others navigate beauty, modesty and modernity.

Piety and the Veil

Modesty is taken up into the acquisition of piety. The requirements of covering before God for formal prayer for Muslim women are the same as the requirement of covering with non-related men: only face and hands can be seen, no wisp of hair should be showing. Conservative Muslim women check the perimeter of the scarf around their face for any strands of hair that might need tucking back, in a frequent, almost unconscious gesture. Mahmoud describes how adopting the veil was used by Muslim women in Cairo to train themselves pious attitudes of modesty or shyness. One woman explained how "In the beginning when you wear it, you're embarrassed and don't want to wear it. ... But you *must* wear the veil, first because it is God's command, and then, with time, because your inside learns to feel shy without the veil." So, the veil becomes both a 'critical marker of piety' and, at the same time, 'the ineluctable means' of training oneself to be pious.[7] For many young women, wearing prayer clothes is their first experience of wearing the veil.[8] Women religious teachers are able to occupy a more public position by operating with the constraints of more conservative conventions of behaviour and clothing.[9]

A common description among conservative Muslim women of the need for modest covering is that they are like a precious jewel that needs to be protected, rather than viewing it as a symbol of oppression. *Bihishti Zewar* (Heavenly Ornaments), written by Mawlana Ashraf 'Ali Thanawi (1864–1943), was written in the early 1900s for Muslim women as an 'instructional guidebook of moral

---

[6] This is discussed in Chapter 18.
[7] Mahmood 2005:157–8.
[8] "Salah" P.M. & M.D. 2020:45.
[9] Kalmbach 2008.

conduct, religious teachings, and daily behaviour.'[10] It was often given to new brides in the Indian sub-continent as a gift and behavioural guide. Fouad Zakaria describes how:

> the view of women among contemporary Muslim fundamentalists suggests a duality of overt praise and flattery on the one hand and covert humiliation and degradation on the other. ... Wearing the veil, therefore, falls at the junction between the repudiation and denunciation of the body ... and excessive concern for the body and the danger it could pose to the woman herself as well as to others.[11]

As a focus on pious behaviour becomes more prominent in a society, its members may experience increased pressure to adhere to religious observance, including women's covering. During the first decade of this century, in the women's carriage of the Cairo metro, I saw increasing numbers of stickers warning passengers, "*al-hijab qabl al-'azab*" ([Wear] *hijab* before [instead of] the torment [of hell]). In a major city in another Middle Eastern country, newspapers reported conservatively-dressed women going into cafes during Ramadan and telling the proprietors that they should close during daylight hours or else face being roasted in hell. Sadaf Ahmed describes the use of peer pressure and the invocation of 'correct' religious practice by Islamists to encourage women to take up more conservative dress.[12] Increasing devoutness is shown by more conformity to an Arab style of modest dress, signalling allegiance to the wider *ummah* which locates its origins and identity in the Middle East. Ahmad describes how women joining the piety movement in Pakistan begin wearing *hijab*s and *abaya*s, and sometimes covering their faces, even though "These practices are largely unheard of in the upper classes these women belong to."[13]

Expressing Modesty

Modesty can encompass clothing, and also voice and behaviour. Girls are socialised into ways of dress, speech and behaviour that protect and affirm their chastity.

> Countless pages are dedicated to the rules and regulations regarding female dress and behaviour, the implicit objective of which is to reconcile the problematic place of woman's physical body in society, given the centrality of her relational role within the family. The consensus is that, other than the woman's face and hands, her body should be covered (*'awrah*). Such an interpretation is derived from

---

[10] Clancy-Smith 2003:108.
[11] Cited by Hadad, in Hadad and Esposito 1998:10.
[12] Ahmed 2011:153.
[13] Ahmad 2009:3.

ambiguous verses of modesty whose meanings are shaped by a view of woman as relational.[14]

Women's perfume and voices can be included in their ʿ*awrah*.[15] Women are taught not to talk or laugh too loudly in public. The inclusion of women's voices in their ʿ*awrah* is the reason that women Qur'anic reciters do not perform in public today in the Middle East, even though their voices were heard in the 1930s and 1940s – most famously, Umm Kulthum.[16] Arab people have told me that if a woman's voice is heard outside her apartment, it is as if she walked outside naked. Even in Indonesia, where women reciters of the Qur'an are common, they may face restrictions in international competitions, and also around the question of whether they can perform if they are menstruating.[17] In a Middle Eastern mosque programme, voices from the main (men's) section of the mosque were frequently broadcast into the women's section, whereas the women were constantly checking to make sure their voices were not audible beyond their own space (in an aural equivalent to the oft-repeated, almost unconscious gesture of ensuring that all their hair was hidden under the enveloping hijab). Modesty may include even close acquaintances not knowing a woman's personal name, or not saying it aloud in public spaces. Fear of people gossiping about dress or behaviour is used to control women's conduct. Modesty as a moral ideal can lead to women experiencing feelings of shame or embarrassment if they find themselves inappropriately dressed or exposed, or insufficiently segregated from unrelated men.

Women show the strong cultural value of modesty (for women, this is sometimes described as 'positive shame') in their clothes and their bodies – how they dress, how (and also where and when) they walk, how they talk (and what they talk about), not letting their voices be heard too loudly, and particularly in not laughing or singing in public. Lama Abud-Odeh suggests that Arab women "are supposed to perform a 'public' virginity with a certain body 'style,' the body moving within a defined and delimited social space. Each one of the above borders, the vaginal, the bodily, and the social is enforced through a set of regulations and prohibitions that the woman is not supposed to violate."[18] Sadaf Ahmad notes that for women in Pakistan, "any activity deemed culturally inappropriate thus results in the loss of honour, and not just hers but also her family's, and eventually her nation's."[19] Family and national honour are protected through ensuring that women keep within carefully prescribed

---

[14] Abugideiri 2007:251.
[15] ʿ*awrah*' – that which must be concealed. See Chapter 5. Also vom Bruck 2002:161–200, esp.172, 178.
[16] Nelson 2001:202–3.
[17] van Doorn-Harder 2006:237–9.
[18] Abu-Odeh 2010:923.
[19] Ahmad 2009:L.681.

community cultural guidelines for modest dress and behaviour.[20] However, expectations of modesty vary across class, age and marital status. "In many societies across the Muslim world, older women behave more assertively, are more relaxed in the company of men, and have more public roles." Being veiled or not, and use of explicit language, may be dependent on gender segregation.[21]

Modesty and Community Honour

Modesty is closely tied to female sexuality and honour. It is defined by appropriate comportment and sexual rectitude. Female modesty demonstrates family and national honour, and so is guarded by both family and state regulations. Muslim morality is closely linked with concepts of female bodily integrity. Mojab describes how "A female, her body, sexuality, name, and fame, is the repository of *namus* (honour). ... A woman's *namus* belongs to the male members of the family, kin, community, tribe, and nation."[22] Because of this link between women's behaviour and community honour, "Female sexuality is often considered as a seriously destabilizing element (*fitna*), hence the need of veiling women in public places."[23] Modest behaviour, or lack of, brings credit or shame to the whole family. So, a family may place pressure on a woman to wear the veil, as a public statement of modesty and piety, but not ask about whether she prays regularly or not. Women's prayer generally happens within the home, and is less exposed to public pressure or gossip. Women's movements may be carefully circumscribed so that no gossip about them will come back to bring shame on their family. Violating the boundaries of where women can be or who they can be with, can bring shame on the family, which must be eradicated by sanctions, and in some communities, by violence.

The movement of women into more public space has led to greater emphasis on modesty – whether in clothing, deportment or language. Stricter forms of modesty and chastity may be enforced than those operating within families. Once women became unveiled and present in public space, national discourses emerged in some countries around the need for modesty and veiling. These discussions developed also in response to the stereotype of western societies as a place where women are sexualised and exploited, so that "the modesty of Muslim women is implicitly or explicitly cast in relationship to the immodesty or immorality of western or non-Muslim women."[24] The political appropriation of modesty values was used to reinforce state power, leading to abuses in some

---

[20] *Purdah* ('curtain') is a term used in the Indian subcontinent to describe the physical seclusion of women, traditionally practised through the division of space into public and private, and domestic space into men's and women's places.
[21] Abu-Lughod 2005:495.
[22] Mojab 2005:214.
[23] Bargach 2006:52.
[24] Abu-Lughod 2005:497; Maududi 1981.

countries including forced virginity examinations and rape as a means of intimidation, and to torture political dissidents.

Circumcision

When God made circumcision a sign of his special covenant relationship with Abraham's family and descendants, Ishmael was circumcised along with his father Abraham and all the male members of the household.[25] Muslim historian Ibn Kathir[26] connects the origins of female circumcision with the story of Hagar. He recounts that Sarah in her jealousy vowed to cut 'three limbs' of Hagar's. So, Abraham told Hagar to pierce both her ears and have herself circumcised.[27] The practice of female circumcision began in the Nilotic regions, which links with Hagar's Egyptian origins.

Female circumcision, or female genital mutilation (FGM), is modesty incised into the flesh. It is practised in some Muslim countries (some parts of Africa, the Middle East and Asia) and also in a number of African Christian communities. It can function as an important rite of passage, which signifies both a woman's purity and also maturity and readiness for marriage. Older women may be the main proponents in the community for perpetuating the custom. There are different forms of severity in the practice. It can range from nicking or cutting the clitoris through to removal of some or all of the external female genitalia.[28] Rulings differ with the various schools of Islamic law: the Shafi'i school declares that circumcision is a duty for both men and women; Hanbali requires it for boys but only advises it for women; and Hanafi

---

[25] Gen 17:23–27.

[26] Qisas, Vol.I, p.202, see Stowasser 1994:47, and 147, note 55.

[27] "After Hagar had conceived, she became haughty toward her mistress, while Sarah grew increasingly jealous. In her jealousy, Sarah vowed to cut 'three limbs' of Hagar's; so Abraham ordered Hagar to pierce her ears and have herself circumcised. 'These customs,' therefore, 'began with Hagar.'"(from Ibn Kathir, *Qisas*, vol.I, p.202), in Stowasser 1994:47).

[28] Female genital mutilation is classified into four major types.
Type 1: this is the partial or total removal of the clitoral glans (the external and visible part of the clitoris, which is a sensitive part of the female genitals), and/or the prepuce/clitoral hood (the fold of skin surrounding the clitoral glans).
Type 2: this is the partial or total removal of the clitoral glans and the labia minora (the inner folds of the vulva), with or without removal of the labia majora (the outer folds of skin of the vulva).
Type 3: Also known as infibulation, this is the narrowing of the vaginal opening through the creation of a covering seal. The seal is formed by cutting and repositioning the labia minora, or labia majora, sometimes through stitching, with or without removal of the clitoral prepuce/clitoral hood and glans (Type I FGM).
Type 4: This includes all other harmful procedures to the female genitalia for non-medical purposes, e.g., pricking, piercing, incising, scraping and cauterizing the genital area.
https://www.who.int/news-room/fact-sheets/detail/female-genital-mutilation.

and Maliki only say it is commendable for both. Female genital mutilation[29] is a form of violent control cut into the bodies of women, to remove any possibility of sexual enjoyment for women. Its practice is justified by the need to control women's chaotic sexuality. In the most extreme form of FGM, both menstruation and sexual intercourse are painful, and childbirth is only possible by cutting the woman open, and sewing her afterwards.

Where circumcision is used to designate a woman as both pure and a (marriageable) adult, communities may need to develop alternative rites of passage which can carry the same meaning. The chapter on Purity and Defilement has discussed how circumcision and baptism can both carry meanings of purity, and entrance into a community of faith. Adult baptism marks the participant as a mature member of their community.

The Bible endorses the need for modest behaviour for both women and men. Decorous conduct can include body posture, attitudes and dress (1 Tim 2:8–9). Appropriate behaviour is determined by that which honours God and strengthens the Christ-community in any context.[30] There are differing verses on the place of women's voices, whether they stay silent, or pray or prophesy in the community. Paul suggests to the early church that when praying or prophesying, men should have their head uncovered, and women cover their heads (1 Cor 11:4–5). This is in contrast to the current belief of many Jews that men should cover their head, particularly when praying, with a skullcap (*kippah/yarmulke*) as a sign of respect to God. The Talmud links the requirement for women to cover their heads with the Old Testament test for adultery, where the woman being examined unbinds her hair (Num 5:18).

Dancing is a particular form of behaviour with particular cultural norms around modesty and appropriateness in each context. These include questioning whether it applies to both genders, or happens more in single-gender gatherings. Types of clothing, music and movements are specified. The Bible records women dancing in public celebration (Ex 15:19–21; Judges 11:32–34; 1 Sam 18:6–7; Jer 31:4; and Judith 15:12–13).

Popular perceptions of the 'veiled Muslim woman' can overlook wider dimensions of modesty, cultural appropriateness, fashion and piety. The New Testament points beyond specific rules around adornments and actions to inner attitudes, appropriate behaviour and good works for women and men.

- What choices are your friends making around what they wear? What signals do their choices send?
- If women are wearing hijab or some other form of head covering, when do they begin the practice?
- What influences are shown by different styles?
- What signals might you be sending through your dress choices?

---

[29] http://www.unfpa.org/resources/female-genital-mutilation-fgm-frequently-asked-questions.
[30] Dale: 2021 (https://www.youtube.com/watch?v=Eh0IQSZOKbQ).

17. Education and Faith

We hear of al-Shaykha Sultana bint 'Ali al-Zubaydy, a female religious scholar of 13th century Hadramawt, Yemen, who was famous for her piety, knowledge, and teachings. A male contemporary of hers, who believed that religious scholarship and teaching were the province of men, challenged her in verse: "But can a female camel compete with a male camel?" Sultana deftly completed the couplet with: "A female camel can carry the same load as a male, and produce offspring and milk as well."[1]

I join the women of the extended family belonging in the building in which I live, as they meet together to read through the Qur'an. Using the popular division of the Qur'an into thirty sections, each woman takes one or two sections to quietly recite, with all murmuring concurrently until the whole Qur'an has been recited.[2] The recitation finishes with a time of *du'a* (supplication), led by one of the women who has gained authority by memorising the whole Qur'an, or who has a particularly affective voice which helps in eliciting the desired tearful attitude of response. At the end everyone enjoys a meal together. Sometimes others outside the group might contribute to the meal, asking for the Qur'an to be read with intercessory intent for someone sick in hospital, or starting a new business.

---

[1] Boxberger 1998:119.
[2] This is the *khitma* (sealing) of the Qur'an through its complete recitation.

Seek Learning

Ta-Ha 20:114 includes the injunction: "and say, 'My Lord! Increase me in knowledge.'"

This verse has been widely used to support the importance of women learning, whether religious knowledge or literacy campaigns. It is supported by a *hadith* attributed to Muhammad:

> Seeking knowledge is an obligation upon every Muslim.[3]

In many cultures, and certainly not only Muslim cultures, girls and boys may be treated quite differently as they grow up. Traditionally, boys have received more opportunities for education than girls. Prominent feminists Huda Shaarawi in Egypt (1879–1947) and Fatima Mernissi in Morocco (1940–2015) both record being discouraged in their desire to learn more of the Qur'an because they were girls.[4] In some societies families prefer to invest their money for education or medicine in sons rather than daughters. If a school is some distance away from the home, families may not send their daughters in case something happens to them. "Spend (money for) education or medicine on a boy, not a girl" is one saying that I sometimes encountered in the Middle East. If the domestic role is seen as women's sphere, it gives them less opportunity for free time or possibilities for education. Expression of their own desires or emotions might be read as not just antisocial, but immodest, bringing the family into disrepute.

However, we find that women scholars have always been present in the history of Islam.

Historical Women Scholars

Muslim women were prominent among the trustworthy transmitters (*muhaddithat*) of the *hadith* that shaped the understanding and practices of the Muslim community over the centuries. Aisha and Umm Salamah were well known among Muhammad's wives as transmitters of *hadith*,[5] and Nasibah and Umm Sulaym were among the Companions.[6] Al-Khansa, and Umara bint Abdel Rahman were famous *muhaddithat* of the first century of Islam, along with Aisha Abdel Hadi in the second century and Nafissah (Muhammad's great

---

[3] Sunan Ibn Mājah 224:
https://www.abuaminaelias.com/dailyhadithonline/2012/08/30/talab-ilm-wajib-faridah/.
Other popular *hadith* include "Seek knowledge even in China," and "Seek knowledge (from the cradle) to the grave." However, these are considered to be of weak authenticity or fabricated.
[4] Shaarawi 1998:40, and Mernissi 1994:102–3.
[5] Deeb 2007:335; Nadwi 2007:248; Roded 2008:49.
[6] 'Ali Qutb 2007:189, 212.

granddaughter) and Rabi'a al-Adawiyya in the third century.[7] The scholars whom Nafissah taught included al-Shafi'i and Ibn Hanbal, founders of two of the four main Sunni schools of jurisprudence. Women have also been jurists and calligraphers. In the seventh century, women were part of a revival in *hadith* scholarship in Syria, learning and teaching *hadith* in some of the main mosques, and in gardens and private houses in seventh-century Damascus.[8] They included Umm al-Darda, a well-known *muhaddithah* and jurist, who taught prominent scholars and others including the caliph Abdul Malik Bin Marwan.[9] As a young woman she used to sit with male scholars in the mosque. She wrote, "I've tried to worship Allah in every way, but I've never found a better one than sitting around, debating with other scholars." She went on to teach *hadith* and jurisprudence (*fiqh*) at the mosque, and the caliph of Damascus attended her lectures.[10] Shuhda the Scribe (d.574/1176) was famous in Baghdad both as a transmitter of *hadith*, and as a calligrapher under whom men studied.

Historians cite examples of women involved in jurisprudence (*fiqh*), Qur'an interpretation (*tafsir*) and issuing legal rulings (*fatwas*). Hence, Nadwi insists that "women scholars acquired and exercised the same authority as men scholars."[11] These women scholars were both students and teachers of men and women. They were often relatives of male clerics, from the *'ulama* (scholar) class.[12] They might be taught by a male relative such as their father, and sometimes also were able to have access to private tutors.[13] There is an impressive collection of historic sources, such as biographies and religious histories, which mention prominent women, which include:[14]

1. Ibn Sa'ad (d. A.H.230/ninth century) *Al-Tabaqat al-kubra*. Volume 8 is devoted to the subject of women.

2. Abi Abdallah Ibn Mus'ab Al-Zubeiri (ninth century) *Kitab Nassab Goraich*.

3. Al-Tabari, Abu Jafar Muhammad Ibn Jarir (d. A.H.310/10th century) *Tarikh al-uman wa al-muluk*. He discusses the role of women in a text inserted at the end of the 13th and final volume.

4. Ibn Hazm al-Andaloussi (d. A.H.456 /11th century*) Jamharat ansab* al-'Arab.

5. Ibn Amir Yusuf-al-Namri al-Qurtubi (Ibn 'Abd al-Barr) (d. A.H.463) *Kitab al-Isti'ab*. His book ends with women's biographies.

6. Al-Khatib al-Baghdadi (d. A.H.463) in his Ta'rikh Baghdad included 29 women in his list of 7831 scholars over a 300-year period.

---

[7] Abdel-Halim 2008:19.

[8] Deeb 2007:335; Nadwi 2007:248 266–7; Roded 2008:49.

[9] https://islamictextinstitute.co.za/umm-darda-may-allah-be-pleased-with-her/.

[10] Nadwi 2007:266–7.

[11] Nadwi 2007:XVIII, ch.10; also Roded 2008:96.

[12] Ahmed 1992:113–4: Nadwi 2007:XII.

[13] Lane 1860/1966:64; Gerner 1984:77; Baron 1988; Hatem 1998:74.

[14] See Mernissi (1996:82–100) for much of this list.

7. Ibn al-Athir (d. A.H.631/13th century) *Usd al-ghaba fi ma'rifat al-Sahaba*. Volume 5, *Kitab al-nisa*, is on women.
8. Al-Dahbi (d. 748/1370) *Siyar a'lam al-nubula*.
9. Ibn Hisham (d. 833 A.D.) *Al-Sira al-Nabawiya*, which describes the active involvement of women around Muhammad.
10.   Sakina Shihabi's editing of the comments of Imam Ibn 'Asakir's (d. 571/1175) special volume on women, *Tarikh Dimashq*, which contains 196 biographies of famous Muslim women who either lived in or visited Damascus: "... it gave Ibn 'Asakir an opportunity to summarise all existing data until his time (12th century A.D.) on some of the most active and forceful women of our civilisation." Ibn Asakir describes women of his time being able to study, earn *ijazahs* and qualify as scholars and teachers (particularly in families of scholars). Lindsay notes that Ibn Asakir himself had studied under eighty different female teachers.[15]
11.   Ibn Hajar, al 'Asqalani (d. 852/1449) *Al-Isaba fi tamyiz al-Sahaba*. Volume 7 acknowledges 1,552 women as disciples.
12.   al-Sakhawi (d. 902/1497) followed the example of al-Asqalani in devoting the final section of his biographical dictionary to women scholars. It included over one thousand, of whom: "38% of these women studied, received licences (ijazahs) to transmit their learning and/or taught others."[16]

The first and second centuries after Muhammad, and the sixth to ninth centuries of the Muslim calendar in particular, were significant times for Muslim women scholars. In the first centuries Islam was expanding and developing, and the later period saw the Muslim world invaded by the Crusaders and the Mongols. Times of disruption can allow women more space to flourish than times of consolidation.

In the 18th to 19th centuries a few girls, mostly of middle-class families, attended the small local Qur'anic schools (*kuttab*) present throughout the Muslim world.[17] Women in wealthier families sometimes had access to tutors. Overall, female literacy was generally low.[18] While each country has its own history of women's access to education, it may be useful to look at one country as a case study. We can take Egypt's timeline for the development of women's education.

---

[15] Lindsay 2005:196–8.
[16] Roded 2008:132. Ahmed 1992:113–114 gives vignettes of some of these women.
[17] Wilks 1968:165; Eickelman 1978:493; Wagner 1993:44.
[18] By comparison, as late as 1792 in the UK, Mary Wollstonecraft was arguing for equal educational opportunities for women in Britain, in her book *A Vindication of the Rights of Women*.

Growing Access to Education for Women

Muhammad 'Ali ruled Egypt from 1805 to 1848, modernising trade and agricultural practices. School for *hakimas* (women doctors) started in 1832. There was some openness to education for women: some upper-class women had European tutors employed for them as well as traditional Arabic teachers. Missionary schools were established in Egypt in the 1830s and 1840s. Coptic Orthodox and other community schools (including Jewish schools) also opened in the 1850s. In 1873, the first Egyptian government girls' primary school was opened, followed by a girls' secondary school in 1874. In 1882, under British occupation, the increasing demand for education led to tuition fees being raised, so Egyptian leaders founded benevolent societies to establish schools. By 1897, there were 11,000 male students in government schools and 181,000 in benevolent schools. And there were 863 female students in government schools, and 1,164 in benevolent schools.

Napoleon's invasion of Egypt in 1798 had introduced the printing press. This contributed towards a *nahda* (awakening or renaissance) in writing and publishing in Egypt and beyond. Towards the end of the 1800s and early 1900s, Arab women were increasingly writing in and publishing magazines for women, initially writing anonymously or with pen names.[19] Some women began to write under their own names. This was like the textual equivalent of unveiling and appearing personally in public spaces.[20] In 1905, in Madras India, Rokeya Sakhawat Hossain wrote *Sultana's Dream*, a novel of a female utopia.[21] In 1908, Nabawiyya Musa (1890–1951) was the first woman to graduate in Egypt with a secondary school certificate.

Early pleas for educating women were based on nationalism and the importance of women's role in the cultural reform of societies. It was at this time that women became a central issue in public discussion about Islam. Qasim Amin (1865–1908) wrote:

> Egyptians … must believe that there is no hope that they will become a vibrant community, one that can play an important role alongside the developed countries, with a place in the world of human civilization, until their homes and their families become a proper environment for providing men with the characteristics upon which success in the world depends. And there is no hope that Egyptian homes and families will become that proper environment unless women are educated and

---

[19] A glance at western women writers shows the same trend of using initials or pseudonyms to publish, including the Bronte sisters and Jane Austen, and far more recently, J.K. Rowling.
[20] Ahmed 1992:140–1; Baron 1994, 1988.
[21] This preceded the similar US novel 'Herland' written by Charlotte Perkins Gilman in 1915. https://en.wikipedia.org/wiki/Herland_(novel); http://digital.library.upenn.edu/women/sultana/dream/dream.html.

unless they participate alongside men in their thoughts, hopes and pains, even if they do not participate in all of their activities.[22]

Amin collaborated with al-Sayyid Jamal al-Din al-Afghani (1838–1897), Muhammad 'Abduh (1849–1905) and Rifa'ah Rafi' al-Tahtawi (1801–1873), also writing on the same topic. These men were influenced by their studies in France, and their concern for the reform of Muslim countries and liberation from western domination, basing their arguments for reform on an appeal to return to the true Islam that had been corrupted over centuries. Other books had been published supporting education for women in 1875 and 1894.[23] In this discussion women's development was promoted, not for their own sake, but because of Muslim children's need for a good mother.[24] Discussions about Muslim women and scholarship were located in ideological discussions of modernisation. Gerarmi and Safiri comment that "The battle of modernity and cultural authenticity has been fought over women's bodies and souls."[25]

In 1925, education was made compulsory for all in Egypt – just forty-five years after Britain in 1880. In 1933, the first graduate degrees were given to women from Egyptian universities (other Egyptian women had already gained degrees from western universities who had opened their doors to women recently).

Learning and Devotion in Community

Women gather for pious activities. Sometimes, reciting a section or all of the Qur'an is used to bring blessing into a life cycle transition, or family crisis such as illness.[26] Groups of women, often linked by extended family or neighbourhood relationships,[27] or through membership of a Sufi *tariqa,* can gather in a household to do *dhikr* together, and at the end people will enjoy the accompanying catch-up with each other over a glass of tea. During the month of *Rabi'a al-Awwal*, the month in which Muhammad was born, a woman may invite family members or friends to gather to sing songs of praise of Muhammad, read the Qur'an and then enjoy food together.[28]

---

[22] 1992:66: First published in Arabic 1899 as *Tahrir al-Mar'a.*

[23] By Mubarak and Fahmi (Ahmed 1992:133–168; Badran 2009:19–21).

[24] This followed global trends of how the role of woman was viewed (Baron 1988; Shakry 1998:138, 149; Abu Lughod 1998:8–9).

[25] Gerami and Safiri, 2007:255.

[26] For example, *al-Na'im* (6) can be recited for its healing power.

[27] The categories of neighbours and extended families can overlap, where neighbours include extended family of sisters and sisters-in-law, mother, aunts and grandmothers, cousins and nieces.

[28] Also in the Gulf, for Muhammad's or for other saints' birthdays: Doumato, 2000:111, 112.

The number of women's programmes in mosques has proliferated, from more established movements such as the *pesantren* in Indonesia and women's mosques among the Hui population of China, to programmes for women in homes and mosques around the world.

The movement of women into official sacred space in mosques (traditionally occupied by men) and into textual hermeneutics has been a notable trend in the last couple of decades. The Muslim women's mosque, or piety movement as it is known, is fuelled by the growth in women's literacy and education, which has combined with the widespread availability of material relating to theological issues and faith duties in popular media such as printed pamphlets and books, tapes and now DVDs and satellite channels, to give women more access to religious discussion and resources. Popular media channels are fed by the development of conservative Islamic movements across the Muslim world, which prioritise religious education, particularly in the context of *da'wa*.[29] In Cairo, during the first years of this century, I increasingly witnessed young women initiating a sermon or leading in Qur'anic recitation in the women's carriage of the Cairo metro. This publicly-defined women's space became a place for the exercise of women's *da'wa*.

Mahmood describes the place of the *da'iyya* (preacher or missionary): "In many ways the figure of the *da'iyya* exemplifies the ethos of the contemporary Islamic Revival, and people now often ascribe to this figure the same degree of authority previously reserved for religious scholars."[30] The teacher in a women's programme in the Middle East described the *da'iyya* as the successor (*khalifa*) to the Prophet (Muhammad). This is a radical shift from women seeing their God-given vocation (*risala*) purely in terms of domestic space and responsibility. In the mosque where I attended her teaching, the extensive upper section was dedicated to the women's programme, with a hall for the larger meetings (often between 80 and 120 women), an office, a number of smaller rooms for classes or *dhikr*, and a library and computer area specifically for the women. Weekly activities included teaching classes, *dhikr* sessions, classes in memorising and correct recitation (*tajwid*) of the Qur'an, and classes on the

---

[29] *Da'wa* means to call or invite. In religious terms it is "the invitation, addressed to men (*sic*) by God and the prophets, to believe in the true religion, Islam (*Ibrahim* 14:44)." It determined the Muslim community's relationship to non-Muslims: "Those to whom the da'wa had not yet penetrated had to be invited to embrace Islam before fighting could take place." Canard 1965:168–170. The contemporary piety movement relates *da'wa* not only to non-Muslims, but also to the duty of every practising Muslim to urge fellow Muslims to correct Islamic practice. The development of *da'wa* links with the principle of 'enjoining (others) in doing good or right and forbidding the evil,' (*al-Imran*: 104, 110: *al-Taubah*:71). The former reference links the two specifically (and let there be from you people inviting to the good, enjoining what is right and forbidding what is wrong.); whereas the latter addresses men and women equally, 'the believing men and believing women.'

[30] Mahmood 2005:58.

fundamentals of Islamic practices and history. In Ramadan, the evening *tarawih* prayers were always attended by hundreds of women (as well as the men in the main downstairs section), even those women who never attended the mosque during the rest of the year. And the women's programme had special times of celebration for the main religious feasts. Only on Fridays when men filled the mosque for the Friday community address and prayers, did they also take over the women's space – on that day, women did their prayers at home.

The women's mosque programme provided a context for learning about official Islamic teaching, but at the same time reinterpreting it to focus more on the place of women in Islamic history, and the place of Islamic teaching in relation to women's everyday lives and concerns. Contrary to what was taught in many other mosques, this programme taught that modern methods of hygiene made it acceptable for women to continue attending the mosque for teaching even during their menstrual period. They could continue to benefit from the teaching and join in *dhikr*, even if they couldn't do the *salah* prayer.

Women's movements can also link women beyond family and neighbourhood associations in wider regional and even inter-country networks across the theological and geographic spectrum.

As Sufism became more institutionalised into orders, women's orders also developed, including convents led by women.[31] Cynthia Strong describes Somali Sufi women belonging to their own order or *tariqah*, and tracing their "spiritual lineage and *barakah* back to Muhammad's daughter, Fatima."[32] Through Sufi orders, women link with one another across nations and internationally. A more recent example, which combines features of Sufism and the piety movement, is the Qubaysi group, a Sunni women's organisation led by Miss Munira al-Qubaysi. Today its adherents number thousands in Syria and beyond. The group met in homes for many years, but their growing influence through numbers, influential family connections and the further spread of their teaching through the elementary schools they run, encouraged the government to give them licences to meet in mosques. Some observers suggest that the movement deliberately recruited women from wealthy and influential families. The group originated from the al-Nur Mosque in Damascus, when Ahmed Muhammad Amin Kuftaro (1915–2004) was Imam and Grand Mufti of Syria. In the Sufi Naqshabandi order (with influential connections in the al-Nur Mosque) the disciple is required to give absolute allegiance to his teacher or *shaykh*.[33] One of the Qubaysi tenets is: "No knowledge can be attained and there is no way to reach God without a mentor."[34] Identifiable by the colour (shades of blue) and

---

[31] Bodman 1998:12.

[32] Strong 2006:184.

[33] http://www.sheiknazim2.com/naqshbandiorder.html.

[34] http://faculty-staff.ou.edu/L/Joshua.M.Landis-1/syriablog/: Thoughts on Syrian politics, history and religion. Tuesday, May 16, 2006. *The Qubaysi Women's Islamic Movement* by Ibrahim Hamidi.

style of tying their *hijab* and the long, dark, typically ankle-length overcoats they wear, it has spread beyond neighbouring countries into Europe and the United States.

The Tablighi Jama'at Islamicist movement begun in the Indian sub-continent, and is now one of the biggest religious reform movements in the world. They are now giving more attention to Muslim women whom they see as "bastions of 'Hinduistic' customs and traditions."[35] They encourage women to take time off from domestic and family responsibilities to form a women's group to preach reformist Islam to other Muslim women in the areas they visit. Beginning with three days every two months, with experience, women are encouraged to go for up to forty days, including visiting other countries. The women are accompanied by male permitted (*mahram*) relatives, who take all the decisions about the working of the whole group and the women's daily programme. As well as spending time praying, reading and listening to lectures (usually from a man) about Islamic faith and practice, women can take this opportunity to share each other's lives, joys and sorrows.

Women's gatherings exist throughout the Muslim world, offering different possibilities to women, including community, and an opportunity to leave their homes; roles of leadership; blessing, or access to God's power; and an opportunity to shape community norms. And religious gatherings give women an acceptable reason to leave their homes and meet with other women, perhaps even to travel beyond their immediate home or village environs for conferences or training. They can provide women with the opportunity for leadership in roles that are not only domestic, but can include organising, leading in prayer, teaching, reciting or singing. In these gatherings women can develop their abilities in new areas and gain recognition. And women's gatherings also offer a way for women who are seeking to grow in religious knowledge or experience.

There is a rich tradition of women scholars existing within Muslim history. Combined with growing possibilities for education for women today, it forms a backdrop for the growing women's mosque movement across the Muslim world today. Alongside state schools, many women are now graduating from state-sponsored religious institutions for women. Some of these institutions have been deliberately developed as a way to combat extremist religious teaching.

Women's Oral Poetry

However, there is another dimension where women have used oral text, songs or poems to influence the societies in which they live. In many Muslim cultures poems are powerful and appreciated, both in love and war. Words are active weapons which can be used to confer honour or hurl shame.

---

[35] SOCIOLOGY_OF_ISLAM@listserv.vt.edu (23/03/2009) *Women and the Tablighi Jama'at*, from Yoginder Sikand.

In the community in which Islam made its appearance, the songs or poetry of women were influential. In pre-Islamic society, women's role was to compose poems of lament with which to incite men to action. Al-Khansa' (d.24/645) was ·a well-known woman poet and public performer. Hind al Hunnud led women in chanting songs to inflame the warriors in battle against Muhammad.[36] Early biographies describe Muhammad's relief when one of his followers killed 'Asma' bint Marwan, who was composing and reciting verses again him. Smith notes that while Muhammad extended amnesty to many of his foes after his final victory, "the only ones he could not forgive… were those (especially women) who had ridiculed him in songs and poems."[37]

In many communities in the Middle East and Central Asia and even further afield, women continue to use poems and songs to elicit reaction. Abu Lughod has described how, among the Bedouin in Egypt's Western Desert, both women's and men's chanted poetry (*ghinnawa*) "moves people and brings about changes in their actions or attitudes."[38] I have heard other examples described in Central and Southeast Asia, where women use rhymed comments to provoke men into action. A woman, Ahlam al-Nasr, described as the "Poetess of the Islamic State," was a powerful contemporary lyricist for ISIS.[39] There has been increased interest recently in Afghani women's use of poetry, particularly landays.[40] This is a translation of some of the poems read in a Pashtun gathering of women poets in 2011:

> You will witness a poetic scene if my voiceless voice is risen
> You will hear thousands of voices kept behind those scenes
> My tragic words will then burst out of my wounded heart
> You will then hear thousands of my unheard poems.
> Oh my sister – lost in the traditional struggle of the society
> Oh my sister – lost in the shadow of pain
> Your heart was full of dreams and hope
> Oh my sister – lost in the darkness of war

---

[36] Uglow and Hendry 1998:260.

[37] Smith 1985:24.

[38] Abu-Lughod 1986:242.

[39] http://www.newyorker.com/magazine/2015/06/08/battle-lines-jihad-creswell-and-haykel.

[40] "Each has twenty-two syllables: nine in the first line, thirteen in the second. The poem ends with the sound "ma" or "na." Sometimes they rhyme, but more often not. In Pashto, they lilt internally from word to word in a kind of two-line lullaby that belies the sharpness of their content, which is distinctive not only for its beauty, bawdiness, and wit, but also for the piercing ability to articulate a common truth about war, separation, homeland, grief, or love. Within these five main tropes, the couplets express a collective fury, a lament, an earthy joke, a love of home, a longing for the end of separation, a call to arms, all of which frustrate any facile image of a Pashtun woman as nothing but a mute ghost beneath a blue *burqa*."
https://www.poetryfoundation.org/media/landays.html.

Likewise I have also experienced the bitterness of life
Likewise I have also experienced miseries and agonies.[41]

Women's Songs and Poems in the Bible

The tradition of women singing (and dancing) in praise of what God has done is well established in the Bible. Miriam takes up her tambourine, and exuberantly leads the other women in song (Exodus 15:21). Hannah also sings in triumph when God answers her prayer and she gives birth to Samuel (1 Samuel 2:1–10). Deborah recounts God's action and victory in song (Judges 5), and Judith also sings to celebrate her victory (Judith 16:1–17). Later we hear the women of Israel singing, celebrating David's victory over the enemy (1 Samuel 18:6–7), and Saul reacts to their songs with anger and envy. In the New Testament, Luke begins his Gospel with the voices of Elizabeth and Mary, as Elizabeth praises God for his saving action, and Mary responds with her song (Luke 1:42–45, 46–55).

In all these songs, women are both announcing to the community of faith what God has done and interpreting it. They tell of national victories in battle together with domestic events of pregnancy, as signs of God's new action in the world. And in most of the songs, the women singing are also the agents through whom God brings salvation. They are not only witnesses to what God is doing, but active participators through whom God acts to bring about his purposes in the world. Richard Bauckham comments that:

> What happens in the domestic and familial sphere of the woman transcends that sphere, achieving in God's purpose, national and even worldwide significance and effect. The combination, in each song in its context, of the individual and the general, the personal and the political, the domestic and the public, is precisely the point of the song.[42]

Conclusion

While women have had overall less access to education than men, the history of Islam includes significant presence of women scholars. This is reflected in the growth of the women's mosque movement today. We also need to be aware of the influence and expression of women's voices through informal means of oral poetry.

- What is the history of women scholars and women's access to education in the community in which you are involved?
- What opportunities do women have today for education, whether state or religious? How are women represented in higher education?

---

[41] https://www.afghanistan-analysts.org/en/reports/rights-freedom/pashto-womens-poetry-a-mirror-of-their-social-status/.
[42] Bauckham 2002:54, 63.

- In what ways do Muslim women gather, formally or informally, in your neighbourhood? What women's gatherings exist, locally or nationally?
- What women poets or singers do you know? Who do they influence? Are there more hidden forms of poetry or songs that women only use in non-public spaces?

18. Women in Society

"Can a woman be a leader of Muslims?" I asked my grocer, who, like most grocers in Morocco, is a true 'barometer' of public opinion. "I take refuge in God!" he exclaimed, shocked, despite the friendly relations between us. Aghast at the idea, he almost dropped the half-dozen eggs I had come to buy. "May God protect us from the catastrophes of the times!" mumbled a customer who was buying olives, as he made as if to spit. My grocer is a fanatic about cleanliness, and not even denouncing a heresy justifies dirtying the floor in his view. A second customer, a schoolteacher whom I vaguely knew from the newsstand, stood slowly caressing his wet mint leaves, and then hit me with a hadith [tradition of the Prophet] that he knew would be fatal: "Those who entrust their affairs to a woman will never know prosperity!" Silence fell on the scene. There was nothing I could say.[1]

The Qur'an includes verses that emphasise the equality of women and men, in their creation and in their promised rewards:

Verily the Muslims men and women, the believers men and women, the men and the women who are obedient, the men and the women who are truthful, the men and the women who are patient, the men and the women who are humble, the men and the women who give alms, the men and the women who observe fasting, the men and the women who guard their chastity and the men and the women who

---

[1] Described by Mernissi 1998:112–3.

remember Allah much with their hearts and tongues. Allah has prepared for them forgiveness and a great reward. *Al-Abzab* 33:35.

Other verses suggesting parity between women and men include *al-Imran* 3:195, *al-Nisa'* 4:1, 32, 124, *al-Taubah* 9:71-72, *al-Nahl* 16:97, and *al-Rum* 30:20. However, there are also verses in the Qur'an which suggest a difference in status and treatment of women and men. *Al-Baqarah* 2:223 describes wives as the property of their husbands; *al-Baqarah* 2:282 categorises women's witness as half that of men; *al-Nisa* 4:11 gives different rules of inheritance; and *al-Nisa* 4:34 describes men as the 'protectors/maintainers' of women, and includes instructions on how to admonish or punish women.

What position do women actually occupy in Muslim societies? This chapter will look at women in state leadership, economics and politics.

Women in Leadership

Despite the *hadith* referred to in Fatima Mernissi's vivid description of the conversation in her local grocer's store, Mernissi and others point to a number of women rulers in Muslim countries.[2]

The Fatimid princess Sitt al-Mulk was a Shi'ite princess, famous for her beauty and intelligence. Respected by her father (caliph al-Aziz) and brother (caliph al-Hakim) for her administrative ability, she exercised power in the Fatimid empire between 1020 and 1024 in the name of her nephew, caliph al-Dhahir. There were also two Shi'ite (Ismaili) queens in Yemen. Asma bint Shihab al-Sulayhiyya was full co-regent with her husband from 1047 to 1087. Her daughter-in-law Arwa bint Ahmad al-Sulayhiyya then held power from 1091 to 1138. Thurlkill[3] comments that Arwa, like the queens of the Safavid dynasty in 16th century Iran, took on many of Fatima's characteristics. He refers to three Safavid queens who exercised power as wives and mothers of Safavid rulers. Shah-Begi Khan (Tajilu Khanum) was influential as the wife of Shah Ismail (married in 1504), and also as mother of Shah Tahmasp (crowned 1524) until her death in 1540. Pari Khan Khanum exercised influence (1576–78) during some of the reign of her brothers, Ismail II and Muhammad Khodabanda. And Khayr al-Nisa Begum (also known as Mahd-i Ulya), wife of Shah Muhammad, governed from 1578 to 1579.

There were two Mamluk sultanas, Razia Sultan and Shajarat al-Durr. Razia Sultan was ruler in India, in the Delhi Sultanate from 1236 to 1240. Shajarat-al-

---

[2] Narrated Abu Bakra: During the days (of the battle) of Al-Jamal, Allah benefited me with a word I had heard from Allah's Apostle after I had been about to join the Companions of Al-Jamal (i.e., the camel) and fight along with them. When Allah's Apostle was informed that the Persians had crowned the daughter of Khosrau as their ruler, he said, "Such people as ruled by a lady will never be successful." (Al-Bukhari, Book #59, *Hadith* #709), Also Book #88, *Hadith* #219).

[3] Thurlkill 2007:4–5.

Durr (ruled 1250–1257) was an enterprising woman who took power in Egypt after her husband died, playing a key role during the seventh crusade. However, contemporary thinking is ambivalent about her legacy. Today her mausoleum stands neglected, and a famous Egyptian dessert (Um Ali) is named after her co-wife and rival who had Shajarat al-Durr assassinated.

The history of the wide-spreading Mongolian empire includes a number of queens. Kutlugh Khan (ruled 1257–1282) was followed by her daughter, Padishah Khan (1291–1295). Padishah's niece, Absh Khan, ruled in Shiraz, Persia (1263–1287). In Luristan (Southwest Persia), Dawlat Khan took power briefly in 1316, before handing over to her brother-in-law. Sati Bek was a Mongol queen who took power in her own name for just nine months in 1339, but maintained herself in power for longer with three different husbands. Tindu was another Mongol queen who governed Baghdad from 1411 to 1219. Mernissi also mentions Fatima Begum, also known as Sultana Sayyidovna, who is said to have ruled in Central Asia between 1679 and 1681. Other women had prominent roles in the Mongol empire, particularly Mandukhai Khan, known for her wisdom and courage,[4] who led the Mongols in Eastern Mongolia from 1479 to 1510.

In the Maldives, three sultanas reigned: Sultana Khadijah (ruled 1347–1379), succeeded by her sister Sultana Myriam (ruled 1379–1383), and then Myriam's daughter Sultana Fatima (ruled 1383–1388). In the 16th century, Amina was a famous Muslim warrior queen of the Hausa Zaria kingdom (today Northwest Nigeria). And in Acheh, the first Muslim kingdom in Indonesia, there were four queens who ruled "despite the fact that their political enemies had imported from Mecca a *fatwa* that declared that 'it was forbidden by law for a woman to rule'."[5] They included Sultana Tadj al-'Alam Safiyyat al-Din Shah (ruled 1641–1675), followed by Sultana Our al-'Alam Nakiyyat al-Din Shah (ruled 1675–1678), then by 'Inayat Shah Zakiyyat al-Din Shah (ruled 1678–1688), and Kamalat Shah (ruled 1688–1699). They were the fourteenth–seventeenth rulers of their dynasty.

With such a history of leading women in many parts of the Muslim world, it is no surprise that in recent times, six Muslim nations have had female heads of government. They include Pakistan (Benazir Bhutto 1993–1996); Senegal (Mame Madior Boye 2001–2002); Turkey (Tansu Ciller 1993–1996); Kosovo (Kaqusha Jashari 1987–1989); Indonesia (Megawati Sukarnoputri 2001–2004); and Bangladesh (Khaleda Zia 1991–1996, 2001-2006 and Sheikh Hasina Wazed 2009–present).

Culture, clan and political (and military) acumen can score as highly as religious rulings in determining the influence and even overt power of women leaders.

---

[4] Weatherford 2010.
[5] Mernissi 1990:110.

Working Women and Entrepreneurs

What of women in the marketplace? Khadijah, first wife of Muhammad, was a trader, and Muhammad was one of her employees. Working-class women have almost always been involved in service and market production in the informal sector. But women also had a place in history as wealthy patrons and entrepreneurs. Because Islamic law permitted women to inherit and own property independently of their husbands or brothers,[6] middle-class women could own property and be involved in buying and selling and other business activities.

Islamic endowments (*waqf*) allow property and its income to be set aside for charitable purposes. Studies of endowment deeds across different areas and times list women as about thirty percent of the founders, administrators or beneficiaries of charitable endowments. This shows that large numbers of women both owned property and were able to dispose of it as they wanted.[7] They created endowments and funds for schools, hospices and mausoleums. Details of the endowment deed could include not only the name of the founder, the foundation and conditions of its endowment, but also the food to be purchased, cooked and distributed.

Studies of women in Turkey, Aleppo and Egypt between the 16th and 19th centuries describe women as involved in up to 40% of property transfers (commercial as well as residential). Wealthier women might invest in trade, such as spices or slaves, whereas middle-class women tended more to real estate. Prior to the entry of European goods, women were also involved in textile production, including sewing, embroidery, weaving and dyeing.[8] Women's influence and involvement varied according to the political and legal climate of the time.

Afaf Marsot[9] describes how, in the chaotic politics of the Mamluk era in 18th century Egypt, women were entrusted with wealth and property of their male relatives, to prevent it being confiscated in the vicissitudes of infighting between the local lords (*beys*) governing Egypt, and their retainers. Women invested accumulated capital in property which could then be rented. Nearly 40% of wills registered during that time were in the names of women. However, with a political shift to centralised power in the 19th century and the introduction of

---

[6] In contrast in the west until recently, married women were not allowed to own property or have any legal rights or existence independent of their husbands. It was not a crime for a husband to beat or rape his wife. And women were disenfranchised. At the time under English law, married women could not own property, all their income belonged to their husbands, and they had no rights over their own children. William Blackstone wrote in his *Commentaries on the Laws of England,* "By marriage... the very being or legal existence of the woman is suspended." It wasn't until the mid to late eighteen hundreds that women gained custody of their children, limited grounds for divorce, and basic legal rights over their own property and earnings.

[7] Roded 2008:142.

[8] Ahmed 1992:110-112.

[9] Marsot 1996:36–45.

trade with Europe, women were excluded, and their legal presence and participation in banks and businesses was denied.

At a more grassroots level, women participate in economic-based gatherings around saving associations and informal credit schemes throughout the Muslim world and beyond. Offering a place for women both to access capital, and also to socialise with one another, they are not profit-making; no interest or fees are given to members or leaders. They exist under different names in different countries, and with slightly different formats.

In Egypt, *gami'yyat* operate as interest-free, rotating saving associations. People choose members to form a group that pools agreed sums on a regular basis, and the total sum of the credit collected is distributed to a single member of the group until all members have had a turn in collecting the credit. Usually led by one person who is well-respected, the leader admits people to the group, receives the instalments, and gives the lump sum to the person whose turn it is to receive it next. As institutions, they are held in place by social rules of honour and shame. If someone defaults, they lose their reputation, and it is hard for them to join another *gam'iyya*. A woman may be a member of more than one *gam'iyya* at the same time, with different amounts, and for different purposes, such as to collect money for a fridge or other house furniture, for a son's school expenses, or a deposit for a husband's business.

In Sudan, women meet to form a *sanduq,* contributing a sum each month, and the total is allocated to one person each time, in an order decided in the first meeting. In Yemen, women, often in poor urban communities, organise themselves in *huqbas*, where the money given to each member in turn helps the women to face family economic crises, and to save money in a shorter time. In Indonesia, the savings clubs are known as *arisans*, where lots are drawn to decide who will get the entire amount each time.

Sharing food or drink is often linked with the credit associations. Groups of women in Turkey organise tea parties with gold coin (*altin gunleri)* or gold dollar (*dolar gunleri*) days, where each guest gives the host a gold coin, so that the parties become credit sources for each host in turn. Iran has lending funds of interest-free loans, meeting in members' houses. Also in Iran is the *shirvara* associations of women, who pool their resources and dairy products in order to satisfy the needs of one woman at a time, each week or month. Uighur women in Kazakhstan meet together for a feast called a *chai, gap* or *messtrap,* provided by the hostess. Each participant puts in a pre-agreed amount of money which the hostess receives at the time. Then the hostess pays it back at other feasts, returning to each participant in turn the same amount she received from her. These groups may continue for years.[10]

Among women throughout Africa, rotating credit associations offer a way to save money to buy a stall or a house: other associations are formed to buy in bulk, or to pay for burials. Women traders in Dar es Salam in Tanzania described

---

[10] Jansen 2000:192.

collectively buying a tiny house so that they could protect the material goods they had bought, from being taken by their husbands' families if they became widows. Custom gives the husband's family the right to take the refrigerator or television from a widow's house: but in the communal house, ownership of goods was less individually obvious and so less vulnerable.

These gatherings help women, who often have limited access to more formal financial institutions. If they do not own identity cards, they are not eligible for most bank or government schemes. They may also encounter antagonism from men, or control by men who want to use women for proxy access to credit. And in facing daily challenges of poverty, household emergencies, or pressure from other household members, it can be difficult to save in their own home context. So, these savings groups are often the only way women can afford to buy a fridge or stove, or to paint or mend their home. Women may start such a gathering at a time of need to support one another, when the first collection is given to the person facing the emergency.

These saving groups thus work to insulate women's savings from husbands who would spend them; enable faster purchase ability for the ones who receive the collection earlier; and provide a way of offering discipline in saving in the face of other pressures that might make them draw on their money. And they also serve an important social function, offering regular meetings with other women that contribute to community solidarity.

We need to be aware of both the economic and social contribution that these groups make to women's daily survival and well-being, and consider their potential role also for women who become followers of Christ and face being cut off from both material and social resources for their decision. Being involved in such a group may help to contribute the physical, social-communal and discipling support that women need.

Women's Voices and Votes

Women's bodies are often at the centre of conflict, or the vehicle for the expression of communal emotion. In many cultures, during a funeral or prolonged time of family mourning, it is the women who wear black. In both colonial and nationalist discourses, women are used as the symbol of family honour, civic order, and of the nation's backwardness or enlightenment.

In the 1800s and 1900s, new movements were changing the face of the nations. The early stirrings of anti-colonialism were making themselves felt in non-western nations. Wealthy women from Muslim countries participated in anti-colonial rallies and boycotts in their own countries, seeking independence from colonial government, and they drew on those learned skills to campaign for education and the vote for women.[11] Some of them took their place attending

---

[11] In the west, the campaigns for emancipation of slaves, education for all, and universal suffrage, including women, were developing. When women in America took up the

international women's meetings. And the place and role of women began to take central place in some of the debates around Islam and modernism. Cromer (British consul general of Egypt, 1883–1907) argued that the veiling and segregation of Muslim women exemplified their degraded position in Islam and need for western civilisation. However, Leila Ahmed points out that, while Cromer was advocating the liberation of women in the Muslim world, he was also arguing strongly against women having the vote in his own country: he was a "founding member and sometime president of the Men's League for Opposing Women's Suffrage".[12] However, the national and international movements seeking emancipation and education, independence and voting, continued. In the twentieth century, women joined in the nationalist movements, and then were involved in social services, and overseeing organisations running hospitals, orphanages, and homes for the blind. Again, Egypt can offer us a case study of women's movements.

In 1908, the 'Society for the Advancement of Women' was founded. This was followed with other women's organisations, and Egyptian women established dispensaries and clinics, nursery schools and charitable associations, for women and also for boys and men. Women involved in resistance to colonial occupation marched in the streets in Egypt in 1919. Public unveiling by upper class women occurred in the context of some of these demonstrations for independence. But it is noticeable that women feminists generally preferred a more gradual approach to unveiling than that promoted by Qasim Amin and Cromer (and later by Ataturk in Turkey and Reza Shah in Iran). Egypt gained independence from Britain in 1923. In the same year Huda Sha'rawi founded the Egyptian Feminist Union. In May that year, Sha'rawi went with Saiza Nabarawi and Nabawiyya Musa to the Rome Conference of the International Women's Alliance. Sha'rawi and Nabarawi removed their veils as they stepped off the train in Cairo on their return from the conference. Also in that year, the minimum marriage age for girls in Egypt was raised to sixteen, and boys to eighteen.

Arab women joining public demonstrations for national independence against colonial occupying forces often faced a fierce backlash for doing so. In 1928, Nazira Zayn al-Din (1908–1976) published a book in Beirut, Lebanon called *al-Sufur wa al-Hijab* (Unveiling and Veiling), noting in the introduction to her book that the events in Damascus in 1927, where Muslim women were harassed and

---

cause of opposing slavery as a moral responsibility, they found that as women, they didn't have the rights that they were seeking for black men. So, they drew on the organising skills they had learned through demonstrations, making speeches, and publishing written materials, towards getting the vote for women. At the same time in some other countries women received voting rights: in New Zealand in 1892, and in Australia between 1894 and 1908 (Australian Indigenous people did not receive the same rights until 1967). Women were able to vote in Canada in 1918; in 1919 women in the UK received limited rights to vote (full rights in 1928), and in the US, women were able to vote in federal elections in 1920.

[12] Ahmed 1992:152-4.

prevented from appearing on the streets unveiled, had stimulated her writing. In arguing against the *ḥijab* and seclusion of women, Zayn al-Din contended for women being able to interpret religious texts. The book aroused a storm of criticism, and after publishing another book the following year called *al-Fatah wa al-Shuyukh* (The Young Woman and the Shayks), Zayn al-Din retired from public view.[13]

In 1928, Hasan al Banna founded Muslim Brotherhood. It grew rapidly, but attracted few women. In 1936, Zeinab al-Ghazali (1918–2005) founded the Muslim Women's Association (after initially working with Huda Sha'rawi in the Egyptian Feminist Union). Al-Ghazali worked closely with Hasan al-Banna, but refused to merge her association with the Muslim Brotherhood. Women's political involvement in Egypt and the wider Arab world continued.

In 1944, the inter-country Arab Feminist Union was founded, with Sha'rawi as its president. One of its actions was to organise support for Palestinians. In 1945, rioting broke out in Damascus against the French occupation, and women went onto the streets to join the protests against occupation. However, again there was a conservative Sunni backlash against their presence. In 1951, Doria Shafik led 1000 women in a demonstration at the Egyptian parliament, disrupting it for three hours. In 1954, Shafik and fourteen other women went on a very public hunger strike, until the governor of Cairo sent to tell her that new Egyptian constitution would guarantee full political rights for women. In the meantime, a military coup on 23rd July 1952, had seen King Farouk exiled and Nasser brought to power. The 1956 Egyptian constitution gave the right to vote to women who asked for it (a condition not applied to men). In 1957, two women were elected to the national assembly; and in 1962, Nasser appointed Dr Hikmat Abu Zaid as minister of social affairs (both of these events occurred less than thirty years after corresponding developments in Britain).

Feminist Movements

The feminist movement gives us a way to look at patterns and contrasts between women's movements in the west and in the Muslim world. In the first wave of feminism (approximately 1840–1920), women sought to be able to vote, and have a say in government decisions that affected their everyday lives. As well as seeking suffrage, they were also involved in movements for freedom from colonial rule or the abolition of slavery. They were setting up organisations and institutions to care for women and others. However, the movements operated from different understandings of the place and nature of women. While in the west women were arguing against being viewed as weaker and less capable, in the Muslim world the view of women was more of a powerful, chaotic force that needed to be controlled for the sake of wider society and the men in it.

---

[13] Shaaban 1995:61–77; Mojab 2001; Keddie 2007:96; Badran 2009:313, excerpts in Kurzman 1998:101–6.

From the 1960s to the 1990s, in what is known as the second wave, women continued to seek social justice. Women in Muslim countries were dealing with issues of sexuality and opportunities for women outside the domestic sphere, including discussion around female genital mutilation, female bodily rights, honour killings, divorce rights, and equity in access to legal rulings for women.[14] Women in the west sought for equal employment opportunities with men, equal pay for equal work, and for legal reform, beyond being defined in terms of their reproductive capacity and traditional gender roles.

Women claimed the right to interpret their own experience of female sexuality, rape, pregnancy and abortion, rather than having it defined by male doctors and psychologists, religious leaders, fathers or husbands. Women of colour and developing nations were included in the growing recognition that race, class and gender oppression are all related. Concepts such as eco-feminism grew out of the description of women as more collaborative, inclusive, nurturing and holistic in their approach to problem-solving and to the environment. In the west, women were involved in the civil rights movement.

The third wave is placed from the late 1980s to about 2010. By now, women in many countries were participating in public life and education in greater numbers. Instead of 'equal rights', the slogan of the third wave was 'my choice', embracing individual empowerment. Third-wavers were more driven by personal statements about their own lives and experiences, rather than mass movements. This wave was both more individual, and more inclusive and boundary-crossing. 'Intersectionality'[15] was used to analyse how different oppressions such as race and gender interacted with one another.[16] Differences of ethnicity, class, gender and sexual orientation were included and celebrated, and categories were perceived as situational and shifting. Gender was seen as a position on a spectrum; being pro-woman did not exclude empathy for men's experiences, including sexual assault. Many third-wavers rejected the term

---

[14] See, for example, Nawal El-Saadawi's ground-breaking book, *The Hidden Face of Eve*, and the work of 'Sisters in Islam' in Malaysia http://www.sistersinislam.org.my/.

[15] Kimberlé Crenshaw developed the term. See:
http://socialdifference.columbia.edu/files/socialdiff/projects/Article__Mapping_the_Margins_by_Kimblere_Crenshaw.pdf or
http://www.racialequitytools.org/resourcefiles/mapping-margins.pdf.

[16] This was vividly expressed earlier in Sojourner Truth's (former slave, and campaigner) famous speech:
"That man over there says that women need to be helped into carriages, and lifted over ditches, and to have the best place everywhere. Nobody ever helps me into carriages, or over mud-puddles, or gives me any best place! And ain't I a woman? Look at me! Look at my arm! I have ploughed and planted, and gathered into barns, and no man could head me! And ain't I a woman? I could work as much and eat as much as a man – when I could get it – and bear the lash as well! And ain't I a woman? I have borne thirteen children, and seen most all sold off to slavery, and when I cried out with my mother's grief, none but Jesus heard me! And ain't I a woman?"
https://sourcebooks.fordham.edu/mod/sojtruth-woman.asp.

'feminism' as too binary, suggesting 'us/them' thinking. Others saw feminism as part of a larger consciousness of oppression together with racism, ageism, classism, ableism, and sexual orientation.

Rejecting a 'victim' perspective, these women were reclaiming their own sexuality as subjects. This period saw the growth of the Muslim women's piety movement, including many young women adopting the *hijab*, that their mothers and grandmothers had taken off, as a statement of resistance, identity or even as a fashion statement. In the west, this wave included re-adopting features such as lipstick, high heels and cleavage, which had been rejected by the first two waves as attributes of male oppression. Even pornography and sex work could be described not as inherently demeaning, but as positive choices for women. An appreciation of the impact of standpoint led to both Christians and Muslims questioning traditional 'male' readings of their scriptures, with a rapid growth in publications around women's readings of the Bible and Qur'an.[17]

The fourth wave emerged from about 2008 onwards. This was the time when a critical mass of younger feminists began expressing themselves; women who were tech-savvy and gender-sophisticated. This wave is defined by technology, which enables women to build online popular mass movements, and by political activism that combines spirituality[18] and social justice, affirming collaboration, female bonds and values of tolerance and ecofeminism as tools against global violence and poverty.[19] In place of zines and songs, young feminists create blogs, Twitter campaigns, and online media. This is when Amina Sboui in Tunisia joined the Femen movement,[20] posting on Facebook a picture of her naked chest inscribed with the defiant slogan, "My body belongs to me: it is not the source of anyone's honour."[21]

Issues that were central to the earliest phases of the women's movement moved into public discussion and media attention, including sexual abuse, rape and violence against women, unequal pay, the pressure on women to conform to a single and unrealistic body type and the recognition of how restricted female

---

[17] An early influential book for Muslim women was Amina Wadud's *Qur'an and Woman: Rereading the Sacred Text from a Woman's Perspective* (1999). A more recent Christian publication is Brittany E. Wilson's *Unmanly Men: Refigurations of Masculinity in Luke-Acts*, exploring how Jesus' teaching redrew cultural understandings of masculinity, femininity and (dis)ability (2015).

[18] See for example, http://www.sacredwomensbusiness.com/the-way-of-the-spiritual-feminist-2/.

[19] V-Day describes itself as "a global activist movement to end violence against women and girls." http://www.vday.org/about.html#.WNzgahJ97eR.

[20] http://femen.org/about-us/ "In the beginning, there was the body, feeling of the woman's body, feeling of joy because it is so light and free. Then there was injustice, so sharp that you feel it with your body, it immobilizes the body, hinders its movements, and then you find yourself your body's hostage. And so you turn your body against this injustice, mobilizing every body's cell to struggle against the patriarchy and humiliation." ... "Our Mission is Protest. Our Weapons are bare breasts!"

[21] http://www.bbc.com/news/magazine-34949413.

representation remains in politics and business. For this generation, 'feminism' no longer indicates just the struggles of women, but encompasses gender equity and inclusiveness. At the same time, it stems from frustration built on women's everyday experiences, because of the way society genders and is gendered. In the Muslim world, the Arab Spring saw women making use of social media to organise demonstrations. Malala Yousafzai, a young Pakistani activist promoting female education, is named one of the fourth-wave pioneers, as her advocacy has grown into an international movement.[22] Other movements have shifted from a focus on women and Islamic law, to defining themselves in terms of justice for all individuals, including women and girls.[23] In the Christian community, women who have not been able to gain a platform in traditional church structures are now making use of the internet to gain wide followings, or share their stories and experiences within communities of similar theologically-thinking women.[24] Traditional descriptors such as 'egalitarian' or 'complementarian' are rejected as too binary.

A Place of Meeting?

Does the struggle for the position of women in society offer any potential common ground? Among both Christian and Muslim women, we find pious conservatives, and libertarian socialists. We share together being women; we all live within and interact with the trends of our time, and we all inhabit a place within a community of faith (as opposed to atheist foundations of belief), as we bring our understanding of our respective 'sacred texts' to engage with the currents of thought around us. We have seen similarities in the related women's movements, but also differences according to the context and issues faced. Embracing the commonalities also allows a greater appreciation of difference. Can we find common cause in issues that concern us all, such as violence against women, and also more contextual issues, whether they be the pervasive sexualising of women in commerce and workplaces, or female genital mutilation (found in Christian as well as Muslim communities), or other issues of concern? Might we find a place of meeting in these issues as we seek to live out with

---

[22] https://www.slideshare.net/SusanGraham5/the-fourth-wave-of-feminism.

[23] Femin Ijtihad was a movement promoting "the critical thinking of gender in Islamic law. Our aim is to increase the accessibility of gender-neutral interpretations of Islamic law and inspiring stories about women in Islamic, Pashtun and Afghan Tales to grassroot organisations and activists in Afghanistan. https://www.idealist.org/en/nonprofit/dbee749bd0044d7faff40a12f79029d7-femin-ijtihad-new-york. It has now become SAHR, a "non-profit human rights and law organization", pursuing "a justice that dignifies and empowers individuals, especially women and girls." http://www.sa-hr.org/.

[24] For example, http://www.fixinghereyes.org/.

integrity amid the injustices or prejudices around us, how we understand who God is and who he has made us to be?[25]

- Do you know of any women who have occupied positions of leadership, historically or currently, in Muslim areas with which you have contact? How might you find out? What kind of role have they played?
- What is the current place of women in politics in your area? Voting? Members of parliament? Heads of local associations?
- Describe the place of working women in the Muslim community with which you are familiar? In what kind of occupations or positions do you find them? Among the working class and among the wealthy, how are they regarded?
- Are there any savings associations in your neighbourhood? What form do they take?

---

[25] https://whenwomenspeak.net/blog/how-do-muslim-women-do-theodicy/, https://whenwomenspeak.net/blog/god-and-us/, and http://www.fixinghereyes.org/single-post/2016/09/07/Feminism-1023---Why-Im-a-Christian-and-a-Feminist.

In Conclusion

In this book I have invited you to consider a different view of Islam and the Muslim world, through the eyes of women. This is not an alternative to traditional perspectives and to male perceptions and readings, but rather a needed addition, offering us a fuller picture of the world of Muslim women and men and of the issues and themes that shape their lives. Sacred texts interact with cultural themes and the concerns of daily life. The domestic and personal spheres interrelate with and help shape theological and political domains.

At the conclusion of this book, it may be helpful to look back to Hagar, described as foremother for Islam. In her life we encounter a number of themes that this book has touched on. Little is known about Hagar and her life before the time she spent as Abraham's concubine and mother of his son, until she was cast out. Like many women in history, her life is largely unwritten. Both the Bible and Qur'an note that she is Egyptian. It is likely that she was one of the female slaves given to Abraham and Sarah by Pharaoh.[1] Although much of her life is hidden, she is a woman who came to see God and be seen by Him.

The name 'Hagar' or 'Hajar' means 'immigrant'. Her name is thus linked with the early name of the Muslim community, '*muhajirin*' 'emmigrants' (*Al-Hashr* 59:8), referring first to the group of about seventy Muslims who fled hostility in Mecca to take refuge in Abyssinia (Ethiopia), and later to the community of Muhammad and his followers who moved from Mecca to Medina. The story of Hagar's flight, and seeking water to save her life and that of her son, is physically re-enacted by millions of Muslims every year in the *Hajj* at Mecca.

The Qur'an does not mention Hagar by name. The comment attributed to Ibrahim in *Ibrahim* 14:37 is taken as an allusion to Ishmael living with his mother Hagar in the desert:

> O our Lord! I have made some of my offspring to dwell in an uncultivable valley by Your Sacred House in order, O our Lord, that they may perform prayer. So fill some hearts among men with love towards them, and provide them with fruits so that they may give thanks.

If there is not much material in the Qur'an, it is abundantly present in the *Hadith*. There is an extended *hadith* in al-Bukhari (Book #55, *Hadith* #583), quoted at length in Appendix 2. This account forms the basis for Muslim understanding about Hagar's role in the antecedents of Islam, and her relationship with Ibrahim. Muslim traditions have continued to add detail to the story.[2]

While in the Bible Genesis devotes several chapters to Hagar,[3] there is surprisingly little teaching about her in the Christian community. Genesis 16 tells of Hagar being given to Abraham, her pregnancy and Sarah's jealous harsh treatment of her until she fled. Then it describes her vivid encounter with God (revealed through the angel of the Lord) in the desert. Hagar is given her son's name, Ishma-el (God hears), the angel using a standard biblical form of birth announcement and naming.[4] She, in turn, gives God a name – *El-Roi:* 'the God who sees me'. The only woman in the Old Testament to give God a name, it reflects her amazement that God revealed Himself to her, a slave girl, and that she remained alive to talk about it. The spring where this dramatic encounter took place was also named in honour of it, *Beer-lahai-roi*: 'the spring of the Living One who sees me'. Hagar returns and gives birth to Abraham's son, and Abraham, following God's instructions to Hagar, names him Ishmael. In Genesis 17, God reiterates his promise to Abraham, and gives him the sign of

---

[1] Gen 12:16. Also suggested by Ibn Kathir, *Qisas*, vol I, p.194, cited in Stowasser 1994:147, note 53.

[2] See Stowasser 1994:46–49, for further discussion.

[3] See Kuhn's (2019) discussion.

[4] Other examples of this pattern include Isaac (Gen 17:19), John the Baptist (Luke 1:13–14), and Jesus (Luke 1:31).

circumcision to mark the relationship between God and between Abraham and his descendants. In the same encounter, God answers Abraham's prayer and gives Ishmael the promise of fruitfulness and of becoming a great nation, confirming to Abraham the promise that God had previously made to Hagar fleeing in the desert. Abraham and his son Ishmael (thirteen years old) are circumcised, together with all the men in the extended household as a sign of the relationship of promise and obedience with God.

In Genesis chapter 21, there is another quarrel between the two wives. Sarah is now jubilantly a mother, and she doesn't want the son of her slave to have any share in her own son's inheritance. Abraham is distressed, but God reiterates (for the fourth time now)[5] his promise of descendants and greatness to Ishmael. So, Abraham sends Hagar off into the desert with some bread and water. When the water runs out, she weeps with despair at the impending death of her child, Isaac. And God again hears the voice of the boy and appears to Hagar, showing her a well of water, and promising His care for her son. So "God was with the boy" (Gen 21:20) as he grew up in the wilderness and became an expert archer. We do not hear again of Hagar, but we see in Genesis chapter 25 that it is Isaac and Ishmael who come together to bury Abraham at his death, although Abraham's other sons through Keturah, his concubine, have been sent away. Isaac settles down after the burial at the well where God first appeared to Hagar. The chapter lists the twelve princes and their tribes who descended from Ishmael.

Hagar's voicelessness in both traditions parallels the place of powerlessness she occupies in Abraham's family as a slave, cut off from her own family and community. In that place of vulnerability, she is given to Abraham to bear children for Sarah, as a surrogate mother. Even when Hagar becomes the mother of Abraham's first son and her status increases, she is still subject to the tensions that commonly arise between co-wives.[6] As Hagar's status increases, Sarah's jealousy flares and she ill-treats Hagar. Later, when Sarah is finally able to give birth to her own son, she demands that Hagar and her son be banished "so that the son of that slave woman will not be an heir along with my son Isaac!"[7] And so (like many women today) Hagar becomes a refugee and a single mother. Her precarious situation of powerlessness echoes that of women in similar situations of marginalisation and isolation, and so her story can offer hope to women.

The vicissitudes of Hagar's life fluctuate around crises of conception, birth and weaning. Later, when her son grows up, Hagar is the one who directs his marriage.[8] While the cousin on the paternal side may be preferred officially,

---

[5] Gen 16:10, 17:20, 21:13, 18. The promise is repeated twice to Hagar and twice to Abraham.

[6] This includes women who fill the function of wives even if they lack official status, such as concubines. We note the jealousy of Muhammad's wives of his Egyptian concubine, Mariam.

[7] Gen 21:10.

[8] Gen 21:21.

mothers often like to arrange marriages with a partner from their own family or community. The *hadith* referred to indicates that Hagar's interaction with the visiting tribe opened up the possibility of her son's marriage from among them, although the same *hadith* reasserts Abraham's authority about which wife Ishmael could keep. And after Hagar's death, it is at the death of Ishmael's father that we hear of Ishmael and Isaac acting together as family.[9] The story of the power imbalance, arguments and abuses of the polygamous relationship between Hagar and Sarah with Abraham is backdrop for the historic and contemporary relationships between Muslim, Jewish and Christian communities today.

Many cultures have a tradition of strong women who, in the face of challenging circumstances of bereavement or oppression, are able to act with God to fulfil His greater purposes through their lives. Some bear difficult or traumatic situations with quiet strength; others, from weakness, regain their strength in response to God's initiative. We see the latter in Hagar. Twice she finds herself in the desert – once as a runaway slave; another as a cast-off concubine. Each time, as she cries out in despair, Hagar is seen by and sees God, who appears to her in two dramatic theophanies (appearances of God), and cares for her. In this way, Hagar prefigures women who are oppressed or victimised, and who experience God's care, enabling them to retake agency and initiative, and rebuild their lives. Her story, with that of other women, points forward to how Jesus honoured marginalised women. Hagar invites women, whatever the cultural attitudes that they encounter, to take up their role as co-image bearers of the Divine, called into relationship with God.

In this book I have invited you to consider the Islamic texts and also the cultural themes that work together to shape the lives of Muslim women and men. We have explored how these play out in some of the issues of everyday life in family and society. I have asked what happens when we bring together Islamic writings, Muslim history and the lived experience of Muslim women into conversation with the Bible and what it teaches us. In doing so, I have sought to open up a way to enable deeper engagement with Muslim women and men in the realities of their daily life, and with how the Word of God revealed in Jesus Messiah and recorded in the Bible might speak into their lives and heart languages.

In joining me on this journey of learning and reflection, I hope that you will find that it enriches your reading of the Bible, widens your understanding and deepens your worship of the God of whom the Bible tells, revealed through Jesus Messiah, Word of God and Lord.

---

[9] Gen 16:2–4, 11, 15; 21:8–10; 25:7.

Appendix 1

Cross-cultural Friend Interview Questions[1]

1. Behavioural: What Do People Do?

a) How many children are there in your family? Is that a big family for your society or a small one?
b) Who looked after you most? Father? Mother? Grandparent? Someone else?
c) Who disciplined you most? Father? Mother? Older sibling? Someone else?
d) What responsibilities did your father have? What responsibilities did your mother have?
e) How are boys treated? What are they expected to do?
f) How are girls treated? What are they expected to do?
g) Who do you go to when you want advice?
h) What were the main foods you ate every day? What was a typical meal?
i) Where did you eat?
j) Did the family eat together?
k) Who prepared the food?
l) Who got served first?
m) Were there some foods you couldn't eat? Why?
n) What foods did you eat on special occasions?
o) Which other people did you eat with on special occasions?

Can you draw a rough map of the house you grew up in, **or** of your local community?

House
a) What were the different spaces?
b) What happened in them?
c) Who could go where? (Family? Non-family?)
d)
OR

---

[1] The inspiration for these interviews came from the work of Geoff Morrow of WBT, although the questions have been changed.

Community
a) Where were the places that people lived?
b) Where were the places that people bought and sold things?
c) What were the central places in the community?
d) Where were the places for Government? Law? Religion? Burial?
e) Were there some places where men went more than women? Or women more than men?

2. Evaluative – Aesthetic:
What Do People Feel is Good or Bad, Beautiful or Ugly?

a) A good person is good because they ... (give 4 or 5 examples)
b) A bad person is bad because they ... (give 4 or 5 examples)
c) What are the most important values or ways of behaving for your community?
d) What are the worst things someone can do in your community?
e) What happens to someone who does those things?
f) What language did you speak in your home when you were growing up?
g) Did your mother and father speak the same languages when they were growing up?
h) What language was used at school?
i) What language was used for buying and selling things?
j) What language was used for religious ceremonies?
k) If there was more than one language, which did you understand most? Which did you understand least?
l) What are the traditional kinds of music and of art in your community?
m) Are those kinds of music or of art still practised? Who by? When?
n) What is the music or songs traditionally about?

3. Cognitive: What Do People Believe is True or False, Right or Wrong?

a) What are the different celebrations that happen in a person's life in your community, from birth to death?
b) What are the main feasts celebrated in your country (national or religious or others)?
c) Which are your favourite celebrations or feasts? Why?
d) What do people do when a baby is born?
   i) Are there any special things they do to protect the mother and the baby, before birth or afterwards?
e) What do people do when someone in the family is sick?
   i) Who decides what to do?
   ii) If the treatment doesn't work, what else might people do?
f) What age do people get married?
   i) Traditionally, who is involved in deciding the marriage partner?
   ii) What happens when someone gets married?

iii)If the marriage has problems, what do people do?
g) What do people do when someone dies?
    i) Is it different for men and women?
    ii) What happens to the body?
    iii) What happens afterwards?
    iv) Is there anything that people do for a month, a few months or a year after someone has died?

4. Reality beyond the Surface

a) What invisible forces did people in your community think existed in the supernatural world?
- Impersonal forces? (e.g., luck, blessing, envy/evil eye?)
- Personal forces? (e.g., God, angels, spirits?)

b) What things did they think would keep evil or danger away?
c) What things did they think would bring power or healing or help?
d) What do you think now? Why?
e) Have you ever had experience of something supernatural? What happened?
f) Were you taught that people could pray to God or gods? If so, how did they pray?
g) What were you taught regarding what made a person impure and unable to pray?
h) What do you believe now about prayer? Why?
i) Were you taught in your community that harm could happen through curses? What did someone do if they were cursed?
j) Were you taught, in your community, that good could be done through blessing? What did people do to get blessing?
k) Were there people who practised magic or witchcraft? Can anyone practise magic or witchcraft?
l) What did people in your community believe happened to a person after they died? Do they believe that someone might go to heaven? Why? If they didn't go to heaven, what would happen to them?

Appendix 2

Various *Hadith*

On Reciting the Qur'an

Narrated Aisha: The Prophet said, "Such a person as recites the Qur'an and masters it by heart, will be with the noble, righteous scribes (in heaven). And such a person exerts himself to learn the Qur'an by heart, and recites it with great difficulty, will have a double reward."[1]

On Prayer

Narrated Abu Huraira: The Prophet said, "The prayer offered in congregation is twenty-five times more superior (in reward) to the prayer offered alone in one's house or in a business center, because if one performs ablution and does it perfectly, and then proceeds to the mosque with the sole intention of praying, then for each step which he takes towards the mosque, Allah upgrades him a degree in reward and (forgives) crosses out one sin till he enters the mosque. When he enters the mosque, he is considered in prayer as long as he is waiting for the prayer and the angels keep on asking for Allah's forgiveness for him and they keep on saying: 'O Allah! Be Merciful to him, O Allah! Forgive him, as long as he keeps on sitting at his praying place and does not pass wind'."[2]

Narrated Malik bin Sasaa: The Prophet said, "While I was at the House in a state midway between sleep and wakefulness, (an angel recognised me) as the man lying between two men. A golden tray full of wisdom and belief was brought to me and my body was cut open from the throat to the lower part of the abdomen and then my abdomen was washed with Zamzam water and (my heart was) filled with wisdom and belief. Al-Buraq, a white animal, smaller than a mule and bigger than a donkey, was brought to me and I set out with Gabriel. When I reached the nearest heaven, Gabriel said to the heaven gate-keeper, 'Open the gate.' The gatekeeper asked, 'Who is it?' He said, 'Gabriel.' The gate-keeper asked, 'Who is accompanying you?' Gabriel said, 'Muhammad.' The

---

[1] Al-Bukhari 006.060.459. https://www.islamicity.org/.
[2] See *Hadith* No. 620. Al-Bukhari, Book #8, *Hadith* #466, also Book #11, *Hadith* #620, and Book #34, *Hadith* # 330.

gate-keeper said, 'Has he been called?' Gabriel said, 'Yes.' Then it was said, 'He is welcomed. What a wonderful visit his is!' Then I met Adam and greeted him and he said, 'You are welcomed, O son and a Prophet.' Then we ascended to the second heaven. It was asked, 'Who is it?' Gabriel said, 'Gabriel.' It was said, 'Who is with you?' He said, 'Muhammad' It was asked, 'Has he been sent for?' He said, 'Yes.' It was said, 'He is welcomed. What a wonderful visit his is!' Then I met Jesus and Yahya (John) who said, 'You are welcomed, O brother and a Prophet.' Then we ascended to the third heaven. It was asked, 'Who is it?' Gabriel said, 'Gabriel.' It was asked, 'Who is with you?' Gabriel said, 'Muhammad.' It was asked, 'Has he been sent for?'. 'Yes,' said Gabriel. 'He is welcomed. What a wonderful visit his is!' (The Prophet added:). There I met Joseph and greeted him, and he replied, 'You are welcomed, O brother and a Prophet!' Then we ascended to the fourth heaven and again the same questions and answers were exchanged as in the previous heavens. There I met Idris and greeted him. He said, 'You are welcomed, O brother and Prophet.' Then we ascended to the fifth heaven and again the same questions and answers were exchanged as in previous heavens. there I met and greeted Aaron who said, 'You are welcomed, O brother and a Prophet.' Then we ascended to the sixth heaven and again the same questions and answers were exchanged as in the previous heavens. There I met and greeted Moses who said, 'You are welcomed, O brother and a Prophet.' When I proceeded on, he started weeping and on being asked why he was weeping, he said, 'O Lord! Followers of this youth who was sent after me will enter Paradise in greater number than my followers.' Then we ascended to the seventh heaven and again the same questions and answers were exchanged as in the previous heavens. There I met and greeted Abraham who said, 'You are welcomed, O son and a Prophet.' Then I was shown Al-Bait-al-Ma'mur (i.e., Allah's house). I asked Gabriel about it and he said, 'This is Al Bait-ul-Ma'mur where 70,000 angels perform prayers daily and when they leave they never return to it (but always a fresh batch comes into it daily).' Then I was shown Sidrat-ul-Muntaha (i.e., a tree in the seventh heaven) and I saw its Nabk fruits which resembled the clay jugs of Hajr (i.e., a town in Arabia), and its leaves were like the ears of elephants, and four rivers originated at its root, two of them were apparent and two were hidden. I asked Gabriel about those rivers and he said, 'The two hidden rivers are in Paradise, and the apparent ones are the Nile and the Euphrates.' Then, fifty prayers were enjoined on me. I descended till I met Moses who asked me, 'What have you done?'. I said, 'Fifty prayers have been enjoined on me.' He said, 'I know the people better than you, because I had the hardest experience to bring Bani Israel to obedience. Your followers cannot put up with such obligation. So, return to your Lord and request Him' (to reduce the number of prayers). I returned and requested Allah (for reduction) and He made it forty. I returned and (met Moses) and had a similar discussion, and then returned again to Allah for reduction and He made it thirty, then twenty, then ten, and then I came to Moses who repeated the same advice. Ultimately, Allah reduced it to five. When I came to Moses again, he said, 'What have you done?'.

I said, 'Allah has made it five only.' He repeated the same advice but I said that I surrendered (to Allah's Final Order). Allah's Apostle was addressed by Allah, 'I have decreed My Obligation and have reduced the burden on My slaves, and I shall reward a single good deed as if it were ten good deeds.'"[3]

On Hospitality

It is reported on the authority of Abu Huraira that the Messenger of Allah (may peace be upon him) observed: He who believes in Allah and the Last Day should either utter good words or better keep silence; and he who believes in Allah and the Last Day should treat his neighbour with kindness; and he who believes in Allah and the Last Day should show hospitality to his guest.[4]

On Family

Narrated Abu Huraira: The Prophet said, "We (Muslims) are the last in the world, but will be foremost on the day of Resurrection." Allah's Apostle also said, "By Allah, if anyone of you insists on fulfilling an oath by which he may harm his family, he commits a greater sin in Allah's sight than that of dissolving his oath and making expiation for it."[5]

On Women Leading Salah

Narrated Umm Waraqah daughter of Nawfal: When the Prophet (peace be upon him) proceeded for the Battle of Badr, I said to him: "Apostle of Allah, allow me to accompany you in the battle. I shall act as a nurse for patients. It is possible that Allah might bestow martyrdom upon me." He said: "Stay at your home. Allah, the Almighty, will bestow martyrdom upon you." The narrator said: "Hence, she was called martyr. She read the Qur'an. She sought permission from the Prophet (peace be upon him) to have a mu'adhdhin in her house. He, therefore, permitted her (to do so). She announced that her slave and slave-girl would be free after her death. One night, they went to her and strangled her with a sheet of cloth until she died, and they ran away. Next day, Umar announced among the people, 'Anyone who has knowledge about them, or has seen them, should bring them (to him).' Umar (after their arrest) ordered (to crucify them) and they were crucified. This was the first crucifixion at Medina."[6]

Al-Qadarawi comments on this: It is reported by Imam Ahmad, Abu Dawud, and others on the authority of Umm Waraqah, who said that the Prophet (peace and blessings be upon him) appointed a muezzin for her, and ordered her to lead the members of her household (who included both men and women) in prayer.[7]

---

[3] Al-Bukhari, Book #54, *Hadith* #429.
[4] Muslim, Book #001, *Hadith* #0075, also 0076, 0078.
[5] Al-Bukhari Book #78, *Hadith* #621.
[6] Book #2, *Hadith* #0591.
[7] http://www.islamopediaonline.org/fatwa/dr-yusuf-al-qaradawi-comments-females-

On Marriage

Narrated Ibn 'Abbas: The Prophet said: "I was shown the Hell-fire and that the majority of its dwellers were women who were ungrateful." It was asked, "Do they disbelieve in Allah?" (or are they ungrateful to Allah?) He replied, "They are ungrateful to their husbands and are ungrateful for the favors and the good (charitable deeds) done to them. If you have always been good (benevolent) to one of them and then she sees something in you (not of her liking), she will say, 'I have never received any good from you.'"[8]

Narrated Abu Huraira: Allah's Apostle said, "If a husband calls his wife to his bed (i.e., to have sexual relation) and she refuses and causes him to sleep in anger, the angels will curse her till morning."[9]

Also, a husband's rights over his wife:

Narrated Qays ibn Sa'd: I went to al-Hirah and saw them (the people) prostrating themselves before a satrap of theirs, so I said: "The Apostle of Allah (PBUH) has most right to have prostration made before him." When I came to the Prophet (PBUH), I said: "I went to al-Hirah and saw them prostrating themselves before a satrap of theirs, but you have most right, Apostle of Allah, to have (people) prostrating themselves before you." He said: "Tell me, if you were to pass my grave, would you prostrate yourself before it?" I said: "No." He then said: "Do not do so. If I were to command anyone to make prostration before another, I would command women to prostrate themselves before their husbands, because of the special right over them given to husbands by Allah."[10]

On Adultery and Stoning

'Abdullah b. 'Abbas reported that 'Umar b. Khattab sat on the pulpit of Allah's Messenger (may peace be upon him) and said: "Verily Allah sent Muhammad (may peace be upon him) with truth and He sent down the Book upon him, and the verse of stoning was included in what was sent down to him. We recited it, retained it in our memory and understood it. Allah's Messenger (may peace be upon him) awarded the punishment of stoning to death (to the married adulterer and adulteress) and, after him, we also awarded the punishment of stoning, I am afraid that with the lapse of time, the people (may forget it) and may say: 'We do not find the punishment of stoning in the Book of Allah,' and thus go astray by abandoning this duty prescribed by Allah. Stoning is a duty laid down in Allah's Book for married men and women who commit adultery when proof is established, or if there is pregnancy, or a confession."[11]

---

leading-co-gender-friday-prayers-and-women-leading-other.
[8] Al-Bukhari, Book #2, *Hadith* #28
[9] Al-Bukhari, Book #54, *Hadith* #460
[10] Abudawud, Book #11, *Hadith* #2135.
[11] Al-Muslim, Book #017, *Hadith* 4192, 4194.
https://www.thereligionofpeace.com/quran/muslim/017-smt.htm#017.4192

On Paradise[12]

A woman's access to Paradise depends on her husband being pleased with her:

Umm Salamah reported: The Messenger of Allah (peace and blessings be upon him) said, "Whoever among women dies while her husband is pleased with her, then she will enter Paradise."[13]

On Mothers

On another occasion, the Prophet said: "God has forbidden for you to be undutiful to your mothers."[14]

On Hagar

These *hadith* from al-Bukhari recount how Hagar came to Abraham, and how she eventually settled with Ishmael in the desert.

Narrated Abu Huraira: Abraham did not tell a lie except on three occasions. Twice for the Sake of Allah when he said, "I am sick," and he said, "(I have not done this but) the big idol has done it." The (third was) that while Abraham and Sarah (his wife) were going (on a journey) they passed by (the territory of) a tyrant. Someone said to the tyrant, "This man (i.e., Abraham) is accompanied by a very charming lady." So, he sent for Abraham and asked him about Sarah saying, "Who is this lady?" Abraham said, "She is my sister." Abraham went to Sarah and said, "O Sarah! There are no believers on the surface of the earth except you and I. This man asked me about you and I have told him that you are my sister, so don't contradict my statement." The tyrant then called Sarah and when she went to him, he tried to take hold of her with his hand, but (his hand got stiff and) he was confounded. He asked Sarah. "Pray to Allah for me, and I shall not harm you." So, Sarah asked Allah to cure him and he got cured. He tried to take hold of her for the second time, but (his hand got as stiff as or stiffer than before and) was more confounded. He again requested Sarah, "Pray to Allah for me, and I will not harm you." Sarah asked Allah again and he became alright. He then called one of his guards (who had brought her) and said, "You have not brought me a human being but have brought me a devil." The tyrant then gave Hajar as a girl-servant to Sarah. Sarah came back (to Abraham) while he was praying. Abraham, gesturing with his hand, asked, "What has happened?" She replied, "Allah has spoiled the evil plot of the infidel (or immoral person) and gave me Hajar for service." (Abu Huraira then addressed his listeners saying,

---

[12] Qur'anic verses on women and paradise include *Al-Taubah* 9:72, *Sad* 38:49–52; *Al-Dukhan* 44:51–57; *Al-Rahman* 55:46–78.

[13] Sunan At-Tirmidhi 1078. Grade: Hasan (fair). https://abuaminaelias.com/dailyhadithonline/2013/01/31/hadith-on-marriage-whoever-dies-while-her-husband-is-pleased-will-enter-paradise/.

[14] Sahih Al-Bukhari. https://insideislam.wisc.edu/2012/05/the-importance-of-the-mother-in-islam/.

"That (Hajar) was your mother, O Bani Ma-is-Sama" (i.e., the Arabs, the descendants of Ishmael, Hajar's son).[15]

Narrated Ibn 'Abbas: The first lady to use a girdle[16] was the mother of Ishmael. She used a girdle so that she might hide her tracks from Sarah.[17] Abraham brought her and her son Ishmael, while she was suckling him, to a place near the Ka'ba under a tree on the spot of Zamzam, at the highest place in the mosque. During those days there was nobody in Mecca, nor was there any water. So, he made them sit over there and placed near them a leather bag containing some dates, and a small water-skin containing some water, and set out homeward. Ishmael's mother followed him saying, "O Abraham! Where are you going, leaving us in this valley where there is no person whose company we may enjoy, nor is there anything (to enjoy)?" She repeated that to him many times, but he did not look back at her. Then she asked him, "Has Allah ordered you to do so?" He said, "Yes." She said, "Then He will not neglect us," and returned while Abraham proceeded onwards, and on reaching the Thaniya where they could not see him, he faced the Ka'ba, and raising both hands, invoked Allah saying the following prayers: "O our Lord! I have made some of my offspring dwell in a valley without cultivation, by Your Sacred House (Ka'ba at Mecca) in order, O our Lord, that they may offer prayer perfectly. So, fill some hearts among men with love towards them, and (O Allah) provide them with fruits, so that they may give thanks." (14.37)

Ishmael's mother went on suckling Ishmael and drinking from the water (she had). When the water in the water-skin had all been used up, she became thirsty and her child also became thirsty. She started looking at him (Ishmael) tossing in agony. She left him, for she could not endure looking at him, and found that the mountain of Safa was the nearest mountain to her on that land. She stood on it and started looking at the valley keenly so that she might see somebody, but she could not see anybody. Then she descended from Safa and when she reached the valley, she tucked up her robe and ran in the valley like a person in distress and trouble, till she crossed the valley and reached the Marwa mountain where she stood and started looking, expecting to see somebody, but she could not see anybody. She repeated that (running between Safa and Marwa) seven times. The Prophet said, "This is the source of the tradition of the walking of people between them (Safa and Marwa). When she reached the Marwa (for the last time) she heard a voice and she asked herself to be quiet and listened attentively. She heard the voice again and said, 'O (whoever you may be)! You have made me hear your voice; have you got something to help me?' And behold! She saw an angel at the place of Zamzam, digging the earth with his heel (or his wing), till water

---

[15] Book #55, *Hadith* #578.

[16] Belt or cord worn round the waist.

[17] This is reminiscent of Abu Bakr's elder daughter (Aisha's older sister) covering her tracks to that she would not lead people to where Muhammad and her father were hiding from the hostile Meccan community.

flowed from that place. She started to make something like a basin around it, using her hand in this way, and started filling her water-skin with water with her hands, and the water was flowing out after she had scooped some of it." The Prophet added, "May Allah bestow Mercy on Ishmael's mother! Had she let the Zamzam (flow without trying to control it) (or had she not scooped from that water) (to fill her water-skin), Zamzam would have been a stream flowing on the surface of the earth." The Prophet further added, "Then she drank (water) and suckled her child. The angel said to her, 'Don't be afraid of being neglected, for this is the House of Allah which will be built by this boy and his father, and Allah never neglects His people.' The House (Ka'ba) at that time was on a high place resembling a hillock, and when torrents came, they flowed to its right and left.

"She lived in that way till some people from the tribe of Jurhum or a family from Jurhum passed by her and her child, as they (the Jurhum people) were coming through the way of Kada'. They landed in the lower part of Mecca where they saw a bird that had the habit of flying around water and not leaving it. They said, 'This bird must be flying around water, though we know that there is no water in this valley.' They sent one or two messengers who discovered the source of water, and returned to inform them of the water. So, they all came (towards the water)." The Prophet added, "Ishmael's mother was sitting near the water. They asked her, 'Do you allow us to stay with you?' She replied, 'Yes, but you will have no right to possess the water.' They agreed to that." The Prophet further said, "Ishmael's mother was pleased with the whole situation as she used to love to enjoy the company of the people. So, they settled there, and later on they sent for their families who came and settled with them so that some families became permanent residents there. The child (Ishmael) grew up and learnt Arabic from them and (his virtues) caused them to love and admire him as he grew up, and when he reached the age of puberty, they made him marry a woman from amongst them.

"After Ishmael's mother had died, Abraham came, after Ishmael's marriage, in order to see his family that he had left before, but he did not find Ishmael there. When he asked Ishmael's wife about him, she replied, 'He has gone in search of our livelihood.' Then he asked her about their way of living and their condition, and she replied, 'We are living in misery; we are living in hardship and destitution,' complaining to him. He said, 'When your husband returns, convey my salutation to him and tell him to change the threshold of the gate (of his house).' When Ishmael came, he seemed to have felt something unusual, so he asked his wife, 'Has anyone visited you?' She replied, 'Yes, an old man of so-and-so description came and asked me about you and I informed him, and he asked about our state of living, and I told him that we were living in a hardship and poverty.' On that Ishmael said, 'Did he advise you anything?' She replied, 'Yes, he told me to convey his salutation to you and to tell you to change the threshold of your gate.' Ishmael said, 'It was my father, and he has ordered me to divorce you. Go back to your family.' So, Ishmael divorced her and married another woman from amongst them (i.e., Jurhum).

"Then Abraham stayed away from them for a period as long as Allah wished and called on them again but did not find Ishmael. So, he came to Ishmael's wife and asked her about Ishmael. She said, 'He has gone in search of our livelihood.' Abraham asked her, 'How are you getting on?' asking her about their sustenance and living. She replied, 'We are prosperous and well-off' (i.e., we have everything in abundance). Then she thanked Allah. Abraham said, 'What kind of food do you eat?' She said, 'Meat.' He said, 'What do you drink?' She said, 'Water.' He said, 'O Allah! Bless their meat and water.' The Prophet added, "At that time they did not have grain, and if they had grain, he would have also invoked Allah to bless it." The Prophet added, "If somebody has only these two things as his sustenance, his health and disposition will be badly affected, unless he lives in Mecca." The Prophet added, "Then Abraham said to Ishmael's wife, 'When your husband comes, give my regards to him and tell him that he should keep firm the threshold of his gate.' When Ishmael came back, he asked his wife, 'Did anyone call on you?' She replied, 'Yes, a good-looking old man came to me.' So she praised him and added, He asked about you, and I informed him, and he asked about our livelihood and I told him that we were in a good condition.' Ishmael asked her, 'Did he give you any piece of advice?' She said, 'Yes, he told me to give his regards to you and ordered that you should keep firm the threshold of your gate.' On that Ishmael said, 'It was my father, and you are the threshold (of the gate). He has ordered me to keep you with me.'

"Then Abraham stayed away from them for a period as long as Allah wished, and called on them afterwards. He saw Ishmael under a tree near Zamzam, sharpening his arrows. When he saw Abraham, he rose up to welcome him (and they greeted each other as a father does with his son or a son does with his father). Abraham said, 'O Ishmael! Allah has given me an order.' Ishmael said, 'Do what your Lord has ordered you to do.' Abraham asked, 'Will you help me?' Ishmael said, 'I will help you.' Abraham said, 'Allah has ordered me to build a house here,' pointing to a hillock higher than the land surrounding it." The Prophet added, "Then they raised the foundations of the House (the Ka'ba). Ishmael brought the stones and Abraham was building, and when the walls became high, Ishmael brought this stone and put it for Abraham who stood over it and carried on building, while Ishmael was handing him the stones, and both of them were saying, 'O our Lord! Accept (this service) from us. Verily, You are the All-Hearing, the All-Knowing.'" The Prophet added, "Then both of them went on building and going round the Ka'ba saying: 'O our Lord! Accept (this service) from us. Verily, You are the All-Hearing, the All-Knowing.'" (2.127)[18]

---

[18] Book #55, *Hadith* #583.

Bibliography

Abdel-Halim, Aziza. *Did You Know? Refuting Rigid Interpretations Concerning the Position of Women in Islam and Muslims' Interactions with Non-Muslims*. Sydney: Muslim Women's National Network of Australia, 2008.

Abudi, Dalya. *Mothers and Daughters in Arab Women's Literature: The Family Frontier*. Women and Gender. The Middle East and the Islamic World. 10. Leiden, Boston: Brill, 2011.

Abugideiri, Hibba. "Qur'an: Modern Interpretations. Arabic and Urdu." In *Encyclopedia of Women & Islamic Cultures*, 5:249–52. Leiden, Boston: Brill, 2007.

Abu-Lughod, Lila. "Modesty Discourses." In *Encyclopedia of Women & Islamic Cultures*, 2:294–98. Leiden, Boston: Brill, 2005.

———, ed. *Remaking Women: Feminism and Modernity in the Middle East*. Cairo: The American University in Cairo Press, 1998.

———. *Veiled Sentiments: Honor and Poetry in a Bedouin Society*. CA: University of California Press, 1986.

Abu-Odeh, Lama. "Honor Killings and the Construction of Gender in Arab Societies." *American Journal of Comparative Law* 58, no. 4 (Fall 2010): 911–52. https://doi.org/10.5131/ajcl.2010.0007.

Afshar, Haleh, Rob Aitken, and Myfanwy Franks. "Feminisms, Islamophobia and Identities." *Political Studies* 53 (2005): 262–83.

Ahmad, Sadaf. *Transforming Faith: The Story of Al-Huda and Islamic Revivalism Among Urban Pakistani Women*. Gender and Globalization. New York: Syracuse University Press, 2009.

Ahmed, Leila. *A Quiet Revolution. The Veil's Resurgence from the Middle East to America*. New Haven & London: Yale University Press, 2011.

———. *Women and Gender in Islam*. New Haven & London: Yale University Press, 1992.

Al-Faisal, Toujan. "They Insult Us … and We Elect Them!!" In *Faith and Freedom: Women's Human Rights in the Muslim World*, 232–37. London & New York: Tauris, 1995.

Ali Atassi, Muhammad. "The Veiling of the City." *Al Jadid*, 2011. http://www.aljadid.com/content/veiling-city.

Ali, Kecia. "Religious Practices: Obedience and Disobedience in Islamic Discourses." In *Encyclopedia of Women & Islamic Cultures*, 5:309–13. Leiden-Boston: Brill, 2007.

'Ali Qutb, Muhammad. *Women Around the Messenger*. Riyadh: International Islamic Publishing House, 2007.

Alison, James. "Girard's Breakthrough." *James Alison. Theology* (blog), 1996. http://www.jamesalison.co.uk/texts/eng05.html.

Al-Qahtani, Sa'id bin Wahf. حصن المسلم. *Fortress of the Muslim. Invocations from the*

Qur'an and Sunnah. 5th ed. Riyadh: Darussalam, 2006.

Alter, Robert. *The Hebrew Bible: A Translation with Commentary*. 1 edition. 3 vols. New York; London: W. W. Norton & Company, 2018.

Amin, Qasim. *The Liberation of Women*. Cairo: The American University in Cairo Press, 1992.

Ammar, Nawal H. "Wife Battery in Islam: A Comprehensive Understanding of Interpretations." *Violence Against Women* 13 (2007): 516. https://doi.org/10.1177/1077801207300658.

Anouar, Majid. "The Politics of Feminism in Islam." In *Gender, Politics and Islam*, 53–94. Chicago and London: University of Chicago Press, 2002.

Anwar, Etin. "Bodily Waste." In *Family, Body, Sexuality and Health*, 3:27–33. Encylopedia of Women & Islamic Cultures (Ed.) Suad Joseph. Leiden, Boston: Brill, 2006.

Aryanti, Tutin. "Shame and Borders: The 'Aisyiyah's Struggle for Muslim Women's Education in Indonesia." In *Gender, Religion and Education in a Chaotic Postmodern World*, 83–92. Netherlands: Springer, 2012.

Azban, Ahmad Kamal. *Diwan Baladna: Arab Culture from an Arab's Perspective*. Amman, Jordan: www.smashwords.com, 2010.

Badran, Margot. *Feminism in Islam. Secular and Religious Convergences*. Oxford: Oneworld, 2009.

Barclay, John M. G. *Paul and the Gift*. Grand Rapids, MI: Eerdmans, 2015.

Bargach, Jamila. "Celibacy." In *Encyclopedia of Women & Islamic Cultures*, 3:52–53. Leiden, Boston: Brill, 2006.

Barlas, Asma. *"Believing Women" in Islam. Unreading Patriarchal Interpretations of the Qur'an*. Austin, TX: University of Texas Press, 2002.

Barlas, Asma, and David Raeburn Finn. *Believing Women in Islam: A Brief Introduction*. Reprint edition. Austin, TX: University of Texas Press, 2019.

Baron, Beth. *The Women's Awakening in Egypt: Culture, Society, and the Press*. New Haven & London: Yale University Press, 1994.

Baron, Beth Ann. "The Rise of a New Literary Culture: The Women's Press of Egypt, 1882–1919." PhD, University of California, 1988.

Bauckham, Richard. *Gospel Women. Studies of the Named Women in the Gospels*. Grand Rapids, MI: William B. Eerdmans, 2002.

Belenky, Mary Field, Blythe Mcvicker Clinchy, Nancy Rule Goldberger, and Jill Mattuck Tarule. *Women's Ways of Knowing: The Development of Self, Voice, and Mind 10th Anniversary Edition*. New York: Basic Books, 1997.

Boddy, Janice. *Wombs and Alien Spirits: Women, Men and the Zar Cult in Northern Sudan*. Madison, WI: University of Wisconsin Press, 1989.

Bodman, Herbert L., and Nayereh Esfahlani Tohidi, eds. *Women in Muslim Societies: Diversity Within Unity*.. Boulder, CO: Lynne Rienner Pub, 1998.

Bowring, Bill. "Law: Customary, in Central Asia." In *Encyclopedia of Women & Islamic Cultures*, 2:416–18. Leiden, Boston: Brill, 2005.

Boxberger, Linda. "From Two States to One: Women's Lives in the Transformation of Yemen." In *Women in Muslim Societies: Diversity Within Unity*, 119–33. Boulder & London: Lynne Rienner Publishers, 1998.

Brooks, Geraldine. *Nine Parts of Desire: The Hidden World of Islamic Women*. North Sydney: Random House, 2008.

Bruck, Gabriele vom. "Elusive Bodies: The Politics of Aesthetics among Yemeni Elite Women." In *Gender, Politics, and Islam*, 161–200. Chicago & London: University of Chicago Press, 2002.

Buckley, Thomas, and Alma Gottlieb, eds. *Blood Magic: The Anthropology of*

Menstruation. Berkley and Los Angeles, CA: University of California Press, 1988.

Buitelaar, Marjo. "Space: Hammam – Overview." In *Encyclopedia of Women & Islamic Cultures*, 4:541–43. Leiden, Boston: Brill, 2007.

Canard, M. "Da'wa." In *Encylopaedia of Islam*, 2:168–70. Leiden: Brill, 1965.

Chheenah, Muhammad Ashraf. *Hagar: The Princess, the Mother of the Arabs ; and, Ishmael, the Father of Twelve Princes*. Edited by Abdus Satta Ghauri. 1st edition. Islamabad, Pakistan Interfaith Study and Research Centre, 2012. https://trove.nla.gov.au/version/182368894.

Chinchen, Delbert. "The Patron-Client System: A Model of Indigenous Discipleship." *Evangelical Missions Quarterly* 31, no. 4 (1995): 446–51.

Churchill, Mary C. "The Oppositional Paradigm of Purity versus Pollution in Charles Hudson's the Southeastern Indians." *American Indian Quarterly* 20, no. 3/4 (Summer/Fall 1996): 563–94.

Clancy-Smith, Julia. "Colonialism: 18th to Early 20th Century." In *Encyclopedia of Women & Islamic Cultures*, 1:100–115. Leiden, Boston: Brill, 2003.

Clarke, Lynda. "Religious Practices: Prophecy and Women Prophets. Overview." In *Encyclopedia of Women and Islamic Cultures*, 5:351–54. Leiden-Boston: Brill, 2007.

Cohick, Lynn H. *Women in the World of the Earliest Christians. Illuminating Ancient Ways of Life*. Grand Rapids, MI: Baker Academic, 2009.

"Comparative Islamic Studies." Accessed May 19, 2021. https://journal.equinoxpub.com/CIS.

Cooper, Barbara M. "Gender and Religion in Hausaland: Variations in Islamic Practice in Niger and Nigeria." In *Women in Muslim Societies: Diversity Within Unity*, 21–37. Boulder, London: Lynne Rienner Publishers, 1998.

Cragg, Kenneth. *The Call of the Minaret*. 2nd ed. London: Collins, 1985.

Crumbley, Deidre Helen. "Patriarchies, Prophets, and Procreation: Sources of Gender Practices in Three African Churches." *Africa* 73, no. 4 (2003): 584–606.

Dale, Moyra. *Biblical Womanhood*, 2021. https://www.youtube.com/watch?v=Eh0IQSZOKbQ.

———. "(Re)Forming Identities and Allegiances." In *When Women Speak...*, 67–88. Oxford: Regnum Books, 2018.

———. *Shifting Allegiances: Networks of Kinship and of Faith: The Women's Program in a Syrian Mosque*. Australian College of Theology Monograph Series. Eugene, OR: Wipf and Stock, 2016.

Dale, Moyra, Cathy Hine, and Carol Walker, eds. *When Women Speak....* Regnum Books International, 2018.

Davies, G. Henton. "Leviticus." In *The Interpreter's Dictionary of the Bible*, 3:117–22. Nashville, TN: Abingdon, 1962.

Davies, Sharyn Graham. "Surveilling Sexuality in Indonesia." In *Sex and Sexualities in Contemporary Indonesia. Sexual Politics, Health, Diversity and Representations*, 29–50. London & New York: Routledge, 2015.

Dawood, N. J., trans. *The Koran*. Revised edition. London; New York: Penguin Classics, 2015.

De Troyer, Kristin, Judith A Herbert, Judith Ann Johnson, and Anne-Marie Korte. *Wholly Woman, Holy Blood: A Feminist Critique of Purity and Impurity*. Harrisburg, PA: Trinity Press International, 2003.

Deeb, Lara. "Religious Practices: Preaching and Women Preachers. Arab States (excepting North Africa and the Gulf)." In *Encyclopedia of Women & Islamic Cultures*, 5:335–36. Leiden, Boston: Brill, 2007.

Dehqani-Tafti, H.B. *The Unfolding Design of My World. A Pilgrim in Exile*. 2nd. Norwich: Canterbury Press, 2000.

deSilva, David A. *Honor, Patronage, Kinship & Purity: Unlocking the New Testament Culture*. IL: IVP Academic, 2000.

———. *The Letter to the Hebrews in Social-Scientific Perspective*. Eugene, OR: Wipf and Stock Publishers, 2012.

DeYoung, Curtiss Paul, Michael O. Emerson, George Yancey, and Karen Chai Kim. *United by Faith: The Multiracial Congregation as an Answer to the Problem of Race*. Oxford: Oxford University Press, 2003.

Dhami, Sangeeta, and Aziz Sheikh. "The Muslim Family." *Western Journal of Medicine* 173, no. 5 (November 2000): 352–56.

Diamant, Anita. *The Red Tent*. Crows Nest, Sydney: Allen & Unwin, 1998.

Doorn-Harder, Pieternella van. *Women Shaping Islam: Reading the Qur'an in Indonesia*. Urbana and Chicago, IL: University of Illinois Press, 2006.

Douglas, Mary. *Natural Symbols: Explorations in Cosmology*. 2nd ed. London & New York: Routledge Classics, 1996.

———. *Purity and Danger. An Analysis of the Concepts of Pollution and Taboo*. London & New York: Routledge, 1966.

Doumato, Eleanor Abdella. *Getting God's Ear: Women, Islam, and Healing in Saudi Arabia and the Gulf*. New York: Columbia University Press, 2000.

D'Souza. "Devotional Practices among Shia Women in South India." In *Lived Islam in South Asia: Adaptation, Accommodation, and Conflict*. New Delhi: Social Science Press, 2004.

Duderija, Adis. "A Case Study of Patriarchy and Slavery: The Hermeneutical Importance of Qur'anic Assumptions in the Development of a Values-Based and Purposive Oriented Qur'an-Sunna Hermeneutic." *Journal of Women of the Middle East and the Islamic World*. 11 (2013): 1–30.

Dunn, Shannon, and Rosemary B Kellison. "At The Intersection of Scripture and Law. Qur'an 4:34 and Violence against Women." *Journal of Feminist Studies in Religion* 26, no. 2 (2010): 11–36.

Edwards, Colin. "Patronage, Salvation, and Being Joined with Jesus: Socio-Anthropological Insights from South Asia." In *Longing for Community: Church, Ummah, or Somewhere In Between*, 79–88. Pasadena, CA: William Carey Library, 2013.

Eickelman, D.F. "The Art of Memory: Islamic Education and Its Social Reproduction." *Comparative Studies in Society and History* 20, no. 4 (1978): 485–516.

El Fadl, Khaled Abou. *Speaking in God's Name. Islamic Law, Authority and Women*. Oxford: Oneworld, 2001.

El Guindi, Fadwa. *Suckling: Kinship More Fluid*. Routledge, 2020.

El Saadawi, Nawal. *Memoirs of a Woman Doctor*. Translated by Catherine Cobham. London: Saqi Books, 1988.

———. *The Hidden Face of Eve: Women in the Arab World*. London: Zed Press, 1980.

Elliott, John H. *Beware the Evil Eye. Volume 1. Introduction, Mesopotamia, and Egypt*. Vol. 1. Eugene, OR.: Cascade Books, 2015.

———. *Beware the Evil Eye. Volume 2: Greece and Rome*. Eugene, OR: Cascade Books, 2016.

———. *Beware the Evil Eye. Volume 3: The Bible and Related Sources*. Eugene, OR: Wipf and Stock Publishers, 2016.

———. *Beware the Evil Eye. Volume 4: Postbiblical Israel and Early Christianity through Late Antiquity*. Eugene, Oregon: Cascade Books, 2017.

———. *Conflict, Community, and Honor: 1 Peter in Social-Scientific Perspective*. Eugene, OR: Wipf & Stock Pub, 2007.

Emerick, Yaya. *What Islam is All About*. Kuala Lumpur, Malaysia: A.S. Noordeen,

2002.

Engineer, Asghar Ali. *The Rights of Women in Islam*. London: C. Hurst & Company, 1992.

Feldman, Shelley, and Lindy Williams. "Development: Family. Overview." In *Encyclopedia of Women & Islamic Cultures*, 4:79–84. Leiden, Boston: Brill, 2007.

Flanders, Christopher L. *About Face: Rethinking Face for 21st Century Mission*. Vol. 9. American Society of Missiology Series. Eugene, OR: Pickwick Publications, 2011.

Foster, George. "Peasant Society and the Image of Limited Good." *American Anthropologist* 67 (1965): 293–315.

Frank, Audrey. *Covered Glory: The Face of Honor and Shame in the Muslim World*. Eugene, OR: Harvest House Publishers, 2019.

Gauvain, Richard. "Ritual Rewards: A Consideration of Three Recent Approaches to Sunni Purity Law." *Islamic Law and Society* 12, no. 3 (2005): 333–93.

Gennep, Arnold van, Monika B. Vizedon, and Gabrielle L. Caffee. *The Rites of Passage*. Chicago: University of Chicago Press, 1961.

Georges, Jayson. *Ministering in Patronage Cultures: Biblical Models and Missional Implications*. Downer's Grove, IL: IVP Academic, 2019.

Georges, Jayson, and Mark D. Baker. *Ministering in Honor-Shame Cultures: Biblical Foundations and Practical Essentials*. Downers Grove, IL: IVP Academic, 2016.

Gerami, Shahin, and Khadijeh Safiri. "Qur'an: Modern Interpretations. Persian." In *Encyclopedia of Women and Islamic Cultures*, 5:255–58. Leiden-Boston: Brill, 2007.

Gerner, Debbie J. "Roles in Transition: The Evolving Position of Women in Arab-Islamic Countries." In *Muslim Women*, 71–99. Beckenham: CroomHelm Ltd, 1984.

Ghadanfar, Mahmood Ahmad. Revised by Sheikh Safium-Rahman Al-Mubarapuri. *Great Women of Islam Who Were given the Good News of Paradise*. Riyadh: Darussalam, 2001.

Ghadially, Rehana. "A Hajari (Meal Tray) for Abbas Alam Dar: Women's Household Ritual in a South Asian Muslim Sect." *The Muslim World* 92, no. 2 (2003): 309–22.

Ghannam, Farha. "Motherhood: Arab States." In *Encyclopedia of Women & Islamic Cultures*, 2:508–9. Leiden, Boston: Brill, 2005.

Gibb, H.A.R, and J.H Kramers. *Shorter Encyclopaedia of Islam*. Leiden: E.J.Brill, 1974.

Gibson, Shimon. *The Final Days of Jesus:. The Archaeological Evidence*. New York: HarperCollins, 2009.

Girard, René. *The Girard Reader*. New York: Crossroad, 1996.

Glaser, Ida, and Napoleon John. *Partners or Prisoners? Christians Thinking about Women and Islam*. Carlisle: Solway, 1998.

Goerling, Fritz. "Baraka (as Divine Blessing) as a Bridge in Manding Languages (Especially in Jula of Cote d'Ivoire)." *Journal of Translation* 6, no. 1 (2010): 1–9.

Greenlee, David, ed. *From the Straight Path to the Narrow Way*. Waynesboro, GA: Authentic, 2006.

———, ed. *Longing for Community: Church, Ummah, or Somewhere In Between*. Pasadena, CA: William Carey Library, 2013.

Guindi, Fadwa El. "Veiling Resistance." *Fashion Theory* 3, no. 1 (February 1, 1999): 51–80. https://doi.org/10.2752/136270499779165626.

Haddad, Yvonne Yazbeck. "Islam and Gender: Dilemmas in the Changing Arab World." In *Islam, Gender & Social Change,* Ed. Yvonne Yazbeck Haddad & John L. Esposito, 3–29. New York & Oxford: Oxford University Press, 1998.

Haddad, Yvonne Yazbeck, and John L Esposito. *Islam, Gender, and Social Change*. New York & Oxford: Oxford University Press, 1998.

Handayani, Dwi. "Veiled: Muslim Women in Modern Mission Strategies: Response 1." In *When Women Speak...*, 19–23. Oxford: Regnum Books, 2018.

Hashmi, Taj. *Women and Islam in Bangladesh: Beyond Subjection and Tyranny.*
    London & New York: Palgrave Macmillan & St. Martin's Press, 2000.

Hatem, Mervat. "A'isha Taymur's Tears and the Critique of the Modernist and Feminist
    Discourses on Nineteenth Century Egypt." In *Remaking Women: Feminism and
    Modernity in the Middle East*, 73–87. Cairo: The American University in Cairo
    Press, 1998.

Hegland, Mary Elaine. "Shi'a Women's Rituals in Northwest Pakistan: The
    Shortcomings and Significance of Resistance." *Anthropological Quarterly* 76, no. 3
    (Summer 2003). Academic Search Premier.

Hekmat, Anwar. *Women and the Koran: The Status of Women in Islam.* New York:
    Prometheus Books, 1997.

Helminski, Camille Adams. *Women of Sufism: A Hidden Treasure: Writings and Stories
    of Mystic Poets, Scholars and Saints.* Boston, MA: Shambhala Publications, 2003.

Hibbert, Richard, and Evelyn Hibbert. "Defining Culturally Appropriate Leadership."
    Missiology 47, no. 3 (July 1, 2019): 240–51.
    https://doi.org/10.1177/0091829619858595.

Hibbert, Richard Y. "Defilement and Cleansing." *Missiology: An International Review*
    XXXVI, no. 3 (July 2008): 343–55.

Hibbert, R.Y., and E.C. Hibbert. "Diagnosing Church Health Across Cultures: A Case
    Study of Turkish Gypsy Churches in Bulgaria." *Missiology: An International Review*
    44, no. 3 (2016): 243–56.

Hiebert, Paul. *Transforming Worldviews: An Anthropological Understanding of How
    People Change.* Grand Rapids, MI: Baker Academic, 2008.

———. "Worldview Transformation." In *From the Straight Path to the Narrow Way*,
    23–34. Waynesboro, GA: Authentic, 2006.

Hiebert, Paul G. *Anthropological Reflections on Missiological Issues.* Grand Rapids,
    MI: Baker Books, 1994.

———. "The Flaw of the Excluded Middle." In *Anthropological Reflections on
    Missiological Issues*, 189–201. Grand Rapids, MI: Baker Books, 1994.

Hiebert, Paul G., R. Daniel Shaw, and Tite Tienou. *Understanding Folk Religion: A
    Christian Response to Popular Beliefs and Practices.* Grand Rapids, MI: Baker
    Publishing Group, 2000.

Hilali, Dr Muhammad Taqi-ud-Din al-, and Dr Muhammad Muhsin Khan. *Translation
    of the Meanings of The Noble Qur'an in the English Language.* Madinah, K.S.A.:
    King Fahd Complex for the Printing of the Holy Qur'an, 1404.

Hofstede, Geert, and Gert Jan Hofstede. *Cultures and Organizations: Software of the
    Mind. Intercultural Cooperation and Its Importance for Survival.* 2nd ed. New York:
    McGraw-Hill, 2005.

Hoskins, Janet. "The Menstrual Hut and the Witch's Lair in Two Eastern Indonesian
    Societies." *Ethnology* 41, no. 4 (Fall 2002): 317–34.

Hudson, Valerie, Bonnie Ballif-Spanvill, Mary Capriolo, and Chad Emmett. *Sex and
    World Peace.* New York: Columbia University Press, 2012.

Jansen, Anne. "Building Community in a Muslim Background Believer Church: A Case
    Study among Uighur Women." In *Ministry to Muslim Women: Longing to Call Them
    Sisters.* Pasadena, CA: William Carey Library, 2000.

Jansen, Willy. "Religious Practices: Ablution, Purification, Prayer, Fasting, and Piety.
    North Africa." In *Encyclopedia of Women & Islamic Cultures*, 5:273–74. Leiden,
    Boston: Brill, 2007.

Jardim, Georgina L. *Recovering the Female Voice in Islamic Scripture: Women and
    Silence.* 1 edition. Farnham, Surrey; Burlington, VT: Routledge, 2014.

Jaschok, Maria. "Sources of Authority: Female Ahong and Qingzhen Nusi (Women's

Mosques) in China." In *Women, Leadership, and Mosques: Changes in Contemporary Islamic Authority*, 11:37–58. Women and Gender. The Middle East and the Islamic World. Leiden, Boston: Brill, 2012.

Jaschok, Maria, and Shui, Jingjun. *The History of Women's Mosques in Chinese Islam*. Richmond: Curzon Press, 2000.

Jawad, Haifaa A. *The Rights of Women in Islam*. Hampshire and New York: Macmillan Press and St. Martin's Press, 1998.

Joseph, Suad, ed. *Encyclopedia of Women and Islamic Cultures: Family, Law and Politics*. Leiden; Boston, Mass: Brill, 2005.

Joseph, Suad (ed). *Gender and Citizenship in the Middle East*. Contemporary Issues in the Middle East. Syracuse, NY: Syracuse University Press, 2000.

———. *Intimate Selving in Arab Families: Gender, Self and Identity*. Gender, Culture, and Politics in the Middle East. Syracuse, NY: Syracuse University Press, 1999.

Julian of Norwich. *Revelations of Divine Love*. Translated by Barry Windeatt. Oxford, New York: Oxford University Press, 2015.

Kahteran, Nevad. "Hafiz/Tahfiz/Hifz/Muhaffiz." In *The Qur'an: An Encyclopaedia*, 231–34. London & New York: Routledge, 2006.

———. "Tajwid." In *The Qur'an: An Encyclopaedia*, 635–38. London & New York: Routledge, 2006.

Kalmbach, Hilary. "Social and Religious Change in Damascus: One Case of Female Islamic Religious Authority." *British Journal of Middle Eastern Studies* 35, no. 1 (April 1, 2008): 37–57.

Kamel, Laila R. Iskandar. *Mokattam Garbage Village, Cairo, Egypt*. Cairo: L.R.I. Kamel, 1994.

Kandiyoti, Deniz. "Bargaining With Patriarchy." *Gender & Society* 2, no. 3 (September 1, 1988): 274–90. https://doi.org/10.1177/089124388002003004.

Katz, Marion. "Scholarly versus Women's Authority in the Islamic Law of Menstrual Purity." In *Gender in Judaism and Islam: Common Lives, Uncommon Heritage*, 73–105. New York & London: New York University Press, 2015.

Keddie, Nikki R. *Women in the Middle East, Past and Present*. Princeton, NJ: Princeton University Press, 2007.

Khan, Muhammad M., trans. *The Translation of the Meanings of Summarized Sahih Al-Bukhari: Arabic-English*. Lahore, Pakistan: Dar-us-Salam Publications, 1995.

Khattab, Huda. *The Muslim Woman's Handbook*. 2nd ed. London: Ta-Ha Publishers, 1994.

Kilinc, Ahmet. *Islam: The Perfect Way of Life*. Translated by Ayse Kilinc. Coburg: AGP Australia, 2011.

Klingorová, Kamila, and Tomáš Havlíček. "Religion and Gender Inequality: The Status of Women in the Societies of World Religions." *Moravian Geographical Reports* 23, no. 2 (June 30, 2015): 2–11. https://doi.org/10.1515/mgr-2015-0006.

Krause, Wanda. *Women in Civil Society: The State, Islamism, and Networks in the UAE*. New York: Palgrave Macmillan, 2008.

Kristor, Nicholas D., and Sheryl WuDunn. *Half the Sky: Turning Oppression into Opportunity for Women Worldwide*. New York: Alfred A. Knopf, 2010.

Kuhn, Michael F. *Finding Hagar: God's Pursuit of a Runaway*. Illustrated Edition. Carlisle: Langham Global Library, 2019.

Kung, Hans. *Islam Past, Present & Future*. Oxford: Oxford University Press, 2004.

Kurzman, Charles, ed. *Liberal Islam: A Source Book*. Oxford, New York: Oxford University Press, 1998.

Lane, E.W. *Manners and Customs of the Modern Egyptians*. 3rd ed. London & New York: Everyman's Library, 1860.

Lather, Patti. *Getting Smart: Feminist Research and Pedagogy With/in the Postmodern.* Hove: Psychology Press, 1991.

Le Renard, Amelie. "From Qur'anic Circles to the Internet: Gender Segregation and the Rise of Female Preachers in Saudi Arabia." In *Women, Leadership, and Mosques: Changes in Contemporary Islamic Authority*, 11:105–26. Women and Gender. The Middle East and the Islamic World. Leiden, Boston: Brill, 2012.

Lenning, Larry G. *Blessing in Mosque and Mission.* Pasadena, CA: William Carey Library, 1980.

Lewis, CS. *The Screwtape Letters.* London: Bles, 1942.

Lewis, Pauline. "Zaynab Al-Ghazali: Pioneer of Islamist Feminism." *Michigan Journal of History* 27, no. 4 (2007): 1–47.

Lewis, Rebecca. "Insider Movements Underground Church Movements: The Surprising Role of Women's Networks." *International Journal of Frontier Missions* 21, no. 4 (Winter 2004): 145.

Lindsay, James E. *Daily Life in the Medieval Islamic World.* Westport, CN: Greenwood Press, 2005.

Love, Fran, and Jeleta Eckheart, eds. *Longing to Call Them Sisters.* Pasadena, CA: William Carey Library, 2000.

Maalouf, Amin, trans. Barbara Bray. *On Identity.* London: The Harvill Press, 2000.

Maghen, Ze'ev. "Close Encounters: Some Preliminary Observations on the Transmission of Impurity in Early Sunni Jurisprudence." *Islamic Law and Society* 6, no. 3 (1999): 348–92.

Maher, Bridget. *Veiled Voices.* DVD, Documentary. Typecast Releasing, 2010.

Mahmood, Saba. *Politics of Piety: The Islamic Revival and the Feminist Subject.* Princeton and Oxford: Princeton University Press, 2005.

Mahmoud, Mohamed. "To Beat or Not to Beat: On the Exegetical Dilemmas over Qur'an, 4:34." *Journal of the American Oriental Society* 126, no. 4 (2006): 537–50.

Malina, Bruce J. *The New Testament World: Insights from Cultural Anthropology.* 3rd ed. Louisville, KY: Westminster John Knox Press, 2001.

Mallouhi, Christine A. *Miniskirts, Mothers and Muslims: A Christian Woman in a Muslim Land.* 2nd ed. Oxford: Monarch Books, 2004.

Malti-Douglas, Fedwa. *Woman's Body, Woman's Word: Gender and Discourse in Arabo-Islamic Writing.* Princeton, NJ: Princeton University Press, 1991.

Marsot, Afaf Lutfi al-Sayyid. "Entrepreneurial Women." In *Feminism and Islam: Legal and Literary Perspectives*, 33–48. Reading: Ithaca Press, 1996.

Mattson, Ingrid. "Adoption and Fostering: Overview." In *Encyclopedia of Women & Islamic Cultures*, 2:1–3. Leiden, Boston: Brill, 2005.

Maududi, Abul A'la. Trans. Ed. Al-Ash'ari. *Purdah and the Status of Woman in Islam.* 2nd ed. Delhi: Markazi Maktabi Islami, 1981. www.al-islamforall.org.

Mauss, Marcel. *The Gift.* Translated by Jane I. Guyer. HAU Books, 1925.

McDonald, Brian. "Violence and the Lamb Slain." *Touchstone* 16, no. 10 (December 2003). http://www.touchstonemag.com/archives/issue.php?id=66.

Meltzer, Julia, and Laura Nix. *The Light in Her Eyes.* DVD, Documentary. Clockshop & Felt Films, 2012. www.TheLightInHerEyesMovie.com.

Mernissi, Fatima. "A Feminist Interpretation of Women's Rights in Islam." In *Liberal Islam: A Sourcebook*, 112–26. New York & Oxford: Oxford University Press, 1998.

———. *Beyond the Veil: Male–Female Dynamics in a Modern Muslim Society.* Cambridge, MA: Schenkman Publishing Company, 1975.

———. *The Forgotten Queens of Islam.* Translated by Mary Jo Lakeland. English translation. Cambridge: Polity Press, 1990.

———. *The Harem Within: Tales of a Moroccan Girlhood.* London: Bantam Books,

1994.

———. *The Veil and the Male Elite: A Feminist Interpretation of Women's Rights in Islam.* Translated by Mary Jo Lakeland. New York: Basic Books, 1992.

———. *Women's Rebellion & Islamic Memory.* London: Zed Books, 1996.

Minesaki, Hiroko. "Gender Strategy and Authority In Islamic Discourses: Female Preachers in Contemporary Egypt." In *Women, Leadership, and Mosques:.Changes in Contemporary Islamic Authority,* 11:393–412. Women and Gender. The Middle East and the Islamic World. Leiden, Boston: Brill, 2012.

Minganti, Pia Karlsson. "Challenging From Within: Youth Associations and Female Leadership In Swedish Mosques." In *Women, Leadership, and Mosques: Changes in Contemporary Islamic Authority,* 11:371–91. Women and Gender. The Middle East and the Islamic World. Leiden, Boston: Brill, 2012.

Moghadam, Valentine M. "Islamic Feminism and Its Discontents: Toward a Resolution of the Debate." In *Gender, Politics, and Islam,* 15–51. Chicago & London: University of Chicago Press, 2002.

Mojab, Shahrzad. "Honor: Iran & Afghanistan." In *Encyclopedia of Women & Islamic Cultures,* 2:215–16. Leiden, Boston: Brill, 2005.

———. "Theorizing the Politics of 'Islamic Feminism'." *Feminist Review* 69 (Winter 2001): 124–56. https://doi.org/10.1080/01417780110070157.

Moon, W. Jay. *Intercultural Discipleship (Encountering Mission): Learning from Global Approaches to Spiritual Formation.* Grand Rapids, MI: Baker Academic, 2017.

Muhammad-Farooq-i-azam-Malik. *English Translation of the Meaning of Al-Qur'an: The Guidance for Mankind.* Houston, TX: Institute of Islamic Knowledge, 1997.

Mullins, Sarah. "Faith on Camelback: Reaching Non-Arabic-Speaking Urban, Less-Educated Muslim Women." In *A Worldview Approach to Ministry Among Muslim Women,* 75–91. Pasadena, CA: William Carey Library, 2006.

Musk, Bill. *Touching The Soul of Islam.* 2nd ed. Oxford: Monarch Books, 2004.

Nadwi, Mohammad Akram. *Al-Muhaddithat: The Women Scholars in Islam.* Oxford, London: Interface Publications, 2007.

Nelson, Kristina. *The Art of Reciting the Qur'an.* Cairo: The American University in Cairo Press, 2001.

"NobleQuran.Com – Simple English Translation of the Qur'an." Accessed May 19, 2021. https://noblequran.com/.

Nomani, Asra Q. *Standing Alone: An American Woman's Struggle for the Soul of Islam,* 2006.

Nurbakhsh, Javad. *Sufi Women.* 3rd ed. London & New York: Khaniqahi Nimatullahi Publications, 2004.

Oduyoye, Mercy. *Introducing African Women's Theology.* Sheffield: Sheffield Academic Press Ltd., 2001.

Osborne, William R. *Divine Blessing and the Fullness of Life in the Presence of God.* Short Studies in Biblical Theology. Wheaton, IL: Crossway, 2020.

Padwick, Constance E. *Muslim Devotions: A Study of Prayer-Manuals in Common Use.* Oxford: Oneworld, 1961.

Parrinder, Geoffrey, and Grace Golden. *A Dictionary of Non-Christian Religions.* 1st Edition. Philadelphia, PA: Westminster John Knox Pr, 1973.

Pemberton, Kelly. "Religious Practices: Ablution, Purification, Prayer, Fasting, and Piety. South Asia." In *Encyclopedia of Women & Islamic Cultures,* 5:274–76. Leiden, Boston: Brill, 2007.

Peters, F. E. *Judaism, Christianity, and Islam, Volume 1: From Covenant to Community.* Princeton, N.J: Princeton University Press, 1990.

Pfluger-Schindlbeck, Ingrid. "Language: Use by Women. The Caucasus." In *Encyclopedia of Women & Islamic Cultures*, 5:233. Leiden, Boston: Brill, 2007.

Philips, Abu Ameenah Bilal. *Islamic Rules on Menstruation and Post-Natal Bleeding*. Kuala Lumpur, Malaysia: A.S. Noordeen, 1995.

Pickthall, Mohammed Marmaduke. "The Meaning of the Glorious Qur'an." Accessed May 19, 2021. https://www.goodreads.com/book/show/462214.The_Meaning_of_the_Glorious_Qur_an.

Pohl, Christine D. *Making Room: Recovering Hospitality as a Christian Tradition*. 59918th edition. Grand Rapids, MI: Eerdmans, 1999.

Power, Bernie. *Challenging Islamic Traditions: Searching Questions about the Hadith from a Christian Perspective*. Pasadena, CA: William Carey Library, 2016.

———. *Engaging Islamic Traditions: Using the Hadith in Christian Ministry to Muslims*. Pasadena, CA: William Carey Library, 2016.

Rahman, Fazlur. *Islam*. 2nd ed. Chicago & London: University of Chicago Press, 1979.

———. *Major Themes of the Qur'an*. Chicago and Minneapolis: Bibliotheca Islamica, 1980.

Richards, E. Randolph, and Richard James. *Misreading Scripture with Individualist Eyes: Patronage, Honor, and Shame in the Biblical World*. Downers Grove, IL: IVP Academic, 2020.

Ripken, Nik. "What's Wrong with Western Missionaries?" Desiring God, September 12, 2016. https://www.desiringgod.org/articles/what-s-wrong-with-western-missionaries.

Rippin, Andrew. "Qur'an: Qur'an and Early Tafsir." In *Encyclopedia of Women & Islamic Cultures*, 5:266–68. Leiden, Boston: Brill, 2007.

Roded, Ruth, ed. *Women in Islam and the Middle East: A Reader*. 2nd ed. New York: I.B. Tauris, 2008.

Ross, Cathy. "Creating Space: Hospitality as a Metaphor for Mission." *Anvil* 25, no. 3 (2008): 167–76.

———. "Without Faces: Women's Perspectives on Contextual Missiology." Presented at the Louis J. Luzbetak SVD Lecture on Mission & Culture, Chicago, Catholic Theological Union, October 3, 2011. https://learn.ctu.edu/without-faces-womens-perspectives-contextual-missiology/.

Roushdy-Hammady, Iman. "Health Policies: Western Europe." In *Encyclopedia of Women & Islamic Cultures*, 6:123–25. Leiden, Boston: Brill, 2007.

Rynkiewich, Michael. *Soul, Self, and Society: A Postmodern Anthropology for Mission in a Postcolonial World*. Eugene, OR: Cascade Books, 2011.

Sabra, Adam. "Poverty." In *Encyclopedia of Women & Islamic Cultures*, 4:490–92. Leiden-Boston: Brill, 2007.

Safran, Janina M. "Rules of Purity and Confessional Boundaries: Maliki Debates about the Pollution of the Christian." *History of Religions* 42, no. 3 (February 2003): 197–213.

HasbunAllah. "Sahih Al-Bukhari (Abridged)," May 28, 2014. https://www.hasbunallah.com.au/sahih-al-bukhari-abridged/.

Saliba, Therese, Carolyn Allen, and Judith A. Howard. *Gender, Politics and Islam*. Chicago and London: University of Chicago Press, 2002.

Saqib, Muhammad Abdul Karim. *A Guide to Salat (Prayer)*. Riyadh: Darussalam, 1997.

Schimmel, Annemarie. Tran. Susan H. Ray. *My Soul Is a Woman: The Feminine in Islam*. New York & London: Continuum, 2003.

Schleifer, Aliah. *Motherhood in Islam*. Islamic Monograph Series. Cambridge: Islamic Academy, 1986.

Scott, Rachel M. "A Contextual Approach to Women's Rights in the Qur'an: Readings of 4:34." *The Muslim World* 99, no. 1 (January 2009): 60–85.

Shaaban, Bouthaina. "The Muted Voices of Women Interpreters." In *Faith and Freedom: Women's Rights in the Muslim World. Ed. Mahnaz Afkhami,* 1995.

Shaarawi, Huda. *Harem Years: The Memoirs of an Egyptian Feminist (1879–1924).* Translated by Margot Badran. Cairo: The American University in Cairo Press, 1998.

Shakry, Omnia. "Schooled Mothers and Structured Play: Child Rearing in Turn-of-the Century Egypt." In *Remaking Women, Feminism and Modernity in the Middle East,* 126–70. Cairo: The American University in Cairo Press, 1998.

Sharabi, Hisham. *Neopatriarchy: A Theory of Distorted Change in Arab Society.* Oxford University Press, 1988.

Shehadeh, Lamia Rustum. *The Idea of Women in Fundamentalist Islam.* Gainesville, FL: University Press of Florida, 2003.

Siddiqui, Mona. *Hospitality and Islam: Welcoming in God's Name.* Reprint edition. Yale University Press, 2016.

Silvers, Laury. "Representations: Sufi Women, Early Period, Seventh–Tenth Centuries." In *Encyclopaedia of Islam,* 5:541–43. Leiden-Boston: Brill, 2007.

Sire, James W. *The Universe Next Door.* 5th ed. Downers Grove, IL: IVP Academic, 2009.

Smith, Jane I. "Women, Religion and Social Change in Early Islam." In *Women, Religion, and Social Change,* 19–35. New York: State University of New York Press, 1985.

Smith, Jane I., and Yvonne Yazbeck Haddad. "The Virgin Mary in Islamic Tradition and Commentary." *Muslim World* 79, no. 3–4 (1989): 161–87.

Smith, Margaret. "Rabi'a al-'Adawiya." In *Shorter Encyclopaedia of Islam,* 462–63. Leiden: Brill, 1974.

———. *Rabi'a the Mystic and Her Fellow-Saints in Islam.* Cambridge: Cambridge University Press, 1928.

Smith, William Robertson. *Kinship and Marriage in Early Arabia.* Cambridge: Cambridge University Press, 1885.

Stark, Rodney. *The Rise of Christianity: How the Obscure, Marginal Jesus Movement Became the Dominant Religious Force in the Western World in a Few Centuries.* Princeton, NJ: Princeton University Press, 1997.

Stewart, Pamela J, and Andrew Strathern. "Power and Placement in Blood Practices." *Ethnology* 41, no. 4 (Fall 2002): 349–64.

Stowasser, Barbara Freyer. "Gender Issues and Contemporary Qur'an Interpretation." In *Islam, Gender & Social Change, Ed. Yvonne Yazbeck Haddad & John L. Esposito,* 30–44. New York & Oxford: Oxford University Press, 1998.

———. *Women in the Qur'an, Traditions, and Interpretation.* New York & Oxford: Oxford University Press, 1994.

Street, Brian. "Cross-Cultural Perspectives on Literacy." In *Functional Literacy,* 95–111. Amsterdam: John Benjamins, 1994.

Strong, Cynthia A. "A Mystic Union: Reaching Sufi Women." In *A Worldview Approach to Ministry Among Muslim Women.* Pasadena, CA: William Carey Library, 2006.

Strong, Cynthia A., and Meg Page, eds. *A Worldview Approach to Ministry Among Muslim Women.* Pasadena, CA: William Carey Library, 2013.

Sullivan, Earl L. *Women in Egyptian Public Life.* Syracuse, NY: Syracuse University Press, 1986.

Syrett, Nicholas L. *American Child Bride: A History of Minors and Marriage in the United States.* Illustrated edition. Chapel Hill, NC: University of North Carolina

Press, 2016.

Tadjbakhsh, Shahrbanou. "Between Lenin and Allah: Women and Ideology in Tajikistan." In *Women in Muslim Societies: Diversity within Unity*. Boulder, CO and London: Lynne Rienner Publishers, 1998.

Talman, Travis. *Understanding Insider Movements: Disciples of Jesus within Diverse Religious Communities*. Pasadena, CA: William Carey Library, 2006.

"The Screwtape Letters," 1942. https://www.goodreads.com/work/best_book/2920952-the-screwtape-letters.

"The Screwtape Letters (Audio Download): Ralph Cosham, C. S. Lewis, Blackstone Audio, Inc.: amazon.com.au: Audible." Accessed May 20, 2021. https://www.amazon.com.au/The-Screwtape-Letters/dp/B00NPB45KC.

Thurlkill, Mary F. *Chosen Among Women: Mary and Fatima in Medieval Christianity and Shi'ite Islam*. Notre Dame, IN: University of Notre Dame Press, 2007.

Tidball, Derek. *The Message of Leviticus*. The Bible Speaks Today. Leicester: Inter-Varsity Press, 2005.

Uglow, Jennifer S., and Maggy Hendry. *The Northeastern Dictionary of Women's Biography*. 3rd ed. Boston: Macmillan, 1998. https://books.google.com.au/books?id=zlQKDvU1WV0C&pg=PA260&dq=hind+al+hunnud&hl=en&sa=X&redir_esc=y#v=onepage&q=hind%20al%20hunnud&f=false.

Wadud, Amina. *Inside the Gender Jihad: Women's Reform in Islam*. Oxford: Oneworld, 2006.

———. *Qur'an and Woman: Rereading the Sacred Text from a Woman's Perspective*. New York & Oxford: Oxford University Press, 1999.

Wagner, Daniel A. *Literacy, Culture and Development: Becoming Literate in Morocco*. New York: Cambridge University Press, 1993.

Walker, Carol. "The Women in the Qur'an." In *Ayesha's Sisters: Some Perspectives on Women in Islam*, 8:31–48. Occasional Papers in the Study of Islam and Other Faiths. Melbourne, Australia: MST Press, 2019.

Walls, Andrew F. *The Cross-Cultural Process in Christian History*. Maryknoll, NY: Orbis Books, 2002.

Wazana, Nili. "A Case of the Evil Eye: Qohelet 4:4–8." *Journal of Biblical Literature* 126, no. 4 (2007): 685–702.

Weatherford, Jack. *The Secret History of the Mongolian Queens: How the Daughters of Genghis Khan Rescued His Empire.* New York: Crown Publishers, 2010.

Wehr, Hans. *A Dictionary of Modern Written Arabic*. 4th ed. Beirut & London: Librairie Du Liban, and Macdonald & Evans, 1974.

Wensinck, A. J. "Salat." In *Shorter Encyclopaedia of Islam*, 491–99. Leiden: E.J. Brill, 1953 1974.

Wilks, Ivor. "The Transmission of Islamic Learning in the Western Sudan." In *Literacy in Traditional Societies*, 161–97. Cambridge: Cambridge University Press, 1968.

Wilson, Brittany E. *Unmanly Men: Refigurations of Masculinity in Luke-Acts*. Oxford, New York: Oxford University Press, 2015.

Wynn, Lisa. "Religious Practices: Ablution, Purification, Prayer, Fasting, and Piety: The Gulf." In *Encyclopedia of Women & Islamic Cultures*, 5:270–71. Leiden, Boston: Brill, 2007.

Index